MW01033827

The Quiet
STORM

Copyright © 2025 Amani Roberts

All rights reserved. No part of this publication may be reproduced, distributed, or transmitted in any form or by any means, including photocopying, recording, or other electronic or mechanical methods, without the prior written permission of the publisher, except in the case of brief quotations embodied in critical reviews and certain other noncommercial uses permitted by copyright law. For permission requests, write to the publisher, addressed "Attention: Permissions Coordinator," at the address below.

www.woodsidemediagroup.com

ISBN: 978-1-7343466-1-9 (paperback)
ISBN: 978-1-7343466-8-8 (ebook)
ISBN: 978-1-7343466-3-3 (hardcover)
ISBN: 978-1-7343466-4-0 (audiobook)

Library of Congress Control Number: 2024922016

Ordering Information:
Special discounts are available on quantity purchases by corporations, associations, and others. For details, contact Amani@amaniexperience.com.

A HISTORICAL AND CULTURAL ANALYSIS OF THE
POWER, PASSION, AND PAIN OF R&B GROUPS

The Quiet
STORM

AMANI ROBERTS, M.A.

I would like to dedicate this book to my dad, Albert Roberts, who first exposed me to music by playing songs on the stereo in the basement and then during the long road trips to soccer games up and down the East Coast.

I also want to dedicate this book to all the R&B lovers worldwide. Keep sharing the stories and let the pain and passion continue to fuel you!

TABLE OF CONTENTS

Part One: The 1950's

Part Two: The 1960s

Part Three: 1970s

Part Four: 1980s

Part Five: 1990s

Part Six : The 2000s

Part Seven: What Happened?

WHAT SHOULD YOU EXPECT WHEN YOU READ THIS BOOK?

THIS BOOK IS NOT JUST A PROJECT FOR me; it's a labor of love that I've been nurturing since 2020. It all began during my time at Berklee College of Music, when I was tasked with choosing a research topic. I found myself drawn to the question, "Why there are no more Black R&B groups in existence?" This wasn't just an academic curiosity; it was a topic that resonated deeply with me, as **my research revealed that 99% of all R&B groups are majority African American.**

Inside the book, the first section gives you a history review of 10 to 12 of the most successful R&B groups per decade. The quantitative research for this section was based on the following:

- Record sales
- *Billboard* Hot 100 charting singles
- Grammy wins
- Notable performances

The second section of the book explores a question that I believe is of great interest to many of you: why have R&B groups disappeared since the mid-2000s? This is not just a financial analysis, it's a qualitative exploration that I'm still actively researching. We'll uncover five main reasons, each one offering a deeper understanding of the complex issues at play.

The final chapter will share my brief thoughts on predictions for the future, where I analyze current signs of what is to come in the world of R&B groups.

That is what you can expect from this book. Feel free to read the book from front to back or skip ahead and read the "What Happened" section. Thanks for reading the book, and let's prepare for our journey.

WHAT DOES THE QUIET STORM TITLE MEAN?

The Quiet Storm title has a substantial meaning, which gives further credence to the journey of R&B groups. In the mid-1970s, a DJ from WHUR 96.3 in Washington, DC (Howard University's signature station), named Melvin Lindsey created this radio format. The music format was love songs from 1950s, 1960s, and 1970s Black artists. When the initial response from listeners was positive, the station manager for WHUR, Cathy Hughes, gave Melvin Lindsey and his classmate Jack Shuler their own show. The show's name came from the Smokey Robinson song "Quiet Storm," which was released in 1975.

Eventually, the show ran for four hours and kept its focus on laid-back, smooth grooves that made for easy listening. Within a short amount of time, every station in the United States with a core Black, urban audience adopted a similar format for its late-night shift. KBLX-FM in San Francisco expanded this concept into a 24-hour quiet storm format. In New York, Vaughn Harper from WBLS-FM adopted a similar format.

The Quiet Storm concept continued on radio stations until the late 1990s, as hip-hop music was the preferred genre for younger listeners, and radio stations underwent a shift in programming to capture these listeners.

I grew up in Washington, DC, listening to *The Quiet Storm*. This book's title allows me to pay tribute to this radio format creation while still recognizing the groups that earned fame based on the exposure from *The Quiet Storm* DJs across the country.

INTRODUCTION
The Love Is Born

MY LOVE FOR R&B GROUPS STARTED ON A Saturday afternoon in my bed-room in Silver Spring, Maryland. I had an old-fashioned tape deck with a radio, and I was waiting for the latest New Edition hit song to come on the radio. Flipping between WKYS (93.9), WHUR (96.3), and OK100 (100.3), I patiently waited for almost three hours before I heard the DJ say that the brand-new New Edition song would be played in a few minutes. My heart started racing, and I prepared my tape deck for recording.

I glanced at the time and realized I had only 45 minutes before dinner (which I could not be late to or risk punishment). I hoped that the DJ was telling the truth and that the song would soon follow. The minutes ticked down, and finally, I heard the beginning of "Candy Girl." The quick bass line and the extended intro with the robotic voice got me excited that my wait had been worth it.

I quickly hit record and listened intently so that I could cut off the song as soon as the new song was blended in. Mission accomplished! I now had a recording of my new favorite song from a young R&B group that would end up having a timeless discography and be the soundtrack to most of my life.

As I was growing up in the Washington, DC, suburbs, my dad would wake my brother and me up on Saturday mornings with his favorite music playing from the stereo downstairs. We had an old-school setup where the speakers were wired downstairs in the basement and upstairs in the living room. Whenever music was played, it was heard throughout the entire house. On any given Saturday, I would be awakened to the sounds of the Isley Brothers, Luther Vandross, the Gap Band, Frankie Beverly & Maze, and so many other prominent R&B groups.

We evolved from vinyl records to cassette tapes and, eventually, when I signed my dad up for Columbia House, to CDs. My very first two 45s were "Cold Blooded" by Rick James and "Gonna Fly Now" from *Rocky*. As I got older, we used to have to drive all over the DC, Maryland, and Virginia area (the DMV, as it is called currently) to travel to my soccer games. The trips were entirely filled with music, first through the radio of a Nissan Datsun, then the stereo of a Toyota Camry, and finally through the speakers of a series of Volvo station wagons. This is where my love of music was confirmed, specifically my love of R&B groups.

As I entered my adolescent years, I began to listen more closely to the lyrics of the songs and determine how each song could be used to help me convince my current crush to go out with me. Guy, After 7, New Edition, and Atlantic Starr were mainstays on my telephone calls where I would call up my crushes and play love songs for them over the phone.

Unfortunately, it never worked out the way I imagined it. Gold stars for me for trying and thinking outside the box, though!

My love for music continued to grow stronger as I went to college at Howard University and used the music of SWV, Jodeci, Boyz II Men, and En Vogue to fill up slow-jam mixtapes that were distributed to select individuals. Once I entered adulthood and began to live and work all over the country, R&B groups continued to serve as the soundtrack to my life.

But by the mid-2000s, suddenly there were no new R&B groups to discover and support—none that I could find, anyway. Only the older groups were around, and they had entered the legacy phase of their careers. The shift was dramatic, but perhaps everyone had just missed the warning signs of what was to come

As we look back over the history of music in the United States, R&B groups have dominated all segments of our country's culture. Many of the notable historical events in the past eight decades have specific songs that trigger memories. The civil rights movement of the 1960s, Reaganomics in the 1980s, and Y2K fears in the late 1990s all had a lasting impact on our culture and were accompanied by music that defined the generation.

In 1965, the Impressions released a song called "People Get Ready" that has been largely recognized as one of the most significant songs in U.S. history. Martin Luther King Jr. named the song the unofficial anthem of the civil rights movement and often used the song to get people marching or to calm and comfort them. The song, written by Curtis Mayfield, had a gospel influence, and the overall composition displayed a growing sense of social and political awareness. In 2015, the song was selected for preservation in the National Recording Registry due to its "cultural, historic, or artistic significance."

In 1987, Prince released "Sign O' the Times," which addressed the state of the world at that time. The song addresses the AIDS epidemic, gang violence, escalating drug addictions, and the Space Shuttle disaster, among other issues. Examining the lyrics more closely shows specific instances of direct social commentary.

In this book, we will take a look at the most popular groups of each decade, starting in the 1950s and moving forward. Each chapter shares a brief story about the group being spotlighted, including how they were formed, the creation of their name, and the inspiration behind a few of their most popular songs. Finally, to close out each chapter, a list of their *Billboard* Hot 100 hits is included (with their top 20 hits bolded), along with a list of Grammy nominations (and wins), my personal take on the group, and my favorite songs and samples from each group.

This project was born in late 2019 as I continued to marvel at the lack of new R&B groups coming on to the music scene. As a DJ, I love to play R&B music, and I feel proud when I see the reaction of crowds of all ages when I drop a classic song from an R&B group. I am fearful of what the future holds for R&B groups, and I feel it is important to create a work of art that highlights their history and keeps the conversation going. When I attended Berklee College of Music for my master's degree in music business, we were tasked with selecting a final project and thesis to culminate our final semester, and it was a no-brainer for me to fully research and write about this topic.

The research in this book combines qualitative and quantitative research into a mixed methods methodology. Examining the quantitative side, I researched all of the R&B groups from the 1950s to the current day. I researched how many top 20 *Billboard* hits the groups earned, how many record sales they earned (gold and platinum singles/albums were the main focus), and then their number of notable performances. In terms of notable performances, when an African American would perform at the White House or on national television (such as on Johnny Carson's late-night show), that was considered a watershed moment and would qualify as a notable performance. Finally, as the last piece of quantitative research, I added the number of Grammy Awards each group received. Please note that the *Billboard* Hot 100 charts were not established until 1958 and *Billboard* pop charts were used in their place.

As we look at the qualitative portion of the book, the assumption is that there are definite reasons for a decline in R&B groups in the *Billboard* Top 20 charts. Very soon after we began the interview and historical review about this segment of the industry, it became obvious that there is a collection of events that led to the disappearance of R&B groups on the charts. The root causes of the decline are very complex and require a narrative approach that is supported by historical facts. The assumption that record labels played a major part in this decline is not completely incorrect. They were part of the worst type of perfect storm within the record industry.

When you look at the popular music of today, the foundation of each genre comes from R&B music. It could be the chords, choreography during live shows, marketing strategies, or how songs make you feel. It all stems from R&B music, and it is crucial that we acknowledge the historical impact and do our part to share the knowledge. As a fan of music, I believe that it is important that no aspects of music disappear from the conversation. This topic requires consistent discussion, as it cannot fade into oblivion and become a sidenote in history.

George Orwell is said to have said, "The most effective way to destroy people is to deny and obliterate their own understanding of their history." The goal is to continue to educate music lovers about R&B music's impact on the culture and historical events across the world. We cannot do that without having uncomfortable conversations reviewing what happened and why it happened. You are at the beginning of a historical review with an uncomfortable conversation at the end.

This book has evolved into an encyclopedic authority on R&B groups with over 60 different stories of risk-taking, struggle, deception, triumph, and resilience. More stories continue to be told in public, which means that this book will continue to grow and mature as more groups step forward to detail their journeys. As you turn each page, the goal is to deliver you alongside each group as they began their voyages into the world of music. Once the stories are complete, I share research-based conclusions on what happened, why it happened, and what the future holds for R&B groups.

It's time to head back to the 1950s and begin.

AUTHOR'S NOTE

IN EACH PART OF THE BOOK, THE GROUPS are listed in alphabetical order. This was the only determination in the order in which each group was listed.

Follow along with the musical journey through the decades via each playlist. One playlist follows my favorite songs and the second playlist follows my favorite samples. Note, the sample playlist will have the original song and the song that uses the sample.

Amani's Favorite
Songs on YouTube

Amani's Favorite
Samples on YouTube

Amani's Favorite
Songs on Spotify

Amani's Favorite
Samples on Spotify

1950's

From Top Left to Bottom Left (clockwise)
The Dominoes, The Chantels, Frankie
Lymon & the Teenagers and The Platters

Part One
THE 1950'S

AS THE 1950S BEGAN, THE WORLD WAS STILL recovering from the end of World War II. Early in the decade, rock and roll as a genre was born, and record companies continued some questionable practices across their entire business units. The solid-body electric guitar became commercially available, and pop, country, and R&B artists quickly adapted to this technological breakthrough. The LP (long playing) vinyl album and the 45 rpm single were introduced, soon becoming the standard for jukeboxes. Yes! Jukeboxes were the predominant way people listened to music in the 1950s, and jukebox plays were used to judge the success of a song and artist.

Rock and roll ruled the day in the 1950s, accounting for approximately 43% of all records sold. By the end of 1956, Elvis Presley would become the first artist to ever have nine singles in the Hot 100 at one time. The trend of white artists covering R&B songs and turning them into pop hits began to emerge and become commonplace.

Radio stations and record labels initially thought that a white face and a white voice were needed to sell records. Therefore, numerous R&B hits were covered by white artists who paid a licensing fee (what is now known as a mechanical license), and mysteriously, none of the licensing fee money made it into the pockets of the Black R&B groups. If you are curious about just how major this was, Google the name "Fred Parris" and the song "In the Still of the Night" (yes, that famous song!). Segregation was still alive and well, and many groups would have a "Black-only show" and a "white-only" show during tours through the South. The groups were instructed to not even look at a white person while performing, let alone dance with them. Groups were not allowed to stay in hotels or eat in most restaurants, and there were numerous instances of tour buses being shot at or stoned.

One of the primary metrics for the selection of the R&B groups featured in each section of the book is how well they performed on the *Billboard* Hot 100 chart. This book focuses on the Hot 100 chart instead of the R&B charts to show the impact that R&B groups had outside of their primary genre and how dominant the genre was on the charts during its peak, but the *Billboard* Hot 100 chart didn't come into existence until approximately August 4, 1958. It was the growing popularity of rock-and-roll music that sparked this change, and in less than a decade, numerous R&B groups appeared on this chart.

Today, the *Billboard* chart rankings are determined using a combination of radio airplay, sales data, and streaming data. Back in the 1950s, rankings were determined by assessing record sales and radio airplay. This method of recognizing hits was not completely foolproof, especially when you factor in the rampant racism, payola, and the plethora of white groups who would immediately rerecord a R&B song that held promise and sell the song off as their own. Despite these facts, the *Billboard* chart is one of the very few ranking sources that covers every decade in this book and remains a respectable and trusted source of historical information within the music business.

Overall, the 1950s were at the genesis of the major R&B group movement. Many groups were able to make it from singing doo-wop music on the corner to the studio and release music. Although record sales were limited and did not reach levels that present-day artists do, these groups must be listed and honored for starting down the pathway to success

📑 **NOTE:** The Grammy Awards did not begin until 1959. Therefore, you will see several groups in this section of the book that received no nominations.

Chapter 1

. . . .

BILLY WARD
AND HIS DOMINOES

Billy Ward and His Dominoes pose for a 1957 portrait. The band includes (L-R) Milton Grayson, Cliff Givens, Billy Ward, Milton Merle, Eugene Mumford. (Photo by Michael Ochs Archives/ Getty Images)

THE DOMINOES ARE REMEMBERED AS MUCH FOR THEIR own music as they are for launching the careers of stars Clyde McPhatter and Jackie Wilson.

The group was founded by Billy Ward, who was raised in the church—his father was a preacher and his mother sang in the choir. After spending much of his childhood in Philadelphia, Ward moved to New York, where he attended the Juilliard School of Music before becoming an arranger and vocal coach.

He was encouraged by songwriter Rose Ann Marks to form a vocal group, and he held public auditions. Those efforts didn't go very far.

As writer Jay Warner wrote, "Ward realized the best way to ensure a stable and motivated group was to assemble the best of his pupils. So it was that in 1950 the Ques were born." The members had gospel backgrounds.

The lead tenor of the Ques was identified as Clyde Ward, Billy's brother, but in fact, it was McPhatter. Other early members included tenor Charlie White, baritone William Joseph Lamont, and Bill Brown on bass.

McPhatter had performed in the Apollo Theater's amateur night, and so did the Ques, who ended up winning. An appearance on *Arthur Godfrey's Talent Scouts* followed, and soon after, buoyed by all of the attention, the group signed with King Records.

With the deal came a new name, one that Ward had previously used: the Dominoes.

The group's first big hit was "Do Something for Me," a song that showcased the Dominoes' prowess in blues and gospel.

But "Sixty Minute Man" propelled the Dominoes to a new stratosphere—and became one of the first R&B crossover hits. The song, written by Ward and

Marks, tells the story of "Lovin' Dan" bragging about his romantic prowess with not at all subtle lyrics.

The song, instead of leading with McPhatter, featured Brown's bass voice. It was edgy and provocative. And it was a smash hit, topping the Black R&B charts and charting on the white-dominated pop charts.

The Dominoes followed up with singles like "I Am With You," "Heart to Heart," and "Have Mercy Baby." Their string of singles and extensive touring raised their national recognition.

But frictions were brewing, fueled in part by Ward's strict leadership and handling of group finances, leading to a series of lineup changes. In 1953, the velvet-voiced McPhatter decided he wanted to strike out on his own—he wound up forming the Drifters. There is speculation that McPhatter was actually fired from the Dominoes, and there has never been a confirmation of what exactly happened.

Ward needed a replacement for McPhatter, and he found his next vocal lead in Wilson, a Michigan native nicknamed "Mr. Excitement," who would achieve solo success in the years to follow. Wilson joined the group after having a successful audition at the Fox Theater in Detroit and soon adopted a new stage name—Jackie Wilson. Wilson's first single with the Dominoes was "You Can't Keep a Good Man Down." Later that year came "Rags To Riches," a remake of the Tony Bennett song, which rose up the pop charts.

Despite Wilson's soaring vocals, the group bounced around from one record label to the next—Jubilee to Decca, then later, Liberty Records.

Wilson left the group in 1957, and Eugene Mumford filled the role on singles like "Star Dust" and "Deep Purple." The group's lineup was constantly evolving into the 1960s, with members endlessly coming and going.

The Dominoes were one of the 1950s' most influential groups—their combination of gospel-influenced harmonies and R&B rhythms helped shape the doo-wop sound and set the stage for the emergence of rock and roll.

Their two most famous lead singers were pretty special, too.

🏆 GRAMMY NOMINATIONS: 0

Photo of Clyde McPhatter, the Dominoes and James Van Loan and Billy Ward and Joe Lamont and David McNeil; Posed group portrait L-R Clyde McPhatter, James Van Loan, Billy Ward, Joe Lamont, and David McNeil (Photo by Gilles Petard/Redferns)

Billboard Hot 100 CHARTING SINGLES

Here is a list of the Dominoes' *Billboard* Hot 100 hits in chronological order.[1]

Song	Year Released	*Billboard* Hot 100/*Billboard* Pop Peak Position
"Sixty Minute Man"	1951	17
"St. Therese of the Roses"	1955	27
"Star Dust"	1957	12
"Deep Purple"	1957	18
"Jennie Lee"	1958	55

My Favorite Billy Ward and His Dominoes Songs

❯ "Sixty Minute Man"   ❯ "Star Dust"

My Favorite Billy Ward and His Dominoes Samples

To date, there are no samples of Billy Ward and His Dominoes. Perhaps as time goes on, some artists will dig into the crates and sample some of their music. If that happens, I will revise this section in future editions.

My Take

This group had several famous lead singers who would go on to be legends in R&B. The skill of identifying these singers to bring into the band is underrated and should be noted. As you will see with many of the bands in the 1950s and 1960s, I learned about them through completing the research for this book.

---

1 The chart position for "Sixty Minute Man" could not be officially confirmed, so an estimate was included.

Chapter 2

. . . .

THE CHANTELS

1957: (L-R) Sonia Goring, Rene Minus, Arlene Smith and Jackie Landry (seated) of the R&B vocal group the Chantels pose for a portrait session in 1957 in New York City, New York. (Photo by Michael Ochs Archives/Getty Images)

THE CHANTELS WERE ONE OF THE FIRST BLACK girl groups to reach national success.

The group formed in the Bronx, New York. Members Arlene Smith, Sonia Goring Wilson, Renée Minus White, Jackie Landry Jackson, and Lois Harris attended high school together. Unlike many 1950s groups, the Chantels didn't have a gospel foundation. The friends just loved singing together.

Their songs dealt with themes like young love and heartbreak.

The Chantels signed with End Records and George Goldner in 1957 after being discovered by Richard Barrett.

"He's Gone," released in 1957, was inspired by a poem penned by Smith. Hits from other female groups were often written by men (and in fact, many Chantels songs written by Smith were credited to others, like Goldner).

They followed up "He's Gone" with their biggest hit, "Maybe," which reached number 15 on the *Billboard* Hot 100 chart in 1958 on the strength of Smith's powerful vocals, which carried sentiments of self-doubt and longing. The song was later listed at number 199 on *Rolling Stone*'s 500 Greatest Songs of All Time.

"At 16, Smith wrote and sang lead on this towering doo-wop song, a template for a generation of girl groups," *Rolling Stone* wrote. "The single was first credited to label owner George Goldner, but now the world knows better."

But the group's success sputtered, and in 1959, the Chantels were dropped by End.

Arlene Smith pursued a solo career—she was replaced by Annette Smith— while Harris went to college. The quartet shifted between record labels and had another big hit with "Look in My Eyes" with Carlton Records in 1961.

The members of the *Chantels* carried forward in the decades that followed, continuing to reach audiences with their doo-wop sound and serving as torchbearers for female groups that followed behind them.

♔ GRAMMY NOMINATIONS: 0

1958: (L-R) Arlene Smith, Sonia Goring, Rene Minus, Jackie Landry and Lois Harris of the R&B vocal group the Chantels pose for a portrait session in 1958 in New York City, New York. (Photo by Michael Ochs Archives/Getty Images)

Billboard Hot 100 CHARTING SINGLES

Here is a list of the Chantels' *Billboard* Hot 100 hits in chronological order.

Song	Year Released	*Billboard* Hot 100/*Billboard* Pop Peak Position
"He's Gone"	1957	71
"Maybe"	1958	15
"Every Night (I Pray)"	1958	39
"I Love You So"	1958	42
"Summer's Love"	1959	93
"Look in My Eyes"	1961	14
"Well I Told You"	1961	29
"Eternally"	1963	77

🔥 *My Favorite The Chantels Songs*

❯ "Maybe" ❯ "Look in My Eyes" ❯ "He's Gone"

🖤 *My Favorite the Chantels Samples*

- •• "Suffocated Love" by Tricky sampled "Look in My Eyes"
- •• "Out for Treats" by Ghettosocks sampled "It's Just Me"

⬇ *My Take*

The Chantels were pioneers as one of the first Black girl groups, *and* they had a songwriter in Arlene Smith. Smith wrote several of their hits, even though she did not get the writing credit or royalties for her work. I believe the Chantels' success (albeit brief) was the inspiration for the Supremes coming a decade later and earning massive success.

Chapter 3

. . . .

THE CLOVERS

Photo of the Clovers; 1951 - Harold Winley, Bill Harris, Harold Lucas, Matthew McQuater and Buddy Bailey (front) (Photo by Gilles Petard/Redferns)

The Clovers had lots of talent and a little bit of luck.

The vocal group formed as a trio in 1946 in Washington, DC, with initial members baritone Harold "Hal" Lucas, tenor Billy Shelton, and bass Thomas Woods. The founding members had all attended Armstrong High School together.

Fellow classmate John "Buddy" Bailey made the group a foursome, so for a while, the group became known as the Four Clovers. A neighborhood friend, Matthew McQuater, joined the Clovers in 1948—Shelton left soon after—while they connected with bass Harold Winley on the amateur radio show circuit. Winley's joining the Clovers meant Woods was out.

The Clovers honed their sound, initially singing pop songs, and solidified their lineup before they were discovered around 1950 by talent scout and producer Lou Krefetz.

"I told them they ought to sing the blues," Krefetz recalled years later.

The producer was able to get the Clovers a recording session in New York with Rainbow Records. From the recording session came "Yes Sir, That's My Baby" and "When You Come Back To Me." Rainbow poorly promoted the record, but as the group was aiming for wider attention, they saw Bill Harris, a blues and classical guitarist, perform at a jazz club and asked him to join the Clovers (he agreed). The addition of Harris brought the Clovers a new edge and musicality.

The Clovers were primed for something big at the same time that Atlantic Records—led by founder Ahmet Ertegun—was looking for new acts. The group signed with Atlantic in 1951, which proved pivotal for their career. At Atlantic, the Clovers began working on more mature material with influential songwriters such as Jesse Stone, aka Charles Calhoun, the writer of "Shake, Rattle and Roll."

The group released a string of successful singles that blended rhythm and blues with elements of doo-wop and rock and roll. Songs like "Don't You Know I Love You," "Fool, Fool, Fool," and "One Mint Julep" propelled them to the forefront of the music scene and solidified their status as a leading vocal group.

Bailey's being drafted into the army created some complications—but by the time he was discharged and rejoined the group in 1954, the Clovers effectively had two lead vocalists in Bailey and Billy Mitchell, who had joined the band in 1953. They leaned into a ballad style. The hits continued through 1956 with songs like "Blue Velvet" and "Devil or Angel" that climbed the charts, and later in the decade they worked with a young Quincy Jones on several tracks.

In fact, many of the group's songs were later covered by other artists. "Blue Velvet," for example, became a smash hit years later for Bobby Vinton.

Things started splintering by 1957, when the Clovers' Atlantic contract wasn't renewed and they joined Krefetz's Poplar Records label. The Clovers recorded an LP for Poplar, and after Krefetz joined United Artists Records, he connected the group with the famed songwriting duo of Jerry Leiber and Mike Stoller. The pair provided a ditty they'd written about a lovestruck lad who keeps striking out with women, so he searches for a potion to make someone fall in love with him. The protagonist visits a Romani woman, Madame Rue, who gives him a bottle of "Love Potion No. 9." However, instead of attracting love, the potion leads the protagonist into a series of unexpected and comical encounters, including kissing a police officer, who winds up breaking his potion bottle.

The quirky song was a smash hit for the Clovers, and they took it to number 23 on the *Billboard* Hot 100 chart in 1959. The song has been covered by numerous artists, including the Searchers, and it remains a beloved classic.

The Clovers were never again able to recapture their chart success of the early 1950s, though, and by the dawn of the 1960s, the group's members were drifting apart.

"They just got tired of each other," Krefetz recalled years later. "You see, I used to be the leader; I called the shots. When they started calling their own shots, that's when they broke up."

Even though the Clovers' time at the top of the charts didn't last, their sustained run of success in the early 1950s—fueled by being one of the first R&B groups to achieve crossover success (appealing to both Black and white audiences) and bridging the gap between gospel and R&B—makes them one of the decade's enduring influences. The crossover success should not be discounted, as the Clovers reached their peak in popularity during a time of racial segregation in the United States. In addition, many of the Clovers' songs were embraced by early rock 'n' roll artists and helped shape the sound of the genre.

♔ GRAMMY NOMINATIONS: 0

Photo of the Clovers; 1956 - Billy Mitchell, Matthew McQuater, Buddy Bailey, Harold Winley, and Bill Harris (Photo by Gilles Petard/Redferns)

billboard hot 100 CHARTING SINGLES

Here is a list of the Clovers' *Billboard* Hot 100 hits in chronological order.[2]

Song	Year Released	/Billboard Pop
"Don't You Know I Love You"	1951	1
"Fool, Fool, Fool"	1951	1
"One Mint Julep"	1952	2
"Ting-A-Ling"	1952	2
"Hey, Miss Fannie"	1952	3
"Crawlin' "	1953	4
"Good Lovin' "	1953	4
"Lovey Dovey"	1954	2
"Little Mama"	1954	7
"Blue Velvet"	1955	14
"In the Morning Time"	1956	25
"Devil or Angel"	1956	37
"Love Potion No. 9"	1959	23

⬤ My Favorite *The Clovers* Songs

❯ "Love Potion No. 9"   ❯ "In the Morning Time"   ❯ "Devil or Angel"

2   Note that research has inconsistent results for the specific peak positions and we used an estimation when including the information.

♥ *My Favorite the Clovers Samples*

→ "The Joker" by Steve Miller Band sampled "Lovey Dovey"

⊙ *My Take*

The Clovers were one of the first groups to experience crossover success, which is cool and notable. I am particularly impressed that early rock-and-roll artists embraced their sound. I do love the witty lyrics for "Love Potion No. 9." Also, look how early Quincy Jones was working with R&B acts and the impact he had over numerous decades.

Chapter 4

....

THE COASTERS

The Coasters (L-R Carl Gardner, Billy Nunn, Leon Hughes and Billy Guy) pose for a studio photo in 1956 in Los Angeles, California. (Photo by Michael Ochs Archive/Getty Images)

THE MEMBERS OF THE COASTERS MAINLY HAILED FROM the West Coast—thus, the group's nickname—but they would find their greatest success after crossing the country and singing about everyday events.

The Coasters achieved crossover popularity in the late 1950s with playful songs such as "Yakety Yak."

The group originated from another vocal group, the Robins, that rose to prominence in California behind hits like "Riot in Cell Block #9." The Robins were managed by Lester Sill, who formed Spark Records with the famed songwriting and producing duo of Jerry Leiber and Mike Stoller, who had a knack for writing catchy, humorous, and narrative-driven songs like "Hound Dog."

Atlantic Records bought up Spark's catalog in 1955, and along with the purchase came Leiber and Stoller—and half of the Robins, Carl Gardner and Bobby Nunn (the other members didn't want to join the East Coast label). So the Coasters were formed with Gardner and Nunn, along with two new members, Leon Hughes and Billy Guy.

Under the guidance of Leiber and Stoller and with the support of Atlantic Records, the Coasters released a series of R&B hits, starting with "Down in Mexico."

After lots of touring, then resettling in New York, the group found their voice with the double-sided hits of "Young Blood" and "Searchin'." Other popular songs followed, including "Yakety Yak," "Charlie Brown," and "Poison Ivy"—songs that showcased their energetic vocal harmonies and whimsical storytelling lyrics.

The Coasters stood out from other 1950s groups because of their teen-focused (rather than love-centered) songs and singing style. As Jay Warner wrote in his book *American Singing Groups*, "While most of the other '50s acts were smoothing out their 'oohs' and 'ahs' behind the lead vocal, the Coasters were often singing in a raunchy unison or backing up the lead with more of a call-

and-response than a doo-wop or blow harmony accompaniment."

"Yakety Yak"—which taps into the rebellious spirit of rock-loving teenagers and the often tense relationship they have with their parents—features silly, simple lyrics describing an exchange between a parent and a child.

The song's most famous lines were delivered by bass vocalist Dub Jones, who joined the group in 1958 along with Cornell Gunter.

Another of the Coasters' enduring hits, "Charlie Brown," was named after the lovable but hapless star of Charles M. Schulz's popular *Peanuts* comic strip.

"Poison Ivy," meanwhile, features lots of innuendos and tongue-in-cheek references to a woman who's trouble, comparing her to the plant that can cause an itchy rash.

As Leiber explained, "Pure and simple, 'Poison Ivy' is a metaphor for a sexually transmitted disease—or the clap—hardly a topic for a song that hit the top 10 in the spring of 1959. But the more we wrote, the less we understood why the public bought what it bought. It didn't make sense, but it didn't matter. We were having fun."

The Coasters' unique style and witty storytelling set them apart from other vocal groups of the era. Their star burned bright during the late 1950s—but as music tastes and the group's lineup continued to change into the 1960s, the Coasters faded from popularity.

While the Coasters did not officially break up, they underwent different iterations and had several lineup changes over the years, while various members continued to perform under the Coasters' name.

In 1987, the Coasters became the first group inducted into the Rock & Roll

Hall of Fame. As the hall notes, "Witty. Engaging. Hilarious. Infectious. The Coasters are in a league of their own."

🏆 GRAMMY NOMINATIONS: 2
🏆 GRAMMY WINS: 0

Studio Photo of Leon Hughes and Carl Gardner and Bobby Nunn and Coasters and Billy Guy, Posed studio group portrait L-R Bobby Nunn, Leon Hughes (front), Carl Gardner and Billy Guy (front) (Photo by Echoes/Redferns)

Billboard Hot 100 CHARTING SINGLES

Here is a list of the Coasters' *Billboard* Hot 100 hits in chronological order.

Song	Year Released	*Billboard* Hot 100 Peak Position
➲ "One Kiss Led to Another"	1956	73
➲ "Searchin'"	1957	3

Song	Year Released	*Billboard* Hot 100 Peak Position
"Young Blood"	1957	8
"Yakety Yak"	1958	1
"Charlie Brown"	1959	2
"Along Came Jones"	1959	9
"Poison Ivy"	1959	7
"What About Us"	1959	17
"Bésame Mucho"	1959	70
"Run Red Run"	1960	36
"Wake Me, Shake Me"	1960	51
"Shoppin' For Clothes"	1960	83
"Wait a Minute"	1961	37
"Little Egypt (Ying-Yang)"	1961	23
"Girls! Girls! Girls!"	1961	96
"T'Ain't Nothin' to Me"	1962	64

My Favorite the Coasters Songs

❯ "Yakety Yak" ❯ "Charlie Brown" ❯ "Poison Ivy"

My Favorite the Coasters Samples

- "Skinz" by Pete Rock & C. L. Smooth feat. Grand Puba sampled "Down Home Girl"
- "Yakety Yak" by 2 Live Crew sampled "Yakety Yak"
- "They Want EFX" by Das EFX sampled "Charlie Brown"

⊙ *My Take*

The Coasters started off strong and five straight top 10 Billboard Hot 100 hits, including two classics. The high profile artists and producers that sampled their music shows just how impactful they were in the music industry. Also, it is import to note that they were the first group inducted into the Rock & Roll Hall of Fame. The is very significant.

Chapter 5

· · · · · · ·

THE DRIFTERS

CIRCA 1970: Photo of Drifters Photo by Michael Ochs Archives/Getty Images

MEMBERS OF THE DRIFTERS WERE CONSTANTLY DRIFTING IN and out of the group. But no other early R&B groups matched their success or longevity.

The Drifters were born in 1953 when Clyde McPhatter left—or was fired from—the Dominoes. Ahmet Ertegun, the head of Atlantic, discovered that McPhatter had left the Dominoes when he went to hear the group perform in New York City and saw that McPhatter was missing.

Ertegun saw an opportunity. "Ahmet went uptown like a shot, found Clyde McPhatter, and signed him up," producer Jerry Wexler said in the book *In the Groove* by author Ted Fox.

The Drifters formed around McPhatter; at the onset they were often identified as Clyde McPhatter & the Drifters or Clyde McPhatter's Drifters, as a result of the singer's popularity. Many of the group's early members—such as tenors David Baughan and William Anderson, baritone David Baldwin, and bass James Johnson—had gospel background similar to McPhatter's.

But after the group's early recordings fell short, McPhatter brought in new singers to back him up. The next iteration of the Drifters included Bill Pinkney, Andrew "Bubba" Thrasher and Gerhart "Gay" Thrasher, and Willie Ferbee.

In September 1953, the group released its first single, "Money Honey." It was a smash, spending 11 weeks at the top of *Billboard*'s R&B chart. The song tells the story of a guy in need of cash who calls the woman he loves and asks for some money. She gets upset, turns his request down, and informs him that the romance is over. She parts by saying she selected another man because he had money.

As the *New York Age* wrote, "In the short span of six months, Clyde McPhatter and his Drifters have made two Apollo appearances, waxed 1953's hottest record [Money Honey] and have edged out virtually every other vocal group in popularity."

A string of hits followed for the Drifters—including "Lucille," the salacious "Honey Love," and "White Christmas," which also crossed over onto the pop charts. But McPhatter's involvement with the group waned after he was drafted for the army, and by 1955 he was out of the Drifters altogether.

In McPhatter's absence, group manager George Treadwell took more and more control of the operations—and money—and due to the low wages, members cycled in and out of the group.

By 1958, McPhatter's Drifters were all but gone. But Treadwell had already made touring commitments in the Drifters' name, and he needed to have a band appear. He struck a deal with a New York-based group, the Five Crowns, to take on the Drifters' name.

The new Drifters—including a tenor lead named Benjamin Earl Nelson—hit the road. This was great publicity for the group and much more money than they had been making as the Five Crowns.

While on tour, Nelson chose to change his stage name to King, his uncle's last name. He became Ben E. King.

When it was time for the new Drifters to record, King brought along a song he had written, "There Goes My Baby." The group—recording for Atlantic—were paired with the songwriting duo of Leiber and Stoller to work on the song.

The production pair relied on a rhythmic Brazilian *baion* beat and scored the song with four violins and a cello. During the recording, "We noticed a kettle drum in the corner of the studio," Leiber and Stoller wrote later. The drummer had never played that type of drum before, so he kept playing the same pitch, "creating a kind of harmonic mud. Then, of course, the baion beat was bringing everything to a boil."

The busy instrumental paired with King's soaring vocals to produce a special sound. But Atlantic executives, especially producer Jerry Wexler, hated the song. "It's dog meat," Wexler told Leiber, calling it "an overpriced production that sounds like a radio caught between two stations." The executive, according to Leiber and Stoller, even spit his tuna fish sandwich against the wall. But the duo wasn't deterred. They spent a few hours remixing the song, and despite Wexler's concerns, the song was released as a single.

The song, as the Rock & Roll Hall of Fame later noted, "not only gave the Drifters a distinctive sound and a radio identity but also represented a milestone in the infiltration of R&B into mainstream American pop."

More timeless hits with more conventional arrangements followed, such as "Save the Last Dance for Me" and "This Magic Moment." King's majestic voice—paired with songwriting by Doc Pomus and Mort Shuman—perfectly captured sentiments of longing and lost love.

"Save the Last Dance for Me" was written by Pomus, who contracted polio as a child, which left him unable to dance. During his wedding reception, he had observed his bride dancing with their guests while he sat in his wheelchair, unable to join her.

King's turn with the group only lasted for about a year—the same frictions about money were always brewing—and he was destined for solo stardom. Into his place stepped Rudy Lewis, who served as lead on successful singles like "Up on the Roof" and "On Broadway."

Lewis was also slated to serve as lead singer on "Under the Boardwalk," a song about summer love, but he died just before the recording session. Johnny Moore recorded the lead vocals in his place. It would be the Drifters' final *Billboard* top 10 hit, but the group—in some arrangement and many splintered forms—would continue on for decades.

The Drifters, encouraged by the group's success in England, even moved across the Atlantic and released four more albums during the 1970s.

The Drifters' innovative sound and style set the standard for the R&B artists who followed. Their two-decade run on the charts and their subsequent international touring success shows the consistency in their music and their ability to evolve while staying relevant as the R&B genre expanded.

♔ GRAMMY NOMINATIONS: 1
♔ GRAMMY WINS: 0

New York - 1967: R&B group The Drifters (clockwise from top) Rick Sheppard, Bill Davis aka Abdul Samad, Johnny Moore, Charlie Thomas and Bill Fredricks pose for a portrait in 1967 in New York City, New York. (Photo by Michael Ochs Archives/Getty Images)

billboard hot 100 CHARTING SINGLES

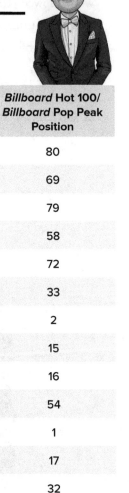

Here is a list of the Drifters' *Billboard* Hot 100 hits in chronological order.

Song	Year Released	*Billboard* Hot 100/ *Billboard* Pop Peak Position
"White Christmas"	1954	80
"Fools Fall in Love"	1957	69
"Hypnotized"	1957	79
"Drip Drop"	1957	58
"Moonlight Bay"	1957	72
"(If You Cry) True Love, True Love"	1957	33
"There Goes My Baby"	1959	2
"Dance with Me"	1959	15
"This Magic Moment"	1960	16
"Lonely Winds"	1960	54
"Save the Last Dance for Me"	1960	1
"I Count the Tears"	1961	17
"Some Kind of Wonderful"	1961	32
"Please Stay"	1961	14
"Sweets for My Sweet"	1961	16
"Room Full of Tears"	1961	72
"Stranger on the Shore"	1961	73
"When My Little Girl Is Smiling"	1962	28

Song	Year Released	Billboard Hot 100/ Billboard Pop Peak Position
➤ "Up on the Roof"	1962	5
➤ "On Broadway"	1963	9
➤ "Rat Race"	1963	71
➤ "Under the Boardwalk"	1964	4
➤ "I'll Take You Home"	1964	25
➤ "I've Got Sand In My Shoes"	1964	33
➤ "Saturday Night at the Movies"	1964	18
➤ "Follow Me"	1965	91
➤ "I'll Take You Where Music's Playing"	1965	51
➤ "At the Club"	1966	43
➤ "Come on Over to My Place"	1966	60
➤ "Baby What I Mean"	1966	62
➤ "Memories Are Made Of This"	1967	48

🔥 My Favorite the Drifters Songs

➤ "Under the Boardwalk" ➤ "On Broadway" ➤ "Up on the Roof"

💜 My Favorite the Drifters Samples

- •• "Sweets for My Sweet" by Super Cat sampled "Sweets for My Sweet"
- •• "Lemon Pound Cake" by Afroman sampled "Under the Boardwalk"
- •• "The Boardwalk" by Jonathan Hay with Twista, Ranna Royce & Mike Smith sampled "Under the Boardwalk"

⊙ My Take

Don't let the lack of *Billboard* Hot 100 hits minimize the impact the Drifters had on R&B. "Money Honey" never charted on the Hot 100 charts but is now on *Rolling Stone*'s top 500 songs of all time. "Under the Boardwalk" is a timeless and classic song. As these charts continued to evolve in the 1950s, this group was experiencing massive success that became timeless as the genre matured over the decades. Another cool accomplishment is the volume of singles that hit the *Billboard* Hot 100 in one single year.

Chapter 6

·······

THE "5" ROYALES

Circa 1955: R&B group the "5" Royales (also known as the "5" Royals) Top: Jimmy Moore, Middle L-R: Obadiah Carter, Eugene Tanner, Johnny Tanner and Bottom: Lowman Pauling pose for a portrait circa 1955. (Photo by Michael Ochs Archives/Getty Images)

You've probably heard lots of "5" Royales songs, but you might not have realized it. Their music has been covered by the likes of Ray Charles, James Brown, Aretha Franklin, and Mick Jagger.

While fame and visibility largely eluded the group, the "5" Royales represent a crucial step in the development of R&B music.

The group formed in Winston-Salem, North Carolina, in the 1940s, focusing on gospel before shifting to secular music. Original members included Lowman and Clarence Pauling, Otto Jeffries, Johnny Tanner, and William Samuels. Lowman Pauling served as the group's songwriter and driving force—and, when he was given the chance, his guitar licks took the group to new heights.

The group formed under the name Royal Sons Gospel Group in Winston-Salem and found regional success before going to New York and recording for Apollo Records. In due time, they shifted from gospel to R&B and became the "5" Royales with a lineup of Lowman Pauling, Tanner, Obadiah Carter, James Moore, and Jeffries, who would later be replaced by Eugene Tanner.

During a portion of the band's run, the group had six members. Despite this fact, the "5" (with the quotes) was included in their name on purpose to help distinguish this group from two other groups with *the Royals* in their names that were releasing music during the same time period.

Some of the group's early singles include "Baby, Don't Do It" and "Help Me Somebody." "Baby, Don't Do It" set a standard for songs by the "5" Royales. It was sexually tinged, gritty, and backed by the Charlie Ferguson Orchestra. The "5" Royales had come a long way from their gospel roots!

" 'Help Me Somebody,' " the Rock & Roll Hall of Fame wrote, "featured the Royales' formidable tenor Johnny Tanner, a treasure of a vocalist who burrowed heart and soul into the gospel-drenched, world-weary plea, with the group draped around him in support. It's the seminal soul moment; in it, you can hear the voice to come of Atlantic-era Ray Charles."

The "5" Royales, more and more, embraced salacious and sultry themes, such as the sexually suggestive "Laundromat Blues," which featured spicy lyrics and *oooohs* from the backing singers. The lyrics included a play on words with dirty clothes and the young lady's laundry machine.

But as the "5" Royales were gaining traction, there always seemed to be other factors chipping away at their progress, such as when another group out of Detroit tried impersonating the group.

After their mentor, Carl LeBow, signed with King Records, the "5" Royales found themselves embroiled in a lawsuit over their song rights. Subsequent singles with session musicians failed to find their stride.

During a 1957 recording session for "Think," Pauling picked up his guitar and started playing; the ensuing sound—explosive and raw—changed the group's direction and shaped popular music.

Another classic, "Dedicated To The One I Love" was recorded months later.

But despite all of the group's musicality, chart success didn't follow. The "5" Royales shifted from one record company to another before splitting up in 1965.

Their legacy lives on through countless other artists who followed their lead— generations of musicians inspired and influenced by an under-the-radar R&B group that shifted popular music forever.

♩ GRAMMY NOMINATIONS: 0

1957: The album cover for The "5" Royales 1957 album *Dedicated To You*
(Photo by Michael Ochs Archives/Getty Images)

Billboard Hot 100 CHARTING SINGLES

The "5" Royales did not have any songs that charted on the *Billboard* Hot 100. They were primarily known for their influence on other artists and their impact on the development of rhythm and blues and soul music.

🔥 *My Favorite "5" Royales Songs*

❯ "Think" ❯ "Laundromat Blues" ❯ "They Don't Know"

💜 *My Favorite "5" Royales Samples*

•• "Think (About It)" by Lyn Collins sampled "Think"

⊙ *My Take*

The "5" Royales were inducted into the Rock & Roll Hall of Fame in 2015, and based on my research, this was a long time coming. The fact that many famous artists who were mentioned in the introduction of this chapter covered their songs lets you know their influence in R&B and other genres (particularly rock and roll). They were innovators who were ahead of their time—the guitar work of Lowman Pauling was particularly innovative.

Chapter 7

....

FRANKIE LYMON & THE TEENAGERS

30th June 1956: Popular young American vocal group Frankie Lymon and The Teenagers; 16-year-old high school students Jimmy Merchant, Joseph Negroni, Sherman Garnes and Herman Santiago, with 13-year-old junior high school pupil Frankie Lymon, second from right, who wrote the lyrics to their hit "Why Do Fools Fall In Love." (Photo by Keystone/Getty Images)

THE METEORIC SUCCESS OF FRANKIE LYMON & THE Teenagers wasn't sustainable—but oh, what voices and impact on popular music.

The trendsetting group formed in 1954 in New York City's Washington Heights section, where they had grown up. Jimmy Merchant and Sherman Garnes, classmates at Edward W. Stitt Junior High School, formed a group together, and they later enlisted two other neighborhood kids, Herman Santiago and Joe Negroni.

The foursome practiced together and started performing at talent shows. At one show, they were approached by Lymon—all of 12 years old—who requested to sing together.

From there, they began performing together more frequently, with Lymon as first tenor (Santiago was initially lead vocalist).

Despite his diminutive size and childlike appearance, Lymon had been forced to grow up fast.

"I never was a child, although I was billed in every theater and auditorium where I appeared as a child star," Lymon told Art Peters for *Ebony* magazine in 1967. "I was a man when I was 11 years old, doing everything that most men do. In the neighborhood where I lived, there was no time to be a child. There were five children in my family and my folks had to scuffle to make ends meet. My father was a truck driver and my mother worked as a domestic in white folks' homes. While kids my age were playing stickball and marbles, I was working in the corner grocery store carrying orders to help pay the rent."

The group, cycling through names like the Earth Angels, the Ermines, the Coup De Villes, and the Premiers, continued practicing together. As the story goes, one night a neighbor—after listening to them practicing the same songs again and again—suggested the boys write some new material and gave them his girlfriend's poems as inspiration.

One of the poems included the words "Why do birds sing so gay?" The teens worked on developing a song.

Pretty soon, the youngsters caught the ear of Richard Barrett, a singer and talent scout for Gee Records. Barrett introduced the group to Gee's president, George Goldner, and the group was signed. At Goldner's suggestion, the title "Why Do Birds Sing So Gay?" was changed to "Why Do Fools Fall in Love."

Goldner was especially taken by the pint-sized Lymon, whose angelic voice and stage presence belied his age. There were lots of teen-centered groups popping up, but this one had something special.

By 1955, the group was recording with saxophonist Jimmy Wright and his instrumental band.

As journalist Marv Goldberg wrote, "They worked on these two tunes all day and far into the night, doing around 25 takes of 'Why Do Fools Fall in Love.' "

But what to call them? The Premiers wouldn't work…the label settled on the Teenagers.

Their first single, "Why Do Fools Fall in Love," became a smash hit, reaching the top of the R&B charts and peaking at number 6 on the *Billboard* pop chart. It catapulted the group—stylized as Frankie Lymon & the Teenagers or Frankie Lymon & *His* Teenagers—to instant stardom. Movies. Bandstand. A national tour and performances in London.

Another hit single, "I Want You to Be My Girl," followed, along with other solid songs like "The ABC's of Love."

But it was all too fast too soon for the teenagers, especially Lymon. The group fractured as a result of all of the attention on Lymon, and the angel-voiced singer began recording solo.

Lymon's career, and soon his life, were undone by a worsening heroin addiction.

The Teenagers continued forward with different lead vocalists, struggling to recapture the magic of their time with Lymon.

Lymon was attempting to make a comeback of his own when, in 1968, he died of an overdose. He was only 25 years old.

While their success was fleeting, Frankie Lymon & the Teenagers left a massive impact on the music industry. Lymon's high-pitched vocals and commanding stage presence inspired and guided a generation of singers that followed him, including Stevie Wonder, Smokey Robinson, and Michael Jackson.

♔ GRAMMY NOMINATIONS: 0

Photo of Frankie Lymon and Teenagers Photo by Michael Ochs Archives/Getty Images

Billboard **Hot 100** CHARTING SINGLES

Here is a list of Frankie Lymon & the Teenagers'
Billboard Hot 100 hits in chronological order.

Song	Year Released	*Billboard* Hot 100/ *Billboard* Pop Peak Position
"Why Do Fools Fall in Love"	1956	6
"I Want You to Be My Girl"	1956	13
"I Promise to Remember"	1956	57
"The ABC's of Love"	1957	77
"Goody Goody"	1957	20

My Favorite Frankie Lymon & the Teenagers Songs

- "Why Do Fools Fall in Love"
- "Fools Rush In (Where Angels Fear to Tread)"
- "Honey Honey (You Don't Know)"

My Favorite Frankie Lymon & the Teenagers Samples

- "This Far" by Mike Dreams sampled "Why Do Fools Fall in Love"
- "Introduction" by Joni Mitchell sampled "I'm Not a Juvenile Delinquent"

⊙ *My Take*

The rapid rise and fall of this group is heartbreaking. If they could have maintained some longevity, they could have preceded groups like the Commodores and the Temptations as the gold standard of R&B groups. In 1957, Frankie Lymon appeared on the famous Alan Freed live ABC TV show *The Big Beat* and danced with a white teenage girl while performing, causing significant issues that included the subsequent canceling of the show. If you search for this on YouTube, you can find some clips. This was an unintentional barrier that Lymon broke through. Keep in mind that ABC executives had previously instructed the white teenagers attending to not dance at all during the performance. The facts and stories further enhance the impact that Frankie Lymon & the Teenagers had on R&B music and the world. Lymon was ahead of his time as a singer and performer. Too bad drugs got the best of him at only age 25!

Chapter 8

....

THE PENGUINS

The Penguins, studio portrait, USA, 1955, top to bottom Bruce Tate, Dexter Tisby, Cleve Duncan, Curtis Williams. (Photo by Gilles Petard/Redferns)

THE PENGUINS RECORDED ONE OF THE MOST FAMOUS—AND most unlikely—hits in music history.

"Earth Angel" captures the longing and yearning of young love in beautiful harmony. The song's impact has transcended generations, and it lives on as an iconic doo-wop song.

The Penguins formed in 1953 in Los Angeles and consisted of four high school students: Cleveland (Cleve) Duncan, Curtis Williams, Dexter Tisby, and Bruce Tate. Williams approached Duncan to inquire about starting a group together, and the pieces fell into place from there.

"We wanted to be cool, so we took our name off Willie the Penguin, the trademark on Kool cigarette packs," Duncan told the *Los Angeles Times* in 1983.

The Penguins were introduced to Walter "Dootsie" Williams, who ran a small production company called Dootone Records.

They wound up recording a demo for "Earth Angel" in a relative's garage. It was crude, with heavy traffic and a dog barking next door that threatened to ruin takes.

After the recording session, Williams stopped at a record store, Dolphin's of Hollywood, which had a DJ on site to play requests on the radio. Williams was asked about the recording, one thing led to another, and the incomplete garage demo wound up being played on the air.

Williams had thought another song, "Hey Senorita," would make a better single. But listeners kept calling and asking for "Earth Angel," and it quickly became a hit.

The song reached number 8 on the *Billboard* Hot 100 chart, even amid cover versions being recorded by white acts.

The Penguins had found something special.

But just as quickly, things fell apart.

Money complicated matters. The singers signed with Mercury Records at the urging of Buck Ram, who would find success as the Platters' manager.

Lawsuits followed over the singers' underage status, the rights to their recordings, and songwriting credits, and in the years after, the Penguins in their initial form were finished.

Although the original lineup of the Penguins did not achieve long-term success, their impact on music lingers. "Earth Angel" sold in excess of 10 million copies; the recording has been inducted into the Grammy Hall of Fame and was added to the Library of Congress National Recording Registry as "culturally, historically, or aesthetically important."

Not bad for an incomplete garage demo recording!

🏆 GRAMMY NOMINATIONS: 0

CIRCA 1958: American doo-wop group "The Penguins" (L-R) Dexter Tisby, Cleve Duncan, Johnny Otis, Teddy Harper and Randy Jones pose for a portrait flanking band leader Johnny Otis circa 1958. (Photo by Michael Ochs Archives/Getty Images)

Billboard **Hot 100** CHARTING SINGLES

The Penguins had two *Billboard* Hot 100 hits during their career. Here is a list of those hits in chronological order.[3]

Song	Year Released	*Billboard* Hot 100/ *Billboard* Pop Peak Position
➔ "Earth Angel (Will You Be Mine)"	1954	8
➔ "Hey Senorita"	1955	27

🔥 *My Favorite the Penguins Songs*

> ❯ "Earth Angel (Will You Be Mine)" ❯ "Hey Senorita"

💜 *My Favorite the Penguins Samples*

•• "The Flying Saucer" by Buchanan & Goodman sampled "Earth Angel (Will You Be Mine)"

⊙ *My Take*

I first heard "Earth Angel" when it was covered by New Edition in 1986 for their *Under the Blue Moon* album, and I loved the song immediately. Eventually, years later, I learned about the original group who first released the song, and I gave the proper respect to the Penguins.

---

3   The official chart position for "Hey Senorita" could not be confirmed. This is the best estimation based on unconfirmed sources.

Chapter 9

. . . .

THE PLATTERS

1954: (Clockwise from bottom left) Herb Reed, Tony Williams, Dave Lynch, Alex Hodge and Zola Taylor of the early rock-and-roll group The Platters pose for a portrait before Alex Hodge left the group and Paul Robi joined what would become the definitive lineup in 1954. (Photo by Michael Ochs Archives/Getty Images)

THE PLATTERS HAD THE MOST CROSSOVER SUCCESS OF any 1950s vocal group. They represented the gold standard—a blend of sharp harmonies, smart songs, and high-quality recordings.

The group's roots were planted in 1953 in Los Angeles.

Tenor Tony Williams, a New Jersey native, had moved to the city of angels hoping to develop a music career like his sister Bertha (known onstage as Linda Hayes). At the onset of his time in California, he washed cars. In time, he connected with quartet of singers, and his sister introduced him to manager, producer, and arranger Buck Ram.

Ram was impressed by Williams's voice and arranged an audition for Williams and his group, the Platters (music records at the time were known as *platters*).

But the Platters had a rocky start. Two members left, and their sound was undefined.

In came two Midwesterners—Herb Reed, a bass singer who'd sung gospel, and tenor David Lynch. Alex Hodge, an original member of the group, stayed on for a while but was replaced as baritone in 1954 by Paul Robi.

The Platters were signed with Federal Records, and Ram wanted them to record a song he'd penned, "Only You." But Syd Nathan, Federal's president, "thought it was so bad he swore he wouldn't issue it," according to writer Jay Warner. So "Only You" was set aside as the Platters released a series of middling singles for Federal.

The Federal songs were selling fine and giving the group a regional following. But the Platters were missing something—or, in this case, *someone*. A female singer, Zola Taylor.

The group continued practicing at Ram's urging. Their opportunity would come soon enough.

Ram—who also represented the Penguins—saw something in the Platters that others didn't quite see yet.

Mercury was interested in the Penguins, and the tactful Ram swung a two-for-one deal for Mercury to take control of the two acts.

The Penguins didn't find much success with the label. The Platters, on the other hand, were primed and ready to break out.

And when the group went to record, they brought along Ram's "Only You." Ram wound up playing piano during the session just to make sure the song was recorded.

Of course, the song that Federal's president had hated became a classic. "Only You" topped the R&B chart and reached number 5 on the pop chart. (Federal later released its own version, but it didn't move the needle.)

Listening to Williams's voice flitter and dance across the song's high notes, it's hard to image how many takes the group had to go through before they got a "good enough" version of the song. It is rumored that lead singer Williams's voice "broke" during the rehearsal for "Only You," but the group decided to keep it in the recording. This song is commonly used in video games to this day as part of story arcs and penultimate scenes.

When Mercury wanted to record more songs with the Platters, Ram scrambled to come up with another hit, writing "The Great Pretender." The song—which centers around a lovelorn man trying to fool himself into believing he's OK amid heartbreak and loneliness—was another top five *Billboard* hit.

Singles like "The Magic Touch," "My Prayer," and "You'll Never Never Know" followed, one after the other, bringing the group sustained popularity in the United States and abroad.

Another hit, "Twilight Time," reflected the magic formula that made the Platters so special. Williams's soaring vocals brought life to Ram's alliterative lyrics. Strings and the group's background vocals provided a majestic feel.

By late 1958, the Platters released their rendition of the classic ballad "Smoke Gets In Your Eyes," and "Enchanted" followed the following year.

But by the end of the 1950s and the dawn of the 1960s, the Platters' magic began to fade. The group's four male members were arrested on a morals charge in 1959 for an encounter involving young women—three of whom were white—at a Cincinnati hotel. They were later acquitted, but the issue impacted the group's radio play.

Williams went out on his own and signed with Reprise Records. His lead vocal role was filled by Sonny Turner. The other members left one by one, starting their own Platters-themed groups while Ram continued touring with his version of the Platters. A flurry of lawsuits—and accolades—followed the group in the decades that followed.

The Platters were inducted into the Rock & Roll Hall of Fame in 1990 and the Vocal Group Hall of Fame in 1998 (its inaugural year). The group had 40 singles reach the *Billboard* Hot 100 charts from 1955 to 1967 and became the first rock-and-roll-era group to have a top 10 album in the United States. In an era when it was difficult to have one *Billboard* Hot 100 hit, they exceeded the possibilities of their time and inspired a generation of groups that followed in their footsteps.

♔ GRAMMY NOMINATIONS: 0

Los Angeles 1956: (L-R) Herb Reed, Dave Lynch, Tony Williams, Zola Taylor and Paul Robi of the early rock-and-roll group The Platters perform onstage in a scene from the movie The Girl Can't Help It which was released in 1956. (Photo by Michael Ochs Archives/Getty Images)

Billboard **Hot 100** CHARTING SINGLES

Here is a list of the Platters' *Billboard* Hot 100 hits in chronological order.

Songs	Year Released	*Billboard* Hot 100/ *Billboard* Pop Peak Position
"Only You (And You Alone)"	1955	5
"The Great Pretender"	1955	1
"(You've Got) The Magic Touch"	1956	4
"My Prayer"	1956	11
"Heaven On Earth"	1956	39
"You'll Never Never Know"	1961	11
"It Isn't Right"	1956	13
"On My Word Of Honor"	1956	20

Songs	Year Released	Billboard Hot 100/ Billboard Pop Peak Position
"One In A Million"	1956	31
"I'm Sorry"	1957	11
"He's Mine"	1957	16
"My Dream"	1957	24
"Only Because"	1957	65
"Helpless"	1957	56
"Twilight Time"	1958	1
"You're Making A Mistake"	1958	51
"I Wish"	1958	42
"It's Raining Outside"	1958	93
"Smoke Gets in Your Eyes"	1958	1
"Enchanted"	1959	12
"Remember When"	1959	41
"Where"	1959	44
"Wish It Were Me"	1959	61
"Harbor Lights"	1960	8
"Sleepy Lagoon"	1960	65
"Ebb Tide"	1960	56
"Red Sails In The Sunset"	1960	36
"To Each His Own"	1960	21
"If I Didn't Care"	1961	30
"Trees"	1961	62

Songs	Year Released	*Billboard* Hot 100/ *Billboard* Pop Peak Position
"I'll Never Smile Again"	1961	25
"It's Magic"	1962	91
"I Love You 1,000 Times"	1966	31
"I'll Be Home"	1966	97
"With This Ring"	1967	14
"Washed Ashore"	1967	56
"Sweet, Sweet Lovin'"	1967	70

My Favorite the Platters Songs

❯ "Only You (And You Alone)" ❯ "Sixteen Tons"
❯ "Unchained Melody"

My Favorite the Platters Samples

•• "Dusk You & Me" by Groove Armada sampled "Twilight Time"
•• "The Flying Saucer" by Buchanan & Goodman sampled "The Great Pretender"

My Take

I vaguely remember first hearing "Only You" while watching the original *Superman* movie as a child. That was my introduction to the Platters. As I was researching this book, I was shocked to learn the number of times the song "The Great Pretender" has been synced (placed in a TV show or movie). As of the time of writing this book, this song has been synced 44 times, ranging in years from 1956 to 2023. A special thank you to Les Brown for first introducing me to "Sixteen Tons" through some of his most famous speeches.

1960's

From Top left to Bottom Left (Clockwise)
Gladys Knight and the Pips, Martha Reeves and the
Vandellas, Sam and Dave and The Commodores

Part Two
THE 1960S

THE UNITED STATES WENT THROUGH MASSIVE SOCIAL CHANGE in the 1960s. The civil rights movement, the assassinations of President Kennedy and Martin Luther King Jr., the Cuban Missile Crisis, and the moon landing were a few of the most impactful events of the decade. The Voting Rights Act of 1965, the first FDA-approved birth control pill, and the U.S. entering the Vietnam War provided inspiration for a new type of music across all genres.

When looking at sports in the United States, the first Super Bowl was played in 1967 in the Los Angeles Coliseum, where the Green Bay Packers defeated the Kansas City Chiefs. UCLA and John Wooden dominated college basketball, outside of a notable victory by Texas Western in 1966, led by legendary coach Don Haskins, who started five Black players for the first time in NCAA history and beat Kentucky, led by coach Adolph Rupp, a known racist who did not recruit or play Black players.

Pop music dominated the majority of the decade, driven by the explosion of youth culture in the U.S. and Europe. The British Invasion of bands like the Beatles and the Rolling Stones helped to develop the sound of the 1960s. Folk-infused rock music also stood tall during the decade as artists such as

Bob Dylan, Joni Mitchell, and Willie Nelson achieved high levels of success.

R&B groups quickly made a mark across the music industry in the 1960s with the emergence of Motown Records, which dominated the R&B sound from this decade. The world experienced a rapid rise to fame from the Supremes, the Temptations, and the Miracles. Toward the end of the decade, we got a glimpse of future starts Stevie Wonder, Marvin Gaye, and the Jackson 5 (thank you, Gladys Knight!).

As the decade ended, the famous Woodstock Music and Art Fair was held in August of 1969. We all remember Jimi Hendrix's rendition of the national anthem during his one-hour performance. Did you know that in the years prior, he was playing with the famous R&B group the Isley Brothers? (See chapter 13 for that story!)

Overall, in the 1960s there was an explosion of musical hits, specifically coming from R&B groups.

Chapter 10

. . . .

BOOKER T & THE MGS

United Kingdom - JANUARY 01: MANCHESTER SQUARE Photo of BOOKER T & THE MGS and Donald Duck Dunn and Al Jackson and Booker T JONES and Steve Cropper, Posed group portrait L-R Donald 'Duck Dunn, Al Jackson Jr. (front), Booker T Jones and Steve Cropper (Photo by CA/Redferns)

BOOKER T & THE MGS SHAPED THE SOUND of southern soul through their own music and by backing other artists.

The group formed in 1962, becoming the house band of Memphis-based Stax Records. Stax, named for its owners, Jim Stewart and Estelle Axton, would keep its studio open for demo recordings, and one day, the assembled musicians—Steve Cropper on guitar, Booker T. Jones on keyboard, Lewie Steinberg on bass, and Al Jackson Jr. on drums—started jamming out after the singer assigned that day had left.

Stewart recorded them. There was something to their sound.

They worked on the arrangement, and the next time they recorded, Jones, the keyboardist and a high school senior, tried out the bluesy riff on a Hammond M-series organ, giving the song grit. After a few takes, they recorded the final version of the song.

Steinberg wanted to name the song "Onions" or "Funky Onions," but *funky* wouldn't work, and onions made people cry…so the group settled on "Green Onions" as the song title.

But what to call the group?

They thought something involving Jones's name—Booker T—had a nice ring to it, and they picked *the MGs* after the British car manufacturer.

"Green Onions" was issued in May 1962 as the B-side to another song, "Behave Yourself," but it got reissued as an A-side. The song made its way to Memphis radio station WOLK, and pretty soon it was being played nationwide. It topped the *Billboard* R&B chart and peaked at number 3 on the Hot 100 chart.

The success of the song drove Booker T & the MGs to release an album later that year, *Green Onions*. The album cover shows bunches of green onions. Notably, the LP art doesn't show the group, which was racially integrated, a rarity for popular music acts of the time.

"Nobody realized this until we started performing in public. We had problems with things like segregated eating, but we survived," Jones told Dave Simpson for the *Guardian* in a 2019 interview.

Recordings were scheduled to accommodate Jones's college course load. At times, Isaac Hayes—himself an eventual star—would record with the group, and in the mid-1960s, Steinberg was replaced on bass by Donald "Duck" Dunn. With Dunn, the foursome clicked fully into gear, both on the group's own songs (such as "Hip Hug-Her") and as a Stax backing band.

And oh, what a lineup of Stax stars. Otis Redding. Wilson Pickett. Sam & Dave. Throughout the 1960s, Booker T & the MGs brought their musicality to such timeless songs as "Try a Little Tenderness," "(Sittin' On) the Dock of the Bay," and "Hold On, I'm Comin'."

As James Cortese wrote in a profile of the group for the *Memphis Commercial Appeal* in 1968, "When you hear Booker T. and the MG's playing together the four merge into such a close unity of sound, it's difficult to consider them as individual personalities. They understand each other and the instruments they play…each is an artist on his instrument as well as being able to produce, write songs, arrange and improvise. Musically they blend into one; but they are individuals."

By the early 1970s, growing increasingly frustrated by Stax's operations, Jones and Cropper wound up leaving the group and heading in separate directions, while Dunn and Jackson stayed at Stax. Jones worked with artists like Bill Withers, while Jackson cowrote Al Green's classic "Let's Stay Together."

The members of Booker T & the MGs discussed a reunion—wrapping up their projects and working together again. But before that could happen,

Jackson, who provided the group's beat, was shot dead.

The surviving members of the group carried forward, playing together in various arrangements and pursuing their own projects. Booker T & the MGs were elected to the Rock & Roll Hall of Fame in 1992, and the ceremony included the likes of Johnny Cash, Keith Richards, Neil Young, and U2's "the Edge" contributing on "Green Onions" alongside Jones, Cropper, and Dunn.

All of these years later, "Green Onions" remains one of the most influential songs in popular music.

"It's still one of my favorite songs," Jones said in 2019. "It's defined my life. But it's deceptively simple. There's a magic in there that's hard to capture. To get it right, I still have to practice."

♙ GRAMMY NOMINATIONS: 4
♙ GRAMMY WINS: 1
♙ BEST POP INSTRUMENTAL PERFORMANCE: "CRUISIN' "

CIRCA 1964: (Clockwise from bottom left) Booker T. Jones, Al Jackson, Steve Cropper and Donald "Duck" Dunn of the R&B band Booker T. & The MG's pose for a portrait with an award in circa 1964. (Photo by Michael Ochs Archives/Getty Images)

Billboard Hot 100 CHARTING SINGLES

Here is a list of Booker T & the MGs' *Billboard* Hot 100 hits in chronological order.

Song	Year Released	*Billboard* Hot 100 Peak Position
"Green Onions"	1962	3
"Boot-Leg"	1965	58
"Groovin'"	1967	21
"Soul Limbo"	1968	17
"Hang 'Em High"	1968	9
"Time Is Tight"	1969	6
"Soul Clap '69"	1969	64
"Mrs. Robinson"	1969	37
"Something"	1970	76
"Melting Pot"	1971	45

My Favorite Booker T & the MGs Songs

"Green Onions" • "Soul Limbo" • "Hip Hug-Her"

My Favorite Booker T & the MGs Samples

- "Don't Curse" by Heavy D & the Boyz, Pete Rock & C. L. Smooth sampled "Hip Hug-Her"
- "Tonight Is the Night" by Betty Wright sampled "Time Is Tight"
- "Love Me or Leave Me Alone" by Brand Nubian sampled "Sing A Simple Song"

⊙ *My Take*

You will notice the mention of the Stax record label for the first time in the book. This will begin a trend of notable producers dominating various eras of R&B music. Stax was huge in the 1960s, and they delivered hit after hit. Another learning through this group is the impact of the song "Green Onions." It is still played on television shows and in movies regularly. I urge you to listen to the opening bars and see if it sounds familiar. "Hip Hug-Her" is full of a bunch of samples that you will recognize when you hear the full song. Oh…I love the piano and organ in "Soul Limbo"!

Chapter 11

. . . .

GLADYS KNIGHT & THE PIPS

Clockwise: Gladys Knight, Edward Patten, William Guest, Merald Bubba Knight of Gladys
Knight & the Pips pose for a portrait in 1964 in New York. (Photo by James Kriegsmann/
Michael Ochs Archives/Getty Images)

EVEN WHEN SHE WAS EIGHT YEARS OLD, GLADYS Knight's voice stood above the rest.

The Georgia native won first prize nationwide on Ted Mack's *The Original Amateur Hour* in 1952, earning herself $2,000 ($23,000 in 2023 dollars) and a gold trophy for her rendition of the Nat King Cole song "Too Young." It was the start of a singing career that would, with her Pips, contribute staples like "I Heard It Through The Grapevine" and "Midnight Train to Georgia."

The Pips began as a family group—founding members included Gladys's siblings Merald "Bubba" Knight and Brenda Knight, as well as cousins Eleanor Guest and William Guest. The relatives had experience singing in the church choir and would participate in talent shows.

By the end of the decade, Brenda Knight and Eleanor Guest departed the Pips. Another cousin, Edward Patten, joined, along with friend Langston George, who stuck with the Pips for a few years.

The Pips' first success came in 1961 with their recording of "Every Beat Of My Heart." At the time, the Pips didn't have a record deal, so Huntom Records, an Atlanta label, signed a distribution deal with Vee-Jay Records. This distribution deal allowed the song to be distributed across the country and increase the awareness of the Pips.

At the same time the song was gaining traction, the Pips signed with New York's Fury Records. The song was rerecorded for the new label, and both versions charted. The Pips, around the time of their signing with Fury, also changed their name to Gladys Knight & the Pips.

But as the group was gearing up for something big, Gladys Knight chose to step away from the Pips and start a family. She returned two years later, and they signed with Maxx Records, releasing a number of strong songs including

"Giving Up."

And then they came onto Berry Gordy's radar. The Motown founder had cultivated an endless roster of talent, and in 1966, he would add Gladys Knight & the Pips. The group was assigned to Motown's Soul Records label.

But for Gladys Knight, it felt like Motown was more focused on other acts, like the Supremes and Marvin Gaye.

Despite the perceived slights, though, nothing could stop their single "I Heard It Through The Grapevine." The up-tempo song showcases Knight's fierce, crystalline vocals and the Pips' perfectly timed harmonies. It was a smash and a revelation and became, up to that point, Motown's biggest selling single (Gaye would later record his own hit version).

Knight was able to recognize talent—and in 1968, she called Motown execs to alert them to a music act she'd just crossed paths with, the Jackson 5.

"We were with Motown at the time, and I went and I called the company and I asked them if they could send a representative out to see these young kids, because they were performing on the talent show that Wednesday night. And I didn't carry a whole lot of weight at the company at that time. And they said, 'Well, we'll do the best we can. We'll see what we can do,' " she told Oprah Winfrey in 1993.

Being overlooked by Motown wore on the group, and after recording hits like "If I Were Your Woman" and "Neither One of Us (Wants To Be The First To Say Goodbye)," they left Motown in 1973 and signed with Buddah Records.

With a reimagined country-themed tune, they found their signature hit.

The Pips had collaborated with songwriter Jim Weatherly before, on "Neither

One of Us (Wants To Be The First To Say Goodbye)," and Weatherly found inspiration in the strangest of ways. He was on a flag football team with actor Lee Majors of *The Six Million Dollar Man*, and when he called Majors one day, Majors's then-girlfriend, actress Farrah Fawcett, answered the phone. Fawcett mentioned taking a "midnight plane to Houston" to visit her family, and for Weatherly, a "bell went off." He scribbled down a song based on that line, imagining it as a country hit.

In time, "Midnight Plane to Houston" became "Midnight Train to Georgia." The song was initially recorded by Cissy Houston—Whitney's mother—but Houston's version was more centered on the country elements Weatherly had anticipated than Gladys Knight and the Pips' version eventually was.

"Never in my wildest dreams did I ever think it would be an R&B record," he said years later.

The song, behind Knight's soaring vocals, captures a sense of yearning and steadfastness in the face of setback—told in the point of view of a woman following her man even after he fell short of his dreams.

"Midnight Train to Georgia" was a smash, a timeless, powerful song that allowed Gladys Knight & the Pips to showcase their talent. In live performances, such as the 1974 Grammy Awards, Knight stood in front of her groupmates, radiant and roaring, while the Pips danced behind her, their moves smooth and well-choreographed.

The song was inducted into the Grammy Hall of Fame and was named on *Rolling Stone*'s list of 500 greatest songs of all time.

"Midnight Train" anchored their album *Imagination*, which marked a commercial and creative high point.

Later in the decade, a contract dispute between Motown and Buddah Records preceded the group recording separate albums before signing with Columbia in 1980. Gladys Knight & the Pips split in the late 1980s, with Knight—the "Empress of Soul"—pursuing a solo career.

♫ GRAMMY NOMINATIONS: 10
♫ GRAMMY WINS: 3

* Best R&B Vocal Performance by a Duo, Group or Chorus: "Midnight Train to Georgia"
* Best R&B Vocal Performance by a Duo, Group or Chorus: "Neither One of Us (Wants To Be The First To Say Goodbye)"
* Best R&B Performance by a Duo or Group with Vocal: "Love Overboard"

Photo of Gladys Knight & the Pips in concert; (Photo by David Redfern/Redferns)

Billboard Hot 100 CHARTING SINGLES

Here is a list of Gladys Knight & the Pips' *Billboard* Hot 100 hits in chronological order.

Song	Year Released	*Billboard* Hot 100 Peak Position
"Every Beat Of My Heart"	1961	6
"Letter Full Of Tears"	1962	19
"Giving Up"	1964	38
"Operator"	1966	38
"I Heard It Through The Grapevine"	1967	2
"The End Of Our Road"	1968	15
"It Should Have Been Me"	1968	40
"Didn't You Know (You'd Have To Cry Sometime)"	1969	33
"Friendship Train"	1969	17
"The Nitty Gritty"	1969	19
"If I Were Your Woman"	1970	9
"I Don't Want To Do Wrong"	1971	17
"Make Me The Woman That You Go Home To"	1971	14
"Help Me Make It Through The Night"	1972	33
"Neither One of Us (Wants To Be The First To Say Goodbye)"	1973	2
"Daddy Could Swear, I Declare"	1973	19
"Midnight Train to Georgia"	1973	1

	Song	Year Released	Billboard Hot 100 Peak Position
→	"I've Got to Use My Imagination"	1973	4
→	"Best Thing That Ever Happened to Me"	1974	3
→	"On and On"	1974	2
→	"I Feel a Song (In My Heart)"	1974	21
→	"Love Finds Its Own Way"	1974	7
→	"The Way We Were/Try to Remember"	1975	11
→	"Part Time Love"	1976	22
→	"Baby, Don't Change Your Mind"	1977	52
→	"Come Back and Finish What You Started"	1977	60
→	"Bourgie', Bourgie'"	1980	31
→	"Taste of Bitter Love"	1980	37
→	"You're Number One (In My Book)"	1983	19
→	"Save the Overtime (For Me)"	1983	66
→	"Love Overboard"	1988	13
→	"Licence to Kill"	1989	79
→	"Men"	1989	95

🔥 My Favorite Gladys Knight & the Pips Songs

❯ "Neither One of Us (Wants To Be The First To Say Goodbye)"

❯ "Love Overboard" ❯ "You're Number One (In My Book)"

♥ *My Favorite Gladys Knight & the Pips Samples*

- •• "Can It Be All So Simple" by Wu-Tang Clan sampled "The Way We Were/Try to Remember"
- •• "Street's Disciple" by Nas feat. Olu Dara sampled "This Child Needs Its Father"
- •• "Yesterday" by J Dilla sampled "Yesterday"

⊙ *My Take*

Initially, I discovered Gladys Knight & the Pips when I heard their mid-'80s hit "Love Overboard" on the radio. My dad used to love this song and played it constantly. As I got older and was able to fully listen to and appreciate their complete discography, I understood how big of an impact they continue to have on R&B music and across the entire music industry. The song "Midnight Train to Georgia" is an amazing story and just shows how genres blend together. Also, the lyrics for "Neither One of Us (Wants To Be The First To Say Goodbye)" are a work of art.

We should keep in mind that in the early 1960s, it was rare for a woman—let alone an African American woman—to lead and be the only female singer in a group of men. Great music crosses numerous barriers. And respect to this group for going strong for over three decades on the charts. That is very rare air!

Chapter 12

. . . .

THE IMPRESSIONS

American soul group The Impressions (American singer-songwriter and musician Curtis Mayfield (1942–1999), American singer Fred Cash, and American singer Sam Gooden) perform live at the Apollo Theater in the Harlem neighborhood of Manhattan, New York City, New York, circa 1965. (Photo by Don Paulsen/Michael Ochs Archives/Getty Images)

THE IMPRESSIONS WERE ONE OF THE MOST SOCIALLY conscious music groups of the 1960s, and their soulful, gospel-infused hits served as a soundtrack for the civil rights era.

The group formed in the late 1950s after Curtis Mayfield and Jerry Butler—who sang gospel together—joined a doo-wop group called the Roosters. The other Roosters members were Arthur and Richard Brooks, who sang a mix of alto and tenor, and baritone Sam Gooden.

By 1958, the group was branded Jerry Butler & the Impressions.

But Butler soon left the group to pursue a solo career, notching hits such as "Only The Strong Survive." Mayfield became the group's songwriter and lead singer, and Fred Cash became the fifth member.

But Vee-Jay kept Butler and let the Impressions go, so the group wound up signing a record deal with ABC Paramount.

Their first ABC single sounded different from other R&B singles of the time. It told a story and featured lots of musicality and Mayfield's "unique, fragile-sounding falsetto," as writer Jay Warner described it. The song climbed up the charts, reaching number 2 on the R&B chart.

Pretty soon, the Brooks brothers departed the group, leaving the Impressions as a trio. They began to work with producer Johnny Pate, and their song "It's All Right" marked a new direction for the Impressions. As Mayfield's website states, "Mayfield perfected the group's singular upper register work and himself remained devoted to the falsetto rather than the more usual model range."

At a time when other Black groups were focused on love songs and dance music, Mayfield guided a series of socially aware, unabashedly Black hits such as "Keep On Pushing" and "People Get Ready," which pulled from gospel influences.

But he did so in a gentle, encouraging manner—something that drew in listeners across all races.

The lyrics for the classic "People Get Ready" include references to the impending arrival of a train, representing the steady movement of progress and urging people to be prepared for the challenges and opportunities ahead.

"We're a Winner," from 1968 has become an anthem of Black pride.

The group joined Mayfield's Curtom label and released additional singles before Mayfield departed the Impressions in 1970 following the release of their *Check Out Your Mind!* LP. But Mayfield continued to produce for the group while juggling soundtracks like *Super Fly* and other collaborations that drove forward soul funk music.

The Impressions continued touring and recording in the late 1970s and 1980s with various lineups, and the group was inducted into the Rock & Roll Hall of Fame in 1991 and the Vocal Group Hall of Fame in 2003.

In 1990, Mayfield was paralyzed from the waist down after wind toppled a lighting rig before a concert in Brooklyn, New York. It was years before he sang again—and when he did, he recorded his final album, *New World Order*.

Fitting, since his music had created a new world order.

🏆 GRAMMY NOMINATIONS: 1
🏆 GRAMMY WINS: 0

American musicians Curtis Mayfield (right), Fred Cash (second right) and Sam Gooden (second left) of The Impressions, backstage at the Apollo Theatre, New York City, circa 1965. (Photo by Don Paulsen/Michael Ochs Archives/Getty Images)

Billboard Hot 100 CHARTING SINGLES

Here is a list of the Impressions' *Billboard* Hot 100 hits in chronological order.

	Song	Year Released	Billboard Hot 100 Peak Position
➔	"For Your Precious Love"	1958	11
➔	"Gypsy Woman"	1961	20
➔	"It's All Right"	1963	4
➔	"Talking About My Baby"	1964	21
➔	"I'm So Proud"	1964	14
➔	"Keep On Pushing"	1964	10

Song	Year Released	Billboard Hot 100 Peak Position
"You Must Believe Me"	1964	15
"Amen"	1964	7
"People Get Ready"	1965	14
"Woman's Got Soul"	1965	29
"I Need You"	1965	61
"You've Been Cheatin' "	1965	33
"We're a Winner"	1968	14
"Fool for You"	1968	22
"Choice Of Colors"	1969	21
"This Is My Country"	1968	25
"Check Out Your Mind"	1970	28
"I'm a Changed Man (Finally Got Myself Together)"	1974	17
"Same Thing It Took"	1975	56

My Favorite the Impressions Songs

"Gypsy Woman" "People Get Ready" "I'm So Proud"

My Favorite the Impressions Samples

- "Go Crazy" by Jeezy feat. Jay-Z sampled "Man Oh Man"
- "One Love/People Get Ready" by Bob Marley and the Wailers sampled "People Get Ready"
- "Love" by J Dilla feat. Pharoahe Monch sampled "We Must Be in Love"

⊙ *My Take*

This was one of the few groups that achieved a modicum of success while singing about socially conscious topics. That is ironic, as the 1960s were an intense time for the civil rights movement. It is also cool to see where Curtis Mayfield got his start. I wonder if many people know that he came from the gospel space. It all blends together for sure.

Chapter 13

....

THE ISLEY BROTHERS

The Isley Brothers (L-R O'Kelly Isley, Ernie Isley, Chris Jasper, Rudolph Isley, Ronald Isley and Marvin Isley) pose for a portrait in February 1978. Photo by Michael Ochs Archives/Getty Images

FEW ARTISTS HAVE HAD SUCH A LONG AND wide-ranging legacy as the Isley Brothers.

The sibling-led group—which began in Cincinnati, Ohio—has drifted from a gospel background to rock and baby-making music, created some of music's most famous beats, and inspired generations of artists.

The Isley Brothers were initially a quartet featuring Ronald, O'Kelly, Rudolph, and Vernon. They were encouraged to perform together by their parents and often sang at churches.

But tragedy struck in 1954 when Vernon, the youngest of the brothers, was riding his bike to school. The bike skidded on gravel, and the boy fell against a truck, killing him. He was only 11 years old.

The trio regrouped, and in 1957 they made their way to New York. Talent scout and producer Richard Barrett helped pair the group with producer George Goldner, who guided their early recordings. The Isley Brothers were trying to find their distinct sound and style.

During performances, they would regularly cover Jackie Wilson's song "Lonely Teardrops," and Ronald began ad-libbing. Here is a quote and description of how the song "Shout" came to be from *Rock & Roll in Kennedy's America*.

One night in 1959 at the Uptown Theater in Philadelphia, the audience really got into the song, jumping up and down and screaming in delight. "The place was packed and the audience was yelling their approval, like at church," remembers Ron Isley. "The energy was so strong that I didn't want to end the song yet." So, he began ad-libbing just the way Wilson did. Ron screamed, "You know, you make me wanna shout!" The band jumped in as the audience went crazy. "I began to ad-lib more lines…I'd wait a second at the end of each line so my brothers and the audience had a chance to answer me with 'Shout.' That song just took over." Encouraged by the response, the group reprised the call-and-response pattern at every performance over the next ten days.

The ad-libbing pulled from the energy of traditional Black gospel—a blending of gospel and rock that was something special, something transformative, something that made people want to dance.

Hey-ey-ey-ey!

In 1959, when the Isley Brothers signed with RCA Records, they wound up recording "Shout" as its own song split over both sides of the record. "Shout" became the group's first single on the *Billboard* Hot 100—and the first of their many ubiquitous songs. It would gain new attention from its usage in the hit 1978 comedy film *Animal House.*

But the group's singles after "Shout" didn't fare so well, and they bounced from Atlantic and then to Wand. There, in 1962, they had a hit with a Bert Berns song called "Twist and Shout." The Beatles would record their smash version of the song two years later.

By 1964, they had moved to New Jersey and launched T-Neck Records. They were continuing to evolve and continuing to find their sound. And they wound up letting their band guitarist, a 22-year-old Seattle native named Jimi Hendrix, stay with them.

"He was the only member of the band permitted to live in our home, and he would play the guitar in his room, and he would play the guitar when [dinner] was prepared. There was something about his spirit that was harmless and gentle. We got a spare room. 'You can stay in our mother's house for a little bit,' " Ernie Isley said in a 2022 interview.

Hendrix appeared on a handful of Isley Brothers songs before striking out on his own.

They signed with Motown Records for a stretch, recording "This Old Heart Of Mine (Is Weak For You)," but they were a secondary act for the label's powerhouse roster. So in 1969, the Isley Brothers left Motown to relaunch T-Neck Records. And they brought on their younger brother, 16-year-old Ernie, on bass.

They recorded the funky, soul-infused "It's Your Thing," and it became a smash hit. The lyrics were full-throated and perfect for a time centered on individuality and self-expression.

"It's Your Thing" reached number 2 on the *Billboard* Hot 100 chart, topped the R&B chart, and earned the group a Grammy. And it set a new sound for the group as the three brothers were joined by their younger brothers Marvin and Ernie and their cousin Chris Jasper, all as full-time members. The Isley Brothers were a full band now—and reaching their creative height.

The group balanced soulful and innovative rock covers like "Summer Breeze" and "Listen to the Music," socially aware songs like "Fight the Power," ballads like "For the Love of You," and sleek, textured songs like "Between the Sheets." Many of their songs would be sampled in the years that followed by hip-hop stars like Public Enemy and the Notorious B.I.G.

The Isley Brothers have been constantly evolving and shifting and changing, and by the mid-1980s, the brothers were splintering. With the oldest brothers facing tax problems and creative differences bubbling over, the youngest members formed a group of their own, Isley-Jasper-Isley.

O'Kelly died of a heart attack in 1986, while Rudolph pursued a life in the ministry and left music behind. The Isley Brothers re-formed in the early 1990s with Ronald, Ernie, and Marvin Isley, and they returned to the charts with 1995's "Down Low (Nobody Has to Know)" with R. Kelly.

They later collaborated on Kelly Price's 1998 single "Friend Of Mine" and 2001's "Contagious," which charted on the *Billboard* chart—making six straight decades in which the Isley Brothers had hit singles.

The Isley Brothers' ability to evolve and adapt to changing music trends—while staying true to their sound—has helped them remain relevant long after their contemporaries. Their influence can be heard in countless other artists who've followed in their footsteps.

♔ GRAMMY NOMINATIONS: 4
♔ GRAMMY WINS: 1
✸ Best R&B Vocal Performance by a Duo or Group: "It's Your Thing"

Circa 1964: American soul vocal pop group the Isley Brothers (left to right) O'Kelly Isley Jr., Ronnie Isley and Rudolph Isley, in Britain to tour. (Photo by Evening Standard/Getty Images)

Billboard Hot 100 CHARTING SINGLES

Here is a list of the Isley Brothers' *Billboard* Hot 100 hits
in chronological order.

Song Title	Year Released	Billboard Hot 100 Peak Position
"Shout"	1959	47
"Twist and Shout"	1962	17
"Nobody But Me"	1962	92
"Twistin' With Linda"	1962	50
"This Old Heart Of Mine (Is Weak For You)"	1966	12
"Take Me In Your Arms (Rock Me A Little While)"	1968	50
"It's Your Thing"	1969	2
"Put Yourself In My Place"	1969	74
"Love the One You're With"	1971	18
"Lay Lady Lay"	1971	61
"Pop That Thang"	1972	24
"Work to Do"	1972	91
"That Lady (Part 1)"	1973	6
"What It Comes Down To"	1973	50
"Summer Breeze"	1974	60
"Live It Up"	1974	4
"Fight the Power (Part 1)"	1975	4

Song Title	Year Released	*Billboard* Hot 100 Peak Position
→ "For the Love of You (Part 1 & Part 2)"	1975	22
→ "Harvest for the World"	1976	63
→ "The Pride (Part 1)"	1977	63
→ "Footsteps in the Dark (Part 1 & Part 2)"	1977	19
→ "Go for Your Guns"	1978	6
→ "Take Me to the Next Phase (Part 1 & Part 2)"	1978	10
→ "I Wanna Be With You (Part 1)"	1979	31
→ "It's a Disco Night (Rock Don't Stop)"	1979	45
→ "Don't Say Goodnight (It's Time For Love) (Part 1 & Part 2)"	1980	39
→ "Lay You Down"	1980	46
→ "Inside You (Part 1)"	1981	59
→ "Choosey Lover"	1983	42
→ "Between the Sheets"	1983	101[4]
→ "Caravan of Love"	1986	51
→ "Smooth Sailin' Tonight"	1987	60
→ "Down Low (Nobody Has to Know)" (with R. Kelly)	1996	4
→ "Let's Lay Together"	1996	93
→ "Floatin' on Your Love" (with Angela Winbush)	1996	47

---

4 OK, so this one technically didn't make the top 100—but it's one of their most sampled songs!

	Song Title	Year Released	*Billboard* Hot 100 Peak Position
➜	"Tears"	1996	55
➜	"Contagious" (with R. Kelly & Chanté Moore)	2001	19
➜	"What Would You Do?"	2003	49

♨ *My Favorite the Isley Brothers Songs*

➤ "Between the Sheets"   ➤ "Voyage to Atlantis"
➤ "Choosey Lover"   ➤ "Caravan of Love" (by Isley-Jasper-Isley, an offshoot of the Isley Brothers[5])

♥ *My Favorite the Isley Brothers Samples*

- •• "Big Poppa" by Notorious B.I.G. sampled "Between the Sheets"

- •• "It Was A Good Day" by Ice Cube sampled "Footsteps in the Dark"

- •• "Shake Your Thang" by Salt-N-Pepa with E.U. sampled "It's Your Thing"

- •• "I" by Kendrick Lamar sampled "That Lady"

---

5   As mentioned earlier, this group was formed due to rumored tensions and fracturing among the original group. Isley-Jasper-Isley released three albums (*Broadway's Closer to Sunset Blvd*, *Caravan of Love*, and *Different Drummer*) before disbanding in 1987. This group was inducted to the Rock & Roll Hall of Fame with the rest of the Isley Brothers in 1992 and received the Grammy Lifetime Achievement Award in January 2014.

⊘ My Take

The Isley Brothers are in my top five favorite groups of all time. My love for them has grown even more as I researched their history and journey for this book. To have *Billboard* Hot 100 charting hits across six decades (1959–2001) is an astonishing feat that may never be duplicated again. The Isley Brothers' music still sounds good today, and hip-hop loves to sample the group, which is a tribute to their timeless music. The power of a sync placement[6] ("Shout" in *Animal House*) is also a prime example of the value of a group's catalog nearly 20 years later. As musical history has shown us, a musical group's catalog (collection) of songs and albums that span over multiple years can increase in value significantly through placements in TV shows and movies that expose a new audience of listeners to their music. I can't say enough about my love for this group. Listen to the lyrics on "Voyage to Atlantis" and enjoy the guitar at the opening of "Choosey Lover"! The Isley Brothers are a mainstay in all of my slow-jam sets ("Between The Sheets" is one of my favorite slow jams), and I encourage anyone who is new to the group to listen to their entire discography from the 1950s to today.

CIRCA 1970: Photo of Isley Brothers. Photo by Michael Ochs Archives/Getty Images

---

6   A *sync placement* is when a song is placed in a movie, television show, advertisement, or video game.

Chapter 14

. . . .

MARTHA AND THE VANDELLAS

Rosalind Ashford, Martha Reeves, and Betty Kelly of Martha and the Vandellas get ready to go onstage circa mid-1964 at the Apollo Theater in Harlem, New York. (Photo by Michael Ochs Archives/Getty Images)

MARTHA AND THE VANDELLAS WERE ONE OF THE fiercest female groups, and hits like "Heatwave" and "Dancing In The Street" proved the perfect way to showcase their talent.

The group was led by Martha Reeves, who was determined to become a music star. She grew up in the church and also sang choir at Detroit's Northeastern High School. She was coached by Abraham Silver, who taught a handful of other soon-to-be stars.

Reeves joined a group with high school friends Gloria Williams, Rosalind Ashford, and Annette Sterling, the Del-Phis, and she made ends meet working odd jobs and serving as a nightclub singer. At one point she showed up at Motown's "Hitsville USA" studios—but instead of recording, she was offered a secretarial job.

As she said in a 1967 interview, "Taking the job gave me a chance to look around and decide if I was headed in the right direction."

One time, when singer Mary Wells missed a recording session, Reeves called on her friends to fill in; soon after, they backed up Marvin Gaye on his song "Stubborn Kind Of Fellow," which became his breakthrough hit.

Then came their chance, and Martha and the Vandellas—with Reeves leading and supported by Ashford and Sterling (later replaced by Betty Kelley)—was born.

Their first major hit was "Come And Get These Memories" in 1963, which reached the top 30 on the *Billboard* Hot 100 chart. The song was written by the famous Motown songwriting team of Holland–Dozier–Holland and was produced by the legendary Motown producer William "Mickey" Stevenson, with the Funk Brothers providing instrumentals.

The song's catchy melody, upbeat tempo, and heartfelt lyrics about reminiscing over past memories struck a chord with listeners and helped establish Martha and the Vandellas as one of the decade's premier girl groups.

They reached a new tier with "Heatwave," which sizzled up the charts. They were soon one of the most popular Motown acts with smash hits like "Quicksand," "Dancing In The Street," and "Nowhere To Run."

As Susan Whitall wrote for the group's Rock & Roll Hall of Fame induction, "In Reeves' voice there were deeper inflections, echoes of the sharp righteousness of gospel and the sultry abandon of R&B. More so than most of her sister Motown singers, Reeves had an earthy and direct quality to her delivery. While the Supremes were adored for their kittenish, airbrushed glamour, Martha and the Vandellas were tough, hip girls down the street. There were intimations of a slight danger in their music, thanks to that interesting, harsh edge of Reeves's alto, a quality that made it slice like a scimitar through layers of background instrumental and vocal accompaniment."

"Dancing In The Street," which became the group's biggest hit, reached number 2 on the *Billboard* Hot 100, and topped the R&B chart. It's since been covered by artists like Mick Jagger and David Bowie.

Another smash hit was 1967's "Jimmy Mack."

But label changes and infighting coincided with the group's chart decline, and in 1972, the group disbanded, with Reeves going solo. She's since dabbled in acting and served on the Detroit City Council. In recent years, she has continued to perform, both by herself and with living members of the Vandellas.

The Vandellas were an influential part of Motown's rise—and the Reeves-led group represents one of the decade's greatest successes. Reeves's determination and distinct voice are both quintessential 1960s Motown and music for all time.

🏆 GRAMMY NOMINATIONS: 1
🏆 GRAMMY WINS: 0

United Kingdom - January 01: Manchester Square (EMI) Photo of Martha Reeves & The
Vandellas and Martha Reeves and Rosalind Ashford, Posed group portrait - Annette Beard,
Rosalind Ashford and Martha Reeves (Photo by RB/Redferns)

Billboard Hot 100 CHARTING SINGLES

Here is a list of Martha and the Vandellas' *Billboard* Hot 100
hits in chronological order.

	Song	Year Released	Billboard Hot 100 Peak Position
➔	"Come And Get These Memories"	1963	29
➔	"(Love Is Like A) Heat Wave"	1963	4
➔	"Quicksand"	1963	8
➔	"Live Wire"	1964	42

	Song	Year Released	Billboard Hot 100 Peak Position
➔	"In My Lonely Room"	1964	44
➔	"Dancing In The Street"	1964	2
➔	"Wild One"	1964	34
➔	"Nowhere To Run"	1965	8
➔	"You've Been In Love Too Long"	1965	36
➔	"Love (Makes Me Do Foolish Things)"	1966	51
➔	"My Baby Loves Me"	1966	22
➔	"I'm Ready For Love"	1966	9
➔	"Jimmy Mack"	1967	10
➔	"Honey Chile"	1967	11
➔	"Love Bug Leave My Heart Alone"	1967	25
➔	"I Promise To Wait My Love"	1968	50
➔	"Forget Me Not"	1968	53

🔥 *My Favorite Martha and the Vandellas Songs*

❯ "I Say A Little Prayer" ❯ "Dancing In The Street"
❯ "Jimmy Mack"

♥ *My Favorite Martha and the Vandellas Samples*

•• "100 Miles And Runnin'" by N.W.A. sampled "Nowhere To Run"

•• "Please Don't Go (Cry Baby)" by Melanie Fiona sampled "Jimmy Mack"

•• "Street Fighting Man" by the Rolling Stones sampled "Dancing In The Street"

⊙ *My Take*

This was another groundbreaking all-female group that I came to appreciate as my music taste matured with life. Until I did the research for this book, I did not know that Martha and the Vandellas were the original artists who performed "I Say A Little Prayer." They did that song justice! I wonder why their version never charted.

Chapter 15

. . . .

THE MIRACLES

Motown group The Miracles Clockwise from left - Pete Moore, Bobby Rogers, Ronald White, Claudette Robinson and Smokey Robinson pose for a portrait circa 1963. (Photo by Michael Ochs Archives/Getty Images)

THE MIRACLES *MADE* MOTOWN, AND THE SILKY VOCALS and smart lyrics of founder and lead singer Smokey Robinson redefined music.

The origins of the Miracles date to the mid-1950s, when Robinson and fellow teens Warren "Pete" Moore (bass), Ronnie White (baritone), and Bobby Rogers and Emerson "Sonny" Rogers (tenors) attended Northern High School in Detroit.

They were initially called the Five Chimes and the Matadors but eventually changed their name. And when Sonny Rogers joined the army, his sister Claudette joined the group. (Smokey and Claudette would later marry.)

Through local shows and performances, the group connected with Berry Gordy, who heard something in the group that others didn't hear. Robinson had big dreams and great work ethic but needed more experience and guidance to take the group to the next level.

Robinson had been writing prolifically—but his songwriting needed refinement.

"I had composed over 100 [songs] by that time," Robinson said in a 1970 interview. "Berry tore each one apart and showed me what was wrong with them. Then, he told me how to develop a basic plot and stick with it. He explained how every song should be a complete story."

Pretty soon, the group recorded a song, "Got A Job," that mirrored the Silhouettes' hit "Get a Job." Before the song's release, the group changed their name to the Miracles.

The song was a national R&B hit, but financially, it didn't make Gordy much money.

The situation made Robinson convince Gordy to start his own label, and Tamla Records was formed, later incorporated as Motown Record Corporation. The Miracles recorded some minor hits. But they—and Gordy—were facing pressure to see the group break through.

They recorded one of Robinson's songs, "Shop Around," which told the story of a woman warning her son to keep his options open before settling down with a woman. The song initially had a blues influence, but Gordy had them rerecord it.

Good idea. It was the label's first million-selling hit. It became clear to Gordy pretty quickly that Robinson was a hitmaking machine, and he tried to bottle that energy by making him Motown's vice president.

In 1962, the Miracles released another iconic top-10 single, "You Really Got A Hold On Me."

Hits and singles followed, even amid lineup changes—Claudette Rogers retired from the group in 1964, while Moore was drafted into the army.

The Miracles' success—and that of other Motown acts—was due in part to Robinson's relentless songwriting, with songs such as "The Tracks Of My Tears." Other standout hits he penned include "My Girl" for the Temptations (cowritten and coproduced with White) and "My Guy" for Mary Wells. Robinson's efforts, along with the Funk Brothers' backing instrumentals and the songwriting talents of Holland–Dozier–Holland, helped create the iconic 1960s "Motown Sound."

The lyrics would click into place.

For "The Tracks Of My Tears," guitarist Marvin Tarplin gave the songwriter riffs on a tape.

"I'm listening to it every day. So after about a week or so, I'd come up with the first three lines of the chorus," Robinson said. The lines of the chorus describe looking at someone who is smiling, but the smile doesn't really fit what is going on in their mind.

Robinson struggled with the last part. *That I'm sad? That I'm missing you so much?*

"One morning, I'm in the mirror and I'm shaving, I'm looking at my face and I'm thinking to myself, I said, 'Golly, what if someone cried so much, so their tears had actually left tracks in their face?' And that was it. And 'Tracks of My Tears' was born." Tarplin's opening guitar riff, the song's lyrics, and Robinson's soaring vocals have made the song timeless and instantly recognizable.

But as the group got more and more airplay and visibility, a shift began to occur. The Miracles became Smokey Robinson and the Miracles.

The hits continued, anchored by pop standards like "I Second That Emotion" and "The Tears Of A Clown," which climbed the British charts before charting stateside.

In 1972, Robinson left the Miracles to begin a successful solo career. Among his biggest solo hits was "Cruisin' " in 1979. The Miracles also continued forward, issuing a number of hits, including "Love Machine" in 1975 (Billy Griffin handled lead vocals).

Smokey Robinson and the Miracles reunited in 1983 for Motown's 25th anniversary TV special.

In 1987, Robinson was inducted into the Rock & Roll Hall of Fame—but for some reason, the Miracles weren't inducted alongside him. The group would finally be honored in 2012, a long overdue honor for one of music's most influential acts.

🏆 GRAMMY NOMINATIONS: 1
🏆 GRAMMY WINS: 0

Motown R&B group Smokey Robinson and The Miracles pose for a portrait circa 1964 in New York City, New York. (Photo by James Kriegsmann/Michael Ochs Archives/Getty Images)

Billboard Hot 100 CHARTING SINGLES

Here is a list of the Miracles' *Billboard* Hot 100 hits in chronological order.

Song	Year Released	Billboard Hot 100 Peak Position
"Shop Around"	1960	2
"Way Over There"	1960	93
"Ain't It Baby"	1961	93
"What's So Good About Goodbye"	1961	61
"I'll Try Something New" (with the Supremes)	1962	39

	Song	Year Released	Billboard Hot 100 Peak Position
➔	"You've Really Got A Hold On Me"	1962	8
➔	"Mickey's Monkey"	1963	8
➔	"I Gotta Dance To Keep From Crying"	1963	35
➔	"Ooo Baby Baby"	1965	16
➔	"The Tracks Of My Tears"	1965	16
➔	"My Girl Has Gone"	1965	14
➔	"Going To A Go-Go"	1966	11
➔	"(Come 'Round Here) I'm the One You Need"	1966	17
➔	"The Love I Saw In You Was Just a Mirage"	1967	20
➔	"More Love"	1967	23
➔	"Special Occasion"	1968	33
➔	"If You Can Want"	1968	33
➔	"Baby, Baby Don't Cry"	1969	8
➔	"Doggone Right"	1969	32
➔	"The Tears Of A Clown"	1970	1
➔	"I Don't Blame You At All"	1970	18
➔	"Do It Baby"	1974	13
➔	"Don't Cha Love It"	1975	47

🔥 *My Favorite the Miracles Songs*

❯ "You've Really Got A Hold On Me" ❯ "The Tracks Of My Tears"
❯ "Ooo Baby Baby"

♥ *My Favorite the Miracles Samples*

- •• "Welcome to Atlanta" by Jermaine Dupri feat. Ludacris sampled "Do It Baby"
- •• "One Eleven" by J Dilla sampled "A Legend In Its Own Time"
- •• "My Struggles" by Missy Elliott feat. Mary J. Blige and Grand Puba sampled "You've Got The Love I Need"

⊙ *My Take*

What stood out for me as I was researching and learning more about this group was Smokey Robinson's pen (songwriting skills). The lyrics for many of his songs were simple, yet so deep. I personally believe lyric writing is a lost art among songwriters nowadays. What I wouldn't give to take a songwriting class with Smokey Robinson! I urge you to listen to the lyrics in "The Tracks Of My Tears." The fact that he wrote hits for some of the most famous artists in history *and* was able to have his own catalog is stunning. He was one of the people who pushed Berry Gordy to start Motown, and we all know the cultural impact it had. Yet he had no Grammy wins, which leads me to shrug my shoulders.

Chapter 16

·······

THE RONETTES

Nedra Talley Ross, Ronnie Spector, and Estelle Bennett Vann of the vocal trio Ronettes pose for a portrait in 1963 in New York City, New York. (Photo by Michael Ochs Archives/Getty Images)

THE RONETTES WEREN'T LIKE THE OTHER GIRL GROUPS of the 1960s.

Where some groups were passive and shy, meek and mild, the Ronettes had a "tough, sexy twist," as the Rock & Roll Hall of Fame described it. Their aggressive, suggestive lyrics drove boys wild.

The group consisted of Veronica "Ronnie" Bennett, later Spector, her sister Estelle, and their cousin Nedra Talley. They grew up together in New York City at a time of much talent, like Frankie Lymon & the Teenagers had.

Ronnie and Estelle's mother worked at a King's Donuts located next door to the famed Apollo Theater, and the girls—along with some friends—entered the theater's talent night.

The Darling Sisters, as they were then known, won. Their relatives encouraged them to continue and helped them get singing lessons, and by 1961, they had signed with Colpix Records as Ronnie and the Relatives. Some of their early work was written by Carole King.

Even when their singles weren't going very far, they knew how to put on a show with their hairdos and sleek outfits. The Ronettes worked as backing artists and lounge performers, and with all of their hustle and gumption, they drew the interest of famed producer Phil Spector, who signed them to his Philles label.

Their first single on the label, released in July 1963, was "Be My Baby," which featured Spector's "wall of sound" instrumental style and house band, later known as the famed Wrecking Crew.

The only Ronette to appear on the record was Ronnie—and many view the song as Spector's love letter to his future wife. Ronnie later admitted that she spent days practicing her *oh-oh-ohs* to get her vocals just right.

The hit shot the Ronettes into a new stratosphere. They toured with Dick Clark's *Caravan of Stars.*

They followed up with another classic, "Baby, I Love You," and the Christmas staple "I Saw Mommy Kissing Santa Claus."

In 1964, traveling to the UK, the Ronettes finally learned the full impact of their stardom, touring with and befriending the Beatles and the Rolling Stones. The British Invasion was dominating the airwaves—but even so, the Ronettes continued to break through, and they stayed popular as other girl groups of the era lost momentum.

A big reason why was their string of powerful songs, including 1964's "Walking In the Rain," a somber ballad penned by Phil Spector, Barry Mann, and Cynthia Weil. Ronnie recorded the vocals on the first take.

The group kept recording songs, but Phil Spector—who would marry and later divorce the group's star singer—wouldn't release them. And the other two members were frustrated about being pushed to the background.

As the decade wore on, with the singers drifting in different directions in their personal lives, the Supremes eclipsed the Ronettes as the decade's most successful girl group.

The members of the Ronettes later sued Philles Records and Spector for unpaid royalties and won a multimillion-dollar settlement.

They were finally inducted into the Rock & Roll Hall of Fame in 2007—a long overdue honor for the music pioneers. They were also inducted into the Grammy Hall of Fame for "Be My Baby" and into the Vocal Group Hall of Fame, and musicians like Brian Wilson of the Beach Boys and Bruce Springsteen have noted Ronnie's—and the group's—influence on them.

♔ GRAMMY NOMINATIONS: 0

Vocal trio Ronettes pose for a portrait in 1964 in Los Angeles, California. (L-R) Estelle Bennett Vann, Ronnie Spector, Nedra Talley Ross. (Photo by Michael Ochs Archives/Getty Images)

Billboard Hot 100 CHARTING SINGLES

Here is a list of the Ronettes' *Billboard* Hot 100 hits in chronological order.

Song	Year Released	Billboard Hot 100 Peak Position
"Be My Baby"	1963	2
"Baby, I Love You"	1963	24
"(The Best Part Of) Breakin' Up"	1964	39
"Do I Love You?"	1964	34

	Song	Year Released	Billboard Hot 100 Peak Position
➔	"Walking In the Rain"	1964	23
➔	"Born To Be Together"	1965	52
➔	"Is This What I Get For Loving You?"	1965	75
➔	"I Can Hear Music"	1966	100

🔥 *My Favorite the Ronettes Songs*

❯ "Be My Baby"   ❯ "Walking In the Rain"
❯ "I Saw Mommy Kissing Santa Claus"

♥ *My Favorite the Ronettes Samples*

❯ "Take Me Home Tonight" by Eddie Money feat. Ronnie Spector sampled "Be My Baby"
❯ "All Star" by Smash Mouth sampled "You Baby"

⬇ *My Take*

The Ronettes were another group who I learned about in more detail while doing the research for this book. I had heard of "Be My Baby" but nothing else. I think it is cool that Carole King wrote some of their earlier songs. The music public and fans of the group fell victim to the record label dispute that prevented the release of several of their songs. This is a consistent theme throughout my research, which is very disappointing.

Chapter 17

....

SAM & DAVE

CIRCA 1970: Photo of Sam & Dave. Photo by Michael Ochs Archives/Getty Images

SAM MOORE AND DAVE PRATER WERE SOUL'S DYNAMIC duo. And together, Sam & Dave inspired artists from Al Green and Bruce Springsteen to the

Blues Brothers.

Moore grew up in the church and forged his singing foundation on gospel music. He connected with Prater, the lead singer of the gospel group the Sensational Hummingbirds, in 1961. They performed Jackie Wilson's "Doggin' Around" that night, and during their performance, Prater tripped.

"He and I went down together, and I caught the mic," Sam told writer Andy Schwartz. "The audience thought that was the act. It wasn't, but they went crazy."

Sam & Dave was born.

The call-and-response style of the group's songs reflected its gospel roots.

After Sam & Dave released a handful of singles, Jerry Wexler of Atlantic Records discovered them in 1964 and paired them with Memphis's famed Stax Records/Volt Studios. There, the duo collaborated with musicians like Isaac Hayes, David Porter, and Booker T & the MGs, fueling hits like "Hold On, I'm Comin' " and, in 1967, the Grammy-winning smash "Soul Man."

The performers were known for their extravagant live shows, which earned them the nickname "the Sultans of Sweat."

But an end to the distribution agreement between Stax and Atlantic brought an end to Sam & Dave's peak.

Despite their success, Prater and Moore had a difficult relationship, and they frequently argued and fought on and off stage. According to various accounts, Prater was often dissatisfied with the level of recognition he received and felt that Moore was getting more attention and credit than he was, which led to tensions between the two. Additionally, Moore struggled with drug addiction (cocaine), which caused problems in their working relationship and may have contributed to some of their arguments.

They first broke up in 1970 but later reconciled and continued touring together. The Blues Brothers' recording of "Soul Man" brought new visibility and attention to the duo, even if that visibility was tinged with bitterness and racism.

Prater died in a car crash in 1988. Moore—who has been public with his struggles with addiction—has kept performing, keeping the memory of one of music's greatest duos fresh.

♙ GRAMMY NOMINATIONS: 4
♙ GRAMMY WINS: 1

✸ Best Rhythm & Blues Group Performance, Vocal or Instrumental: "Soul Man"

United Kingdom - JANUARY 01: Photo of Sam Moore and SAM & DAVE and Dave Prater; Posed portrait of Sam Moore (L) and Dave Prater, (Photo by CA/Redferns)

Billboard Hot 100 CHARTING SINGLES

Here is a list of Sam & Dave's *Billboard* Hot 100 hits
in chronological order.

Song	Year Released	Billboard Hot 100 Peak Position
"You Don't Know Like I Know"	1966	90
"Hold On, I'm Comin' "	1966	21
"You Got Me Hummin' "	1966	78
"When Something Is Wrong with My Baby"	1967	42
"Soul Man"	1967	2
"I Thank You"	1968	9
"Wrap It Up"	1968	92
"Soul Sister, Brown Sugar"	1969	23
"Born Again"	1973	97

My Favorite Sam & Dave Songs

"Soul Man" ⊘ "Hold On, I'm Comin' " ⊘ "I Thank You"

My Favorite Sam & Dave Samples

→ "Slam" by Onyx sampled "Rich Kind of Poverty"

→ "Clap Yo Hands" by Naughty By Nature sampled "I Thank You"

→ "Soul on a Roll" by M.A.C. 10 sampled "Soul Man"

⊙ *My Take*

I think of Sam & Dave as a group whose flame burned too brightly, one that was done before it hit its stride. "Soul Man" is a timeless song that continues to be heard across all mediums. I first heard the song in the movie of the same name and I recently heard the song in a video game set in the future, which made me laugh.

Chapter 18

·······

SLY & THE FAMILY STONE

Psychedelic soul group Sly & The Family Stone pose for a portrait in 1968. (L-R) Freddie Stone, Sly Stone, Rosie Stone, Larry Graham, Cynthia Robinson, Jerry Martini, Gregg Errico. (Photo by Michael Ochs Archives/Getty Images)

SLY & THE FAMILY STONE REPRESENTED A MELTING pot of music styles and influences—funk, soul, R&B, rock, and psychedelic music; Black and white; male and female.

They were the most progressive 1960s group and remain one of the most influential groups in music history.

As Don Was wrote for *Rolling Stone*, "Sly and the Family Stone didn't have to say, 'Why can't we all just get along?' Looking at the band members and listening to their shared sound made the statement. Seeing this group that embraced so many elements of society sort of drew you in as an extended family member. This was a joyous noise and a joyful vision. Without Sly, the world would be very different. Every R&B thing that came after him was influenced by this guy."

"Sly" was Sylvester Stewart, a Texas native whose parents encouraged him and his siblings—including his brother Freddie and sister Rose—in music. The family later moved to California.

Stewart joined bands in high school and studied music and theory in college. By 1964, now going as Sly Stone, he became a radio DJ known for his eclectic tastes. He also became a record producer for Autumn Records.

By 1966, Sly formed a band—Sly & the Stoners—while Freddie had a band of his own, Freddie & the Stone Souls. Pretty soon, the bands merged, and their names were mixed together, Sly & the Family Stone. The blended group included Freddie on guitar, Rose on piano, Greg Errico on drums, Jerry Martini on saxophone, Cynthia Robinson on trumpet, and Robinson's cousin Larry Graham on bass guitar.

A&R (artist & repertoire) exec David Kapralik was tipped off to this blended group with its unique sound, and he signed them to Epic Records. The group started a Las Vegas residency and recorded their first album, *A Whole New Thing*.

And it was a whole new thing—maybe a little too much. Audiences didn't quite catch on.

CBS exec Clive Davis insisted that the group record something more commercially viable, and they reluctantly released "Dance to the Music."

The song didn't sound like anything on the radio, and it launched the group's sound. It shifted the sound of popular music away from Motown and the British Invasion to something funkier, more progressive, more radical.

Sly & the Family Stone continued touring and recording music, and in late 1968, they released the song "Everyday People," which topped the R&B and *Billboard* Hot 100 charts and became a defining song during a turbulent time.

One of the group's iconic performances came at Woodstock in 1969, during a rain-soaked overnight set.

"I was thinking what would happen if I said something and they all said it back. What would that sound like? So I tried it. I took the microphone and spoke to everyone," Stone told the *Guardian* in a 2023 interview.

He said "higher," the last word of the band's song "I Want to Take You Higher."

"Higher went out. Higher came back. What the word meant widened. It wasn't just keeping yourself up with a good mood or good drugs. It was defeating anything that could bring you down."

The release of their hit "Thank You (Falettinme Be Mice Elf Agin)" in late 1969 marked the end of the decade—and a shift in Sly & the Family Stone's sound.

As the 1970s opened, Stone's life and drug use were spiraling, and friction within the band was boiling over. The group began exploring darker themes and sounds, including funk and overdubbing. The good vibes of the '60s had faded to apathy and disappointment.

Their iconic release *There's a Riot Goin' On* has been hailed as a classic album, and they followed it with *Fresh* in 1973.

But by the release of the gold album *Small Talk* in 1974, Sly & the Family Stone were all but finished. Stone continued releasing new music, first with Epic and later with Warner Brothers. Freddie joined Graham Central Station.

At the band's Rock & Roll Hall of Fame induction in 1993, Stone wasn't expected to appear, but midway through the speech, there he was, getting serenaded by "Thank You (Falettinme Be Mice Elf Agin)." "I believe everything's been said, probably," he said. Not in the least, but the ceremony would have been incomplete without him.

♟ GRAMMY NOMINATIONS: 0

Psychedelic soul group Sly & The Family Stone performs on the TV show "The Midnight Special" on in 1971in Burbank, California. (Photo by Michael Ochs Archives/Getty Images)

Billboard Hot 100 CHARTING SINGLES

Here is a list of Sly & the Family Stone's *Billboard* Hot 100 hits in chronological order.

Song	Year Released	Billboard Hot 100 Peak Position
"Dance to the Music"	1968	8
"Everyday People"	1969	1
"Hot Fun in the Summertime"	1969	2
"Thank You (Falettinme Be Mice Elf Agin)"	1969	1
"Sing A Simple Song"	1969	89
"Stand!"	1969	22
"I Want to Take You Higher"	1970	60
"Everybody Is a Star"	1970	1
"Family Affair"	1971	1
"Runnin' Away"	1972	23
"If You Want Me to Stay"	1973	12
"Frisky"	1974	95

My Favorite Sly & the Family Stone Songs

❯ "Everyday People" ❯ "Family Affair"
❯ "Thank You (Falettinme Be Mice Elf Agin)"

My Favorite Sly & the Family Stone Samples

•• "Deep Cover" by Dr. Dre and Snoop Dogg sampled "Sing A

Simple Song"
- •• "Insane in the Brain" by Cypress Hill sampled "Life"
- •• "Sittin' Up In My Room" by Brandy sampled "Thank You (Falettinme Be Mice Elf Agin)"

⊙ *My Take*

This blended group was amazing. I really began to understand the impact of the group while at Howard University in the early 1990s (1992–1996), where I heard their music everywhere, even though some songs were 20 years old. One of my favorite love songs, "One in a Million You," is by Larry Graham, who was in this group from the start. It blew my mind when I found that out.

Look at how creative the song title "Thank You (Falettinme Be Mice Elf Agin)" is. I love it!

Sly & the Family Stone wrote the book that many groups of today follow on how to build a community and grow it organically. We studied their grassroots marketing while I was attending Berklee. Again, no Grammy wins? How, Sway? How?

Chapter 19

·······

THE SUPREMES

Motown singing group The Supremes pose for a portrait with Diana Ross, Cindy Birdsong, and Mary Wilson circa 1967 in New York. (Photo by James Kriegsmann/Michael Ochs Archives/ Getty Images)

THE SUPREMES REIGN SUPREME.

The girl group is among the most successful acts in music history, had the most commercial success of any Motown group, launched the career of the iconic Diana Ross, and served as torchbearers for future musical groups like

Destiny's Child and En Vogue.

The Supremes began in Detroit in 1959 as the Primettes, a sister group to the Primes. Florence Ballard was asked to put together the group, and she recommended her friend Mary Wilson. They then brought on Betty Travis. One of the members of the Primes, Paul Williams (later a member of the Temptations) recommended a 15-year-old named Diane Ross.

Yes, *Diane*. That was the name her mother chose for her, but her birth certificate mistakenly listed her name as *Diana*, which she would begin going by during the 1960s.

Travis didn't last long in the group, and Barbara Martin joined for a time. The Primettes performed at talent shows and sock hops. Notably, the group's three main singers—Ballard, Wilson, and Ross—could all sing lead. They also worked with guitarist Marvin Tarplin.

As the group gained success and found its pop, R&B, and doo-wop-inspired style, they looked to record an album. They wanted to be part of the upstart Motown label, and they auditioned for Ross's old neighbor Smokey Robinson—yes, the lead singer of the Miracles.

Motown's founder, Berry Gordy, thought the high schoolers were still a little too young. But they kept showing up, and he enlisted them to help with hand claps and singing backup.

In 1961, Gordy decided he wanted to sign the Primettes…but he also wanted them to change their name. Ballard suggested *the Supremes*, and the name stuck. They began recording singles for Motown's Tamla label, but throughout 1961, 1962, and 1963, the hits weren't coming.

In early 1964, the Supremes recorded a song that another Motown group, the

Marvelettes, had rejected—"Where Did Our Love Go," written by Holland–Dozier–Holland. The Supremes weren't big on the song, but it was released as a single, and it soon became a smash hit and their first number 1 single.

With the hit, Ross established herself as the group's lead vocalist.

More hits followed.

"Baby Love."

"Come See About Me."

"Stop! In The Name Of Love." For that chart-topper, the Supremes developed their iconic hand motions, and all you could do when watching them perform was pause and observe the syncopated movements and the intricate choreography. The Supremes stood out from other contemporary groups in part because they embraced their femininity, coordinated their outfits, and developed that top-notch choreography.

The Supremes attained true crossover success, something that eluded many early Black groups. During the mid-1960s, they were bigger than any other American singing group.

But changes were afoot.

The production and writing trio of Holland–Dozier–Holland departed Motown, and Ballard drifted, missing shows and recording sessions, until she was replaced in the group by Cindy Birdsong. The Supremes' success was also grating on other Motown acts.

By the end of the decade, Ross was ready to embark on solo stardom, and the Supremes continued forward with a new lead singer, Jean Terrell.

The Terrell-led Supremes had a handful of hits, including 1970's "Stoned Love" and a remake of "River Deep, Mountain High" with the Four Tops. Amid lineup changes and shifting music styles, the Supremes continued forward until the group disbanded in 1977.

By then, Ross had achieved individual superstardom, recording classics like "Ain't No Mountain High Enough" and crossing into movie acting.

The Supremes entered the Rock & Roll Hall of Fame in 1988.

"The Supremes were more of a women group than a girl group. Beautiful, glamorous and mature, the Supremes were so popular that they rivaled even the Beatles," the hall noted.

♫ GRAMMY NOMINATIONS: 2
♫ GRAMMY WINS: 0

CIRCA 1960: Photo of Supremes. Photo by Michael Ochs Archives/Getty Images

Billboard Hot 100 CHARTING SINGLES

Here is a list of the Supremes' *Billboard* Hot 100 hits in chronological order.

	Song	Year Released	Billboard Hot 100 Peak Position
➔	"When The Lovelight Starts Shining Through His Eyes"	1963	23
➔	"Where Did Our Love Go"	1964	1
➔	"Baby Love"	1964	1
➔	"Come See About Me"	1964	1
➔	"Stop! In The Name Of Love"	1965	1
➔	"Back In My Arms Again"	1965	1
➔	"Nothing But Heartaches"	1965	11
➔	"I Hear A Symphony"	1965	1
➔	"My World Is Empty Without You"	1965	5
➔	"Love Is Like An Itching In My Heart"	1966	9
➔	"You Can't Hurry Love"	1966	1
➔	"You Keep Me Hangin' On"	1966	1
➔	"Love Is Here And Now You're Gone"	1967	1
➔	"The Happening"	1967	1
➔	"Reflections"	1967	2
➔	"In And Out Of Love"	1967	9
➔	"Forever Came Today"	1968	28

Song	Year Released	Billboard Hot 100 Peak Position
"Some Things You Never Get Used To"	1968	30
"Love Child"	1968	1
"I'm Gonna Make You Love Me" (with the Temptations)	1968	2
"I'm Livin' In Shame"	1969	10
"The Composer"	1969	27
"No Matter What Sign You Are"	1969	31
"Someday We'll Be Together"	1969	1
"Up the Ladder to the Roof"	1970	10
"Everybody's Got the Right to Love"	1970	21
"Stoned Love"	1970	7
"River Deep, Mountain High" & The Four Tops	1970	14
"Nathan Jones"	1970	16
"You Gotta Have Love in Your Heart"	1971	55
"Touch"	1971	71
"Floy Joy"	1971	16
"Automatically Sunshine"	1972	37
"Your Wonderful, Sweet Sweet Love"	1972	59
"I Guess I'll Miss The Man"	1972	85
"Bad Weather"	1972	87
"I'm Gonna Let My Heart Do the Walking"	1976	40
"You're My Driving Wheel"	1976	85

♨ *My Favorite the Supremes Songs*

❯ "Stop! In The Name Of Love" ❯ "You Can't Hurry Love"
❯ "Baby Love"

♥ *My Favorite the Supremes Samples*

•• "Poor Georgie" by MC Lyte sampled "My World Is Empty Without You"

•• "You Want This" by Janet Jackson sampled "Love Child"

•• "If" by Janet Jackson sampled "Someday We'll Be Together"

⊙ My Take

Outside of the Supremes' many hits and their crossover success, what really struck me was the number of times they had consecutive top 10 hits on the *Billboard* Hot 100 charts. Every year from 1964 to 1969, they had a number 1 hit, including multiple number 1s back-to-back-to-back. Looking over the research, I don't think there is another R&B group that has a condensed run of success like that of the Supremes. They were on fire for almost all of the 1960s. Amazing run. They won a Grammy Lifetime Achievement Award in 2023 (late!) but were never awarded a Grammy for a song or album. That seems crazy to me!

American Motown pop vocal trio The Supremes; Mary Wilson, Cindy Birdsong, and Diana Ross, center. Original Publication: People Disc - HL0212 (Photo by George Stroud/Getty Images)

Chapter 20

....

THE TEMPTATIONS

CIRCA 1970: Photo of Temptations. Photo by Michael Ochs Archives/Getty Images

THE TEMPTATIONS EMBODIED MOTOWN. AND THEIR BIGGEST HITS, like "My Girl," are instantly recognizable.

"With style to spare, drop-dead dance moves and voices that had been nurtured in the deep South and seasoned in the cities of the North, the Temptations captured in their work the pleasure of the street-corner serenade as well as the flash of the Sixties soul revue," Michael Hill wrote to commemorate the group's Rock & Roll Hall of Fame induction.

The group was founded in 1960 when two other groups merged—the Cavaliers (later the Primes) and the Elegants (later the Questions and the Distants). The groups met at a house party, and pretty soon they had a lineup consisting of Otis Miles, Melvin Franklin, Eddie Kendricks, Paul Williams, and Elbridge "Al" Bryant.

The new group was initially called the Elgins. They began touring on the local club circuit and were spotted by Motown founder Berry Gordy. They were signed to the subsidiary Miracle Records and changed their name to the Temptations.

The Temptations, despite their gospel-infused harmonies, couldn't break through at the onset, and a series of singles failed to climb very high on the charts.

Bryant departed in 1963, to be replaced by a tenor from Whynot, Mississippi, whose big, raspy voice had been nurtured on gospel: David Ruffin. With the addition of Ruffin, the Temptations had found their classic lineup.

From there, the hits fell into place. Their first was "The Way You Do The Things You Do," on which Kendricks and his falsetto guided the Smokey Robinson–written track. Robinson—the Miracles' lead vocalist—had Ruffin in mind for the group's next big hit.

As Robinson told NPR in 2009, "David Ruffin, I knew, was like this sleeping giant in this group because he had this—it's sort of like a mellow gruff-sounding voice. And all I needed was the right song for his voice and I felt like I would have a smash hit record. So I sat down at the piano to write a song for David Ruffin's voice. So I wanted to make it something that he could belt out, but yet make it melodic and sweet."

They began practicing the track while the Miracles and the Temptations were touring together, and they recorded it upon returning to Detroit.

The song was called "My Girl." And it became the Temptations'—and Ruffin's—signature song.

"It's a pulsating, shuffle-wobble ballad…that the artists serve up in very tempting style," the publication *Cashbox* wrote, noting its "striking arrangement" and "inviting, blues-styled ballad hip-swinger."

Successful singles piled up, and in time, Norman Whitfield and Brian Holland took over production, bridging the group an edgier sound on songs like "Ain't Too Proud To Beg."

Those hits reinforced the Temptations' identity for their five-part harmonies and elaborate stage shows, which featured the group members wearing matching outfits and doing intricate dance routines.

By 1968, Ruffin was ready to depart the group and record solo; the breakup had been brewing for some time. Ruffin was becoming more and more addicted to cocaine, isolated from his bandmates, and undependable. Dennis Edwards took over for Ruffin. Ruffin left to pursue a solo career.

The Temptations embraced the change while also embracing a new sound—psychedelic rock—with the song "Cloud Nine." The Whitfield-produced track won Motown its first Grammy Award.

Other progressive hits followed like the classic soul song "Papa Was A Rollin'

Stone" and the ballad "Just My Imagination (Running Away With Me)," which features a lush orchestral arrangement.

The Temptations' lineup changed many times over the years. Kendricks, with his smooth falsetto, departed in 1971, just as Ruffin had three years earlier, to pursue solo stardom.

Despite the lineup changes and shifting music tastes from funk to disco and adult contemporary, the Temptations continued to release music and tour, and they were inducted into the Rock & Roll Hall of Fame in 1989.

Ruffin, Kendricks, and Edwards—the group's former leads—embarked on a tour and planned to release an album, but it never came to fruition. Ruffin died of a drug overdose in 1991, while Kendricks died from lung cancer the following year. While their voices were silenced too soon, their impact lives on in the timeless classics they recorded.

♔ GRAMMY NOMINATIONS: 9
♔ GRAMMY WINS: 4

- ✹ Best Rhythm & Blues Performance by a Duo or Group, Vocal or Instrumental: "Cloud Nine"
- ✹ Best R&B Instrumental Performance: "Papa Was A Rollin' Stone"
- ✹ Best R&B Vocal Performance by a Duo, Group or Chorus: "Papa Was A Rollin' Stone"
- ✹ Best Traditional R&B Vocal Album: *Ear-Resistible*

American Motown vocal group The Temptations, UK, April 1972. From left to right, they are singers Otis Williams, Richard Street (1942–2013), Melvin Franklin (1942–1995), Damon Harris (1950–2013), and Dennis Edwards (1943–2018). (Photo by Evening Standard/Hulton Archive/Getty Images)

Billboard Hot 100 CHARTING SINGLES

Here is a list of the Temptations' *Billboard* Hot 100 hits in chronological order.

	Song	Year Released	Billboard Hot 100 Peak Position
➲	"The Way You Do The Things You Do"	1964	11
➲	"My Girl"	1965	1
➲	"It's Growing"	1965	18
➲	"Since I Lost My Baby"	1965	17
➲	"My Baby"	1965	74
➲	"Get Ready"	1966	29

	Song	Year Released	Billboard Hot 100 Peak Position
➡	"Ain't Too Proud To Beg"	1966	13
➡	"Beauty Is Only Skin Deep"	1966	3
➡	"(I Know) I'm Losing You"	1966	8
➡	"All I Need"	1967	8
➡	"You're My Everything"	1967	6
➡	"(Loneliness Made Me Realize) It's You That I Need"	1967	14
➡	"I Wish It Would Rain"	1968	4
➡	"I Could Never Love Another (After Loving You)"	1968	13
➡	"Please Return Your Love To Me"	1968	27
➡	"Cloud Nine"	1968	6
➡	"I'm Gonna Make You Love Me" (with Diana Ross & the Supremes)	1969	2
➡	"Runaway Child, Running Wild"	1969	6
➡	"I Can't Get Next To You"	1969	1
➡	"Psychedelic Shack"	1970	7
➡	"Ball Of Confusion (That's What The World Is Today)"	1970	3
➡	"Just My Imagination (Running Away With Me)"	1971	1
➡	"Superstar (Remember How You Got Where You Are)"	1971	18
➡	"Take A Look Around"	1972	27
➡	"Papa Was A Rollin' Stone"	1972	1
➡	"Masterpiece"	1973	7

Song	Year Released	Billboard Hot 100 Peak Position
"Plastic Man"	1973	40
"Hey Girl (I Like Your Style)"	1973	35
"Let Your Hair Down"	1973	27
"Happy People"	1974	40
"Shakey Ground"	1975	26
"Power"	1980	81
"Sail Away"	1980	51
"Standing On The Top"	1982	66
"Treat Her Like A Lady"	1984	48
"Lady Soul"	1986	53
"Look What You Started"	1986	49
"Some Enchanted Evening"	1986	66
"Stay"	1988	91
"Special"	1989	91
"The Jones' "	1990	77
"My Love Is True (Truly For You)"	1991	88

My Favorite the Temptations Songs

"Papa Was A Rollin' Stone" "Ain't Too Proud To Beg" //
"I Wish It Would Rain"

♥ *My Favorite the Temptations Samples*

- •• "Welcome To The Terrordome" by Public Enemy sampled "Psychedelic Shack"
- •• "Eazy-Duz-It" by Eazy-E sampled "Ball Of Confusion (That's What The World Is Today)"
- •• "Super Freak" by Rick James sampled "Standing On The Top"

⬇ *My Take*

It is ironic that a song with a new sound ("Cloud Nine") was the song that got Motown its first Grammy. This group had so much talent. It is a shame they couldn't stay together for longer and produce even more classic hits.

Chapter 21

....

HONORABLE MENTION—1960S

THE CHIFFONS

Producer Ronnie Mack was shopping a song called "He's So Fine" in 1962, and the producers asked if he had a group to sing it. "Yes, a great group," he told them.

Mack scrambled to get a girl group he knew, the Chiffons, to sing his song. The group had formed a few years earlier—the Chiffons members went to James Monroe High School in the Bronx together.

So it was that Judy Craig, Patricia Bennett, and Barbara Lee, along with an additional singer added by Mack, Sylvia Peterson, recorded the song. "He's So Fine," with its *doo-lang doo-lang doo-lang* intro, topped the pop and R&B charts.

The Chiffons had a handful of other hits, including "One Fine Day," but none has had the impact of "He's So Fine." The song was even the subject of a lawsuit against ex-Beatle George Harrison, who was found to have unintentionally plagiarized the song in "My Sweet Lord."

🏆 **GRAMMY NOMINATIONS: 0**

Billboard Hot 100 CHARTING SINGLES

Here is a list of the Chiffons' *Billboard* Hot 100 hits in chronological order.

Song	Year Released	Billboard Hot 100 Peak Position
"He's So Fine"	1963	1
"One Fine Day"	1963	5
"Lucky Me"	1964	95
"I Have A Boyfriend"	1964	36
"Sailor Boy"	1964	80
"A Love So Fine"	1965	40
"Nobody Knows What's Going On (In My Mind But Me)"	1965	49
"Sweet Talkin' Guy"	1966	10
"Out Of This World"	1966	94
"Up On The Bridge"	1966	85

⬇ My Take

Add this to the list of groups I discovered while doing the research for the book. Their first single was their best-performing single, and the story about how Mack quickly put together the group is a great one.

THE MARVELETTES

The Marvelettes—not the Miracles or the Supremes or the Temptations—secured Motown's first number 1 single with "Please Mr. Postman."

The girl group auditioned for Berry Gordy in 1961 as the Marvels; the label wanted them to come up with an original song. Singer Georgia Dobbins asked a songwriting friend, William Garrett, for help, and he'd written a blues song, "Please Mr. Postman."

Dobbins kept the title and rewrote the lyrics, but after finishing the song, she dropped out of the group. Motown's writing team worked on the song further, and in the summer of 1961, the Marvelettes recorded it.

And then it climbed all the way up the charts.

The Marvelettes churned out hits throughout the 1960s, including "Playboy," "Beechwood 4-5789" and "Don't Mess With Bill." But they notably passed on a song given to them in 1964 that would be recorded by the Supremes: "Baby Love."

Billboard Hot 100 CHARTING SINGLES

Here is a list of the Marvelettes' *Billboard* Hot 100 hits in chronological order.

Song	Year Released	Billboard Hot 100 Peak Position
● "Please Mr. Postman"	1961	1
● "Twistin' Postman"	1962	34
● "Playboy"	1962	7

	Song	Year Released	Billboard Hot 100 Peak Position
➤	"Beechwood 4-5789"	1962	17
➤	"Someday, Someway"	1963	8
➤	"Strange I Know"	1963	49
➤	"Locking Up My Heart"	1963	44
➤	"Too Many Fish In The Sea"	1964	25
➤	"You're My Remedy"	1964	26
➤	"Danger! Heartbreak Dead Ahead"	1965	61
➤	"Don't Mess With Bill"	1966	7
➤	"The Hunter Gets Captured By The Game"	1967	13
➤	"When You're Young And In Love"	1967	23
➤	"My Baby Must Be A Magician"	1967	17

⬇ *My Take*

I would love to learn what the Marvelettes' reasoning was for opting not to record "Baby Love." That song could have continued their momentum during the mid-'60s.

THE SHIRELLES

The Shirelles, hailing from Passaic, New Jersey, were among the first breakout all-female groups and set a high bar for future performers.

The group—which included schoolmates Shirley Owens, Doris Coley, Addie "Micki" Harris, and Beverly Lee—broke through on the strength of a song penned by Carole King and Gerry Goffin, "Will You Love Me Tomorrow." The song was released in late 1960 and became an international hit. The group also became a favorite of the Beatles.

Other smash singles included "Dedicated To The One I Love," "Mama Said," and "Soldier Boy."

The Shirelles were known for their smooth harmonies and crossover appeal at a time when all-Black groups still weren't getting visibility on national programs like *The Ed Sullivan Show*.

As Paul Shaffer wrote for *Rolling Stone,* "The Shirelles had a 'sound,' a word that people from the Sixties vocal-group era use with a lot of reverence. Shirley Alston Reeves [née Shirley Owens], who did most of the group's lead vocals, wasn't a gospel shouter like Arlene Smith of the Chantels. Shirley was more sentimental and street. When she said, 'Baby, it's you,' you thought, 'Baby, it *is* me.'"

The Shirelles were inducted into the Rock & Roll Hall of Fame in 1996, and their music continues to inspire artists today.

Billboard Hot 100 CHARTING SINGLES

Here is a list of the Shirelles' *Billboard* Hot 100 hits in chronological order.

Song	Year Released	Billboard Hot 100 Peak Position
"I Met Him On A Sunday"	1958	49
"Tonight's The Night"	1960	39

Song	Year Released	Billboard Hot 100 Peak Position
"Will You Love Me Tomorrow"	1960	1
"Dedicated To The One I Love"	1961	3
"Mama Said"	1961	4
"A Thing of the Past"	1961	41
"Big John"	1961	21
"Baby It's You"	1962	8
"Soldier Boy"	1962	1
"Welcome Home Baby"	1962	22
"Stop The Music"	1962	36
"Foolish Little Girl"	1963	4
"Don't Say Goodnight And Mean Goodbye"	1964	26
"Thank You Baby"	1965	63

⊙ My Take

Note that the Shirelles were one of the first all-Black groups to appear on
The Ed Sullivan Show. I love the song "Will You Love Me Tomorrow." I feel
a current artist should remake that song.

1970's

From Top left to Bottom left in clockwise order:
Earth Wind and Fire, The Jackson 5, The O'Jays and The
Temptations and Supremes together.

Part Three
1970S

IF THE 1960S WERE THE TIME OF THE rock group, disco ruled the 1970s. That light shone very bright before burning out quickly as we entered the 1980s. The Bee Gees were one of the biggest musical acts of the decade, dominating all types of sales (albums and singles) while living on the charts for months at a time. The release of the movie *Saturday Night Fever*, whose soundtrack album was the biggest selling album of all time before the release of *Thriller*, sparked a cultural revolution in nightclubs around the world. Stevie Wonder picked up momentum as he won Grammy Awards in three different years. Roberta Flack became the first female artist to win back-to-back Grammy Awards for Record of the Year. The Beatles broke up, and Diana Ross left the Supremes. Jim Morrison, Elvis Presley, Janis Joplin, and Jimi Hendrix all passed away in the 1970s.

Looking at the popular news stories of the 1970s, the world continued to move at a rapid pace. The Vietnam War ended early in the 1970s, while there was some madness going on at the Watergate Hotel in 1972. The *Roe v. Wade* decision was made in 1973, serial killer Ted Bundy was on the loose from 1974 to 1978, and the gay liberation movement gained steam in the '70s. The Pittsburgh Steelers won four Super Bowls in this decade, Mr. October

(Reggie Jackson) earned his nickname during this time, and Secretariat won the Triple Crown in record fashion in 1973.

The 1970s started an unprecedented run of success for R&B groups. The next three decades would see R&B evolve into one of the most dominant genres in music. Hip-hop music would catch fire in the 1990s, and artists would sample many of the famous R&B groups from the 1970s as a way of bridging the age demographical gap. Record sales began to match the popularity of the groups of this decade, and several legendary groups came to prominence.

Reflection offers us the chance to review the beginnings of many 1970s groups that changed music forever. The Jackson 5, Earth, Wind & Fire, the Commodores, and Kool and the Gang lead the way.

Chapter 22

. . . .

THE COMMODORES

Photo of Commodores; Back: Walter Orange, Ronald La Pread and Milan Williams. Front: Thomas McClary, Lionel Richie and William King. (Photo by Gilles Petard/Redferns)

THE COMMODORES COULD SLIP BETWEEN FUNK DANCE TRACKS and soul ballads better than just about any group.

Their greatest fame came during the late 1970s and early 1980s, when smooth-sounding Lionel Richie was their co-lead singer, but even without

Richie, the Commodores have proven their mettle with hits like the Grammy-winning "Nightshift."

The group was formed in 1968; its members attended Tuskegee Institute (now Tuskegee University) in Alabama together. They had previously been involved in two different groups, the Mystics and the Jays. They settled on a name in the most random of ways—flipping open the dictionary and picking a random word.

"We lucked out," William King told *People*. "We almost became 'The Commodes.' "

In short order, the Commodores had their classic lineup—Lionel Richie on saxophone, Milan Williams on keyboards, King on trumpet, Walter "Clyde" Orange on drums, Ronald LaPread on bass, and Thomas McClary on guitar.

They aimed to appeal to all audiences with an eclectic sound—so they listened to the Temptations and the Rolling Stones, even Elton John. They performed at different parties and clubs and were managed in those early years by Benny Ashburn.

It wasn't until 1972—when they were opening for the Jackson 5—that the Commodores came onto Berry Gordy and Motown's radar.

In 1974, under Motown Records, the Commodores released their debut studio album, *Machine Gun*, which featured their hit single of the same name. But the Commodores really found their groove with 1975's *Caught in the Act*. The album included their first top 10 hit, "Slippery When Wet."

In the years that followed, the Commodores churned out one hit album after another—and a string of massive hits like "Brick House," "Easy," "Three Times A Lady," and "Sail On." Orange and Richie shared lead singer duties.

Richie described the meaning for "Brick House" in a later interview.

"A brick house means she's stacked," he said. "When you have these wonderful measurements, 36-24-36 or variations of that in any form and you got these legs and this body and guys turn around and go 'aww'…that's a brick house!"

The song features a funky guitar riff, an infectious horn section, and playful lyrics celebrating a confident and attractive woman. "Brick House" was written by Richie, Williams, Orange, and LaPread. The inspiration behind the song was reportedly a woman they had seen walking down the street in downtown Atlanta, Georgia. According to the band, they were driving through Atlanta when they noticed an attractive woman with a curvaceous figure. Her confident and powerful presence left a lasting impression on them. Inspired by this encounter, the band members came up with the idea for the song. The lyrics celebrate the beauty, strength, and allure of the "brick house" woman. The song became one of the Commodores' biggest hits, reaching the top five on the *Billboard* Hot 100 chart in 1977. "Brick House" has since become a classic funk and R&B anthem, known for its captivating groove, catchy melody, and memorable lyrics.

Where the group was more oriented to funk, Richie was best recognized for his slow, heartfelt ballads, and as the 1970s wore on, the Commodores became known more and more for soft, soulful Richie-led hits like "Three Times A Lady."

Their string of singles, the Vocal Group Hall of Fame later wrote, "moved an entire generation." Success, however, was not enough to save them from the changes in the music scene, or most especially, the music business.

Richie left the Commodores in 1982 to pursue solo superstardom.

Lesser groups might have folded or faded. But the Commodores continued forward through various lineup changes. The current iteration of the Commodores consists of Orange, James Dean "J.D." Nicholas, and King.

♔ GRAMMY NOMINATIONS: 9
♔ GRAMMY WINS: 1
✸ Best R&B Performance by a Duo or Group with Vocal: "Nightshift"

CIRCA 1970: Photo of Commodores. Photo by Michael Ochs Archives/Getty Images

Billboard Hot 100 CHARTING SINGLES

Here is a list of the Commodores' *Billboard* Hot 100 hits in chronological order.

Song	Year Released	Billboard Hot 100 Peak Position[7]
"Machine Gun"	1974	22
"Slippery When Wet"	1975	19
"Sweet Love"	1976	5
"Just To Be Close To You"	1976	7
"Fancy Dancer"	1976	39
"Easy"	1977	4
"Brick House"	1977	5
"Too Hot Ta Trot"	1978	24
"Three Times A Lady"	1978	1
"Sail On"	1979	4
"Still"	1979	1
"Wonderland"	1981	25
"Lady (You Bring Me Up)"	1981	8
"Oh No"	1981	4
"Why You Wanna Try Me"	1981	77 *
"Painted Picture"	1982	45 *

---

7   While doing the research, there was conflicting information on the exact peak position on the charts for "Why You Wanna Try Me" and "Painted Picture." The best estimation was used in placing the songs in the chart.

	Song	Year Released	Billboard Hot 100 Peak Position[7]
➤	"Only You"	1983	54
➤	"Nightshift"	1985	3

🔥 *My Favorite the Commodores Songs*

➤ "Easy" ➤ "Brick House" ➤ "Zoom"

💜 *My Favorite the Commodores Samples*

- •• "Let The Rhythm Hit 'Em" by Eric B. & Rakim sampled "The Assembly Line"
- •• "Hey Ma" by Cam'ron & Guests sampled "Easy"
- •• "Ill Na Na" by Fox Brown & Method Man sampled "Brick House"

⬇ My Take

The singles above charted on the *Billboard* Hot 100, representing a selection of the Commodores' most successful and well-known songs. Additionally, the Commodores achieved considerable success on the *Billboard* R&B chart with several of their other releases. The Commodores have sold over 75 million records worldwide, received multiple Grammy nominations, and won numerous awards for their contributions to music. They are considered one of the most successful funk and soul bands of all time, and their music continues to be enjoyed by fans worldwide.

Several of the Commodores' songs remain timeless and are must-plays at any large gatherings of people where there is a wide age demographic (weddings, birthday parties, anniversaries, etc.). It is very hard to imagine this group opening for the Jackson 5, when both groups became such legendary groups.

I feel that "Brick House" could be a hit if it was released today. Also, listen closely to the lyrics of "Easy," which I give a chef's kiss! I am also personally surprised that their hit "Zoom" never even charted on the *Billboard* Hot 100 charts.

Chapter 23

. . . .

EARTH, WIND & FIRE (EWF)

CIRCA 1970: Photo of Earth Wind & Fire. Photo by Michael Ochs Archives/Getty Images

EARTH, WIND & FIRE BRIDGED THE GAP BETWEEN white and Black music, between R&B and pop, and, in the process, the group created a distinct, African- and Caribbean-infused sound that appealed to audiences worldwide—a sound that was as commercially successful as it was artistically groundbreaking.

EWF was founded and led by Maurice White, who joined his church choir at a young age before being drawn to drumming. He soon began getting gigs and performed with Booker T. Jones, of Booker T & the MGs fame. After attending the Chicago Conservatory of Music, White became the studio percussionist for Chess Records—giving him the chance to play with performers like Etta James. There, he connected with Ramsey Lewis, and he joined Lewis's band.

By 1969, White and two friends—Wade Flemons and Don Whitehead—began composing songs and commercials together. White handled vocals, percussion, and kalimba, an African thumb piano that he'd learned about while playing with the Ramsey Lewis Trio.

The trio moved to Los Angeles and signed with Warner Brothers. White decided to name the band Earth, Wind & Fire after the elements—a name that commanded a spiritual, elemental feel. White recruited a cadre of musicians to round out EWF, and they released two albums before White shifted the group's lineup.

The group now consisted of his brother Verdine White on bass, Jessica Cleaves and Philip Bailey on vocals, Ronnie Laws on flute and saxophone, Roland Bautista on guitar, Larry Dunn on keyboard, and Ralph Johnson on percussion.

"Maurice became disillusioned with Warner Brothers, which had signed the group primarily as a jazz act. Maurice, in contrast, was more interested in combining elements of jazz, rock, and soul into an evolving form of fusion, a truly universal sound," EWF's website states.

Amid White's disillusionment, the group came onto Columbia exec Clive Davis's radar, and he bought out their contract.

With Columbia, EWF started coming into its own, and after a few well-received albums, the group hit its stride with 1975's *That's the Way of the World*. The album contained the hit "Shining Star"—imagined as White walked under a star-filled sky—and the title track, which both climbed the R&B charts.

The album also contained the ballad "Reasons," which explores the complexities and depth of relationships and carries a sense of longing. The song, like many of EWF's hits, is characterized by its lush arrangement and soaring vocal harmonies.

Later that year, and after touring Europe, EWF returned to the studio and completed *Gratitude*, an album featuring lots of live concert material. The triple-platinum album spoke to the group's renown for its dynamic and visually stunning live performances, which featured elaborate stage productions, pyrotechnics, laser lights, and magic—in fact, magician David Copperfield worked on some of the group's tours.

The hits continued with 1976's *Spirit* album, which featured the hits "Getaway" and "Saturday Nite," and 1977's *All 'n All*. Songs like the soaring, funky "Fantasy" were unlike anything else any other music act was developing at the time.

By 1978, EWF was looking back—and looking forward—with a greatest hits album, *The Best of Earth, Wind & Fire, Vol. 1*. The album contained some of the group's biggest hits, along with a handful of new tracks, including a cover of the Beatles' "Got To Get You Into My Life." The album's other single was the timeless "September," which carries a joyful feeling—joy for love, joy for youth, joy for joy.

The group's hits continued through the 1970s and into the 1980s, one song after another full of rhythm and tempo changes and horn arrangements.

But music was changing.

"The soulful black pop that dominated the '70s was being pushed out by glam rock, synth pop, and New Wave," Jackson Howard wrote in a 2019 essay for the Ringer.

"In an effort to stay put, *I Am* went for broke, functioning as a stubborn commitment to purpose and pulling out every trick in Earth, Wind & Fire's book—all-star collaborators, outlandish arrangements, torch songs, ballads, and dance-floor fillers—to stave off change. They wouldn't come close to reaching these heights again. But what's left behind from the twilight of the band's peak is an album that is, ironically, bigger than its time and more than the sum of its parts: It's an album by some of the greatest musicians in America hoping that music will save them."

EWF released the LP *Faces* in 1980, one of its best albums, and shifted to an electronic sound for 1981's *Raise!*

In 1984, following the release of *Electric Universe*, White put the band on hiatus. During the downtime, he produced albums for others and his own solo album.

EWF re-formed in 1987 and released the album *Touch the World*, another hit. It spawned the number 1 R&B single "System of Survival."

The band continued producing high-quality albums throughout the 1990s, but White stopped regularly touring after being diagnosed with Parkinson's disease. The band was inducted into the Rock & Roll Hall of Fame in 2000 and performed at a White House state dinner.

Later releases focused on collaborations with contemporaries like will.i.am from the Black Eyed Peas and Big Boi from Outkast.

While White died in 2016, EWF has continued to record and perform, and the group has continued to move people with its soaring, joyful, spiritual, eclectic music. EWF's beginnings as a fusion of musical styles, its spiritual foundation, its spectacular live performances, and its chart-topping hits have propelled the group to become one of the most iconic and revered bands in the music industry. Its music continues to inspire and uplift audiences, cementing its enduring legacy.

🏆 GRAMMY NOMINATIONS: 17
🏆 GRAMMY WINS: 6

- Best R&B Vocal Performance by a Duo, Group or Chorus: "Shining Star"
- Best R&B Instrumental Performance: "Runnin'"
- Best R&B Vocal Performance by a Duo, Group or Chorus: "All 'N All"
- Best R&B Instrumental Performance: "Boogie Wonderland"
- Best R&B Vocal Performance by a Duo, Group or Chorus: "After the Love Has Gone"
- Best R&B Performance by a Duo or Group with Vocals: "Wanna Be with You"

Photo of Earth Wind & Fire; (Photo by Echoes/Redferns)

Billboard Hot 100 CHARTING SINGLES

Here is a list of EWF's *Billboard* Hot 100 hits in chronological order.

Song	Year Released	Billboard Hot 100 Peak Position
"Shining Star"	1	1975
"Sing a Song"	5	1976
"Getaway"	12	1976
"Saturday Nite"	21	1976
"Fantasy"	32	1978
"September"	8	1978
"Boogie Wonderland" (with The Emotions)	6	1979
"After the Love Has Gone"	2	1979
"Let Me Talk"	39	1980
"Can't Let Go"	39	1980
"You"	48	1975
"Serpentine Fire"	13	1977
"Got to Get You Into My Life"	9	1978
"In the Stone"	58	1979
"And Love Goes On"	50	1980
"Wanna Be with You"	15	1981
"Fall in Love with Me"	17	1983
"Side by Side"	50	1983
"Thinking of You"	28	1988

Song	Year Released	Billboard Hot 100 Peak Position
"System of Survival"	60	1987
"Sunday Morning"	39	1993
"Spend the Night"	50	1989
"All In The Way"	65	1999
"Show Me the Way"	44	1990

🔥 *My Favorite Earth, Wind & Fire Songs*

❯ "Reasons" ❯ "Would You Mind" ❯ "After the Love Has Gone"

♥ *My Favorite Earth, Wind & Fire Samples*

- "Still Not a Player" by Big Pun feat. Joe sampled "Brazilian Rhyme (Beijo Interlude)"
- "You Can't Play With My Yo-Yo" by Yo-Yo feat. Ice Cube sampled "Devotion"
- "Paper Thin" by MC Lyte sampled "Shining Star"

⊙ My Take

I am not sure we will see another group like EWF in our lifetimes. The vocals, instrumentation, and live shows have been unmatched since they hit stages in the early 1970s. The fact that they enlisted the help of David Copperfield for their shows is an example of how serious they were about the live performance aspect. Maurice White could have been an amazing solo artist, but his mission was to use the group as a vehicle to spread their music around the world. His mission continues to be quite successful. And once again, Clive Davis shows us how good his ear for talent was, as he had the foresight to buy their contract out and let them be them. Amazing instincts.

Chapter 24

·······

THE FOUR TOPS

Vocal quartet The Four Tops perform onstage in circa 1965. (L-R) Levi Stubbs, Ronaldo Obie Benson, Abdul Duke Fakir, Lawrence Payton. (Photo by Michael Ochs Archives/Getty Images)

THE FOUR TOPS ARE ONE OF THE LONGEST enduring R&B/soul groups— and their peaks, valleys, and reinventions paralleled those of Motown.

The group traces its roots to mid-1950s Detroit. Boyhood friends Levi Stubbs (lead vocals), Abdul "Duke" Fakir (baritone vocals), Renaldo "Obie" Benson (tenor vocals), and Lawrence Payton (tenor vocals) started singing together and called themselves the Four Aims.

They soon rebranded as the Four Tops—and famously, the foursome stuck together without a lineup change for more than 40 years.

It took years for the group to find success; they bounced around from one label to another before coming onto Berry Gordy's radar.

At first, the Four Tops backed up other Motown artists like the Supremes and worked in a jazz vein. But by 1964, the Four Tops recorded a song from the pen of the songwriting team of Holland–Dozier–Holland: "Baby I Need Your Loving." The song set a foundation for hits to come.

The following year, they released their first number 1 pop hit, "I Can't Help Myself," which is known more for its alternate title, "Sugar Pie Honey Bunch." The song speaks to a man's yearning and longing—he can't stop loving the woman who's stolen his heart. Their follow-up, "It's The Same Old Song," was another top five hit.

The group reached its peak with 1966's "Reach Out I'll Be There," an instantly iconic song. The Four Tops were releasing lots of substantive songs, not bubblegum pop.

The Four Tops recorded standards and Broadway tunes. And when the songwriting team of Holland–Dozier–Holland left Motown in 1967, the Four Tops turned to other artists for inspiration, covering hits like the Left Banke's "Walk Away Renee."

The 1970s saw the Four Tops' legacy cemented, from their pairing with the

Supremes for the *Magnificent 7* LP and "River Deep, Mountain High" to a shift to Dunhill, where the hits continued—such as "Ain't No Woman (Like The One I've Got)."

The original Four Tops continued together until the 1997 death of Payton; Benson and Stubbs have also since died. Fakir remained a member of the Four Tops into the 2020s, alongside Ronnie McNeir, Lawrence "Roquel" Payton Jr., and Alexander Morris.

🏆 GRAMMY NOMINATIONS: 1
🏆 GRAMMY WINS: 0

R&B vocal group The Four Tops pose for a **portrait** in 1975. Clockwise from left: Lawrence Payton, Abdul "Duke" Fakir, Ronaldo "Obie" Benson, Levi Stubbs. (Photo by Michael Ochs Archives/Getty Images)

Billboard Hot 100 CHARTING SINGLES

Here is a list of the Four Tops' *Billboard* Hot 100 hits in chronological order.

Song	Year Released	Billboard Hot 100 Peak Position
"Baby I Need Youvr Loving"	1964	11
"Without The One You Love (Life's Not Worthwhile)"	1964	43
"Ask The Lonely"	1965	24
"I Can't Help Myself (Sugar Pie, Honey Bunch)"	1965	1
"It's The Same Old Song"	1965	5
"Something About You"	1965	19
"Shake Me, Wake Me (When It's Over)"	1966	18
"Loving You Is Sweeter Than Ever"	1966	45
"Reach Out I'll Be There"	1966	1
"Standing In The Shadows Of Love"	1966	6
"Bernadette"	1967	4
"7-Rooms of Gloom"	1967	14
"You Keep Running Away"	1967	19
"If I Were A Carpenter"	1968	20
"Walk Away Renee"	1968	14
"Yesterday's Dreams"	1968	49
"What Is A Man"	1969	70

Song	Year Released	Billboard Hot 100 Peak Position
"Don't Let Him Take Your Love From Me"	1969	43
"It's All In The Game"	1970	24
"Still Water (Love)"	1970	11
"River Deep, Mountain High"	1971	14
"A Simple Game"	1972	77
"Keeper Of The Castle"	1972	10
"Ain't No Woman (Like The One I've Got)"	1973	4
"Are You Man Enough?"	1973	15
"Sweet Understanding Love"	1973	33
"One Chain Don't Make No Prison"	1974	41
"Midnight Flower"	1974	52
"Catfish"	1976	44
"When She Was My Girl"	1981	11
"I Just Can't Walk Away"	1983	79
"Sexy Ways"	1985	58

My Favorite the Four Tops Songs

- "I Can't Help Myself (Sugar Pie, Honey Bunch)"
- "Reach Out I'll Be There"
- "Ain't No Woman (Like The One I've Got)"

♥ *My Favorite the Four Tops Samples*

- ·· "Ain't No Nigga" by Jay-Z feat. Foxy Brown sampled "Ain't No Woman (Like The One I've Got)"
- ·· "Cha Cha Cha" by MC Lyte sampled "I Can't Live Without You"
- ·· "The Hours" by Slum Village sampled "I Found The Spirit"

⬇ *My Take*

One of my very first 45s was "I Can't Help Myself (Sugar Pie, Honey Bunch)." I can't seem to find it nowadays though. I respect The Four Tops so much because they were able to thrive across three decades where music changed dramatically. Their music continues to be sampled at a high rate.

Chapter 25

. . . .

THE JACKSON 5/THE JACKSONS

R&B quintet Jackson Five pose for a portrait in 1970 in Los Angeles, California. Clockwise from lower left: Marlon Jackson, Tito Jackson, Jermaine Jackson, Jackie Jackson, Michael Jackson (seated, with hat). (Photo by Michael Ochs Archives/Getty Images)

THE JACKSON 5 WERE ONE OF THE MOST celebrated soul groups of the 1970s and introduced the world to the "King of Pop," Michael Jackson.

The group formed in the mid-1960s in Gary, Indiana, around the Jackson brothers. At first, it featured Tito, Jermaine, and Jackie. Younger brothers Marlon and Michael, who were five years old, joined soon after.

Family patriarch Joe Jackson managed his sons. They started out performing at midwestern talent shows and nightclubs—and after seeing success, Joe took his sons to New York City to play at the Apollo Theater's amateur night contest.

In August 1967, they won that night's contest. Little Michael was only nine years old. Everything—success and fame, lots and lots of fame, and eventually turmoil and heartbreak—was ahead of the family.

They signed to the Steel-Town label in 1968, and their first single, "Big Boy," started getting airplay regionally, which allowed them to work at clubs and theaters in Chicago, which is where bigger acts—namely, Gladys Knight, and Bobby Taylor of the Vancouvers—told Berry Gordy about these little kids who were going to transform the music world.

In general, Gordy was apprehensive about signing a group that was composed primarily of kids. The additional stress and needs of a group full of minors were more challenging for an up-and-coming label like Motown. Even though Motown already had little Stevie Wonder on the label, Gordy was not a fan of kid acts for the reasons mentioned above. But Gordy finally relented, and he recognized the same thing everyone who saw the group did—this group, and especially little Michael, with his high, powerful treble voice, was special. Michael's star power and musicality at such a young age paralleled that of Frankie Lymon from a generation earlier.

As Gordy told UPI in 1970, "The Jackson 5 are five loveable boys well brought up. And Michael Jackson has that rare star quality everyone looks for. The minute I saw Michael and the group I knew they had the potential."

On Motown's roster, the Jackson 5 were taken under superstar Diana Ross's wing. And in late 1969 they were handed a piece of music to record—"I Want You Back," a desperate plea for a female to give her guy one more chance.

The song became a smash hit—the group's first chart-topper—and an instant classic. As *Rolling Stone* wrote when naming the song one of the 500 best songs of all time, " 'I Want You Back' was the song that introduced Motown to the futuristic funk beat of Sly Stone and James Brown. It also introduced the world to an 11-year-old Indiana kid named Michael Jackson."

One of those first introductions came in a December 1969 appearance on *The Ed Sullivan Show*. Michael, wearing a purple hat, was dwarfed onstage by his older brothers. The Jackson siblings danced and shuffled across the stage.

And then Michael started singing with a smile across his face—*Uh-huh huh huh huh*—and you just knew you were listening to something you'd never heard before.

Their next song, "ABC," like many early hits, was written by the Motown collective known as The Corporation, and like "I Want You Back," it also leaped up the charts, unseating the Beatles' "Let It Be."

Next came "The Love You Save," followed by "I'll Be There."

Four singles, four number 1 hits. The slow-tempo ballad "I'll Be There" showcased the group's heart and versatility—and the flecks of vulnerability in Michael's voice. Barely 12 years old, Michael had a command of his voice that few musicians could ever have.

THE JACKSONS WERE STARS, AND BY THE FALL of 1971, they had their own animated TV series.

Michael followed with his own hit album, *Got to Be There*. He also recorded the smash single "Ben," making him, at 14, one of the youngest solo artists to ever hit the top of the *Billboard* Hot 100.

The hits continued for the Jackson 5, and various group members embarked on successful tours, but amid frustrations with the label over royalties and creative control, the Jackson 5 chose to depart Motown for Epic.

Because Motown owned the rights to the group's name, the Jackson 5 re-branded as the Jacksons. It was a more apt name anyway, since the Jackson "5" had expanded to include fellow siblings like Rebbie, Latoya, and, later, the youngest sibling, Janet. The Jacksons also starred in a variety show.

The Jacksons' first two albums under Epic underperformed, but for 1978's *Destiny*, they were allowed more creative control. It reestablished the Jacksons behind the strength of songs like "Shake Your Body (Down to the Ground)."

As the 1970s wound down, and off of his role in the movie *The Wiz*, Michael wanted to explore his own musical tastes separate from the Jacksons. He chose to work with producer Quincy Jones to help him come up with a distinct sound.

The album was called *Off the Wall*.

Little Michael had become a full-fledged pop star with songs like "Don't Stop 'Til You Get Enough," "Rock with You," and "She's Out of My Life."

As Michael became a superstar, the Jacksons continued to produce and release new music—1980 saw the release of *Triumph*. And then came Michael's release of *Thriller*, the best-selling album of all time.

The brothers all came together again to perform on Motown's 25th anniversary TV special in 1983. It was a meaningful moment for the Jacksons.

And then Michael, again, stole the show. During a performance of his song "Billie Jean," Michael—clad in a sequined jacket and single white glove—debuted a dance move he'd been practicing, with heels sliding backward to his toes.

The moonwalk.

He moonwalked backward, spun on his heels, and landed en pointe.

Michael had become an icon.

As Michael cemented his status as the King of Pop, the Jacksons trudged along, breaking up for the first time in 1989. They reunited briefly in 2001.

In 2009, the brothers began collaborating again in hopes of a full-blown reunion. But a cloud was cast over their efforts—and the music world—in June of that year, when Michael died at the age of 50.

GRAMMY NOMINATIONS: 2
GRAMMY WINS: 0

R&B quintet Jackson 5 perform on a Bob Hope Special on September 26, 1973. (L-R) Tito Jackson, Marlon Jackson, Jackie Jackson, Michael Jackson, Jermaine Jackson. (Photo by Michael Ochs Archives/Getty Images)

Billboard Hot 100 CHARTING SINGLES

Here is a list of the Jackson 5 and the Jacksons' *Billboard* Hot 100 hits in chronological order.

THE JACKSON 5

Song	Year Released	Billboard Hot 100 Peak Position
"I Want You Back"	1969	1
"ABC"	1970	1
"The Love You Save"	1970	1
"I'll Be There"	1970	1
"Mama's Pearl"	1971	2
"Never Can Say Goodbye"	1971	2

Song	Year Released	Billboard Hot 100 Peak Position
"Maybe Tomorrow"	1971	20
"Sugar Daddy"	1971	10
"Little Bitty Pretty One"	1972	13
"Lookin' Through The Windows"	1972	16
"Doctor My Eyes"	1972	9
"Hallelujah Day"	1973	28
"Skywriter"	1973	25
"Get It Together"	1973	28
"Dancing Machine"	1974	2
"I Am Love (Pts. I & II)"	1975	15
"Forever Came Today"	1975	60

THE JACKSONS

Song	Year Released	Billboard Hot 100 Peak Position
"Enjoy Yourself"	1976	6
"Show You the Way to Go"	1977	28
"Dreamer"	1977	22
"Goin' Places"	1977	26
"Enjoy Yourself" (re-release)	1977	6
"Blame It on the Boogie"	1978	54
"Shake Your Body (Down to the Ground)"	1979	7

	Song	Year Released	Billboard Hot 100 Peak Position
➡	"Lovely One"	1980	12
➡	"This Place Hotel" (originally "Heartbreak Hotel")	1981	22
➡	"Can You Feel It"	1981	77
➡	"Walk Right Now"	1981	73
➡	"State of Shock" (with Mick Jagger)	1984	3
➡	"Torture"	1984	17

🔥 *My Favorite the Jackson 5 and the Jacksons Songs*

- ➤ "I Want You Back"   ➤ "Can You Feel It?"
- ➤ "This Place Hotel" (originally "Heartbreak Hotel")

♥ *My Favorite the Jackson 5 Samples*

- ·· "One More Chance" by the Notorious B.I.G. sampled "I Want You Back"
- ·· "O.P.P." by Naughty By Nature sampled "ABC"
- ·· "Hold On" by En Vogue sampled "Who's Lovin' You"

⊙ *My Take*

Can you imagine if a group like the Jackson 5 came along in today's era of music, with social media and videos so important to a group's status? I am not old enough to personally remember the early stories of the Jackson 5, but my older relatives still have strong feelings and sentiments when they discuss the first time they heard or saw the Jackson 5. It would be interesting to learn more about the specific issues the group had with Motown over royalties, because that surely slowed down their momentum and ended up being the beginning of the end of Motown's historic run. Oh, and speaking from a professional DJ, "I Want You Back" still works in the club!

Chapter 26

. . . .

KOOL & THE GANG

CIRCA 1970: Photo of Kool & the Gang. Photo by Michael Ochs Archives/Getty Images

KOOL & THE GANG WERE THE FUNKIEST GROUP of the 1970s, with an instantly recognizable horn sound—and much like their name suggests, they were *cool.*

The roots of the group were planted in New Jersey in 1964. That's when

Robert "Kool" Bell joined his brother Ronald and friends Robert "Spike" Mickens, Dennis "Dee Tee" Thomas, Ricky Westfield, George Brown, and Charles Smith and formed a band together.

They first called themselves the Jazziacs due to their early focus on jazz.

Other names included the New Dimensions, the Soul Town Band, and Kool & the Flames.

But by the late 1960s, they settled on Kool & the Gang, and the name just worked—as it has for the next half century.

The group cut their chops on the East Coast music scene and released their debut album in 1969—an album focused on the theme that music is the message. It was released on their manager Gene Redd's label, De-Lite Records.

"The instrumental album was an expression of their deep love of music," the group's website states. "It was also an introduction to their signature sound and the fierce horn arrangements created by Khalis, Dee Tee, and Spike."

They followed up with the album *Live at the Sex Machine* in 1970, as well as a few other releases. But it took until 1973's album *Wild and Peaceful* for Kool & the Gang to find their groove. They'd paired their fierce horns with infectious lyrics that made you smile and dance. That album spawned their breakout hits "Funky Stuff" and "Jungle Boogie."

Their songs were fun and suggestive, full of background noise and chants and riffs and bass lines. You wanted to be at whatever party Kool & the Gang were at.

But even though Kool & the Gang was becoming more comfortable writing lyrics, they remained an instrumentals-focused band at heart. Case in point was 1974's song "Summer Madness," one of the most heavily sampled songs in music history.

That song, which appeared in *Rocky*, was one of many Kool & the Gang songs to appear on movie soundtracks—including "Open Sesame" (*Saturday Night Fever*) and "Jungle Boogie" (1994's *Pulp Fiction*). In *Pulp Fiction*, the song's horns kick in, setting off the opening credits, and when Vincent (John Travolta) and Jules (Samuel L. Jackson) are driving. Later, when Jules is trying to calm down a riled-up Jimmy (Quentin Tarantino), Jules tells Jimmy, "Hey, that's Kool and the Gang." Based on my knowledge of the movie and context of the characters, Jimmy was a big Kool and the Gang fan and hearing the song would calm him down.

But as the 1970s wore on, the group hit a wall. Geoff Hines, writing for *Rolling Stone*, noted how "the disco era frowned on Kool & the Gang's loose and greasy approach to dance music."

So the band brought in reinforcements—vocalist James "J.T." Taylor and producer Eumir Deodato. With the right lineup in place, Kool & the Gang entered its commercial and artistic peak.

"Ladies Night," with flourishes of pop and disco, brought in new fans for the group and became one of their enduring hits. Another was "Celebration," which became a theme for sports champions and was played as American hostages returned from Iran.

The emergence of hip-hop music, and its reliance on sampling from earlier artists, made Kool & the Gang music royalty. Not only did they create the party soundtrack for the 1970s and 1980s, but they also influenced the generations that followed.

The group, through various lineup changes, has continued to tour and record new music, including a Christmas album and various singles. And they remain active by to having a steady slate of concerts scheduled.

The party is still going, and Kool & the Gang is still supplying the jams.

🏆 **GRAMMY NOMINATIONS: 3**
🏆 **GRAMMY WINS: 1**

✳ Album of the Year: *Saturday Night Fever* **soundtrack**

CIRCA 1970: Photo of Kool & the Gang. Photo by Michael Ochs Archives/Getty Images

Billboard Hot 100 CHARTING SINGLES

Here is a list of Kool & the Gang's *Billboard* Hot 100 hits in chronological order.

Song	Year Released	Billboard Hot 100 Peak Position
"Jungle Boogie"	1973	4
"Hollywood Swinging"	1974	6

	Song	Year Released	Billboard Hot 100 Peak Position
➔	"Higher Plane"	1974	37
➔	"Spirit Of The Boogie"	1975	35
➔	"Love & Understanding (Come Together)"	1976	87
➔	"Open Sesame"	1976	55
➔	"Dazz"	1976	3
➔	"Slippery When Wet"	1979	16
➔	"Ladies Night"	1979	8
➔	"Too Hot"	1979	5
➔	"Celebration"	1980	1
➔	"Take My Heart (You Can Have It If You Want It)"	1981	17
➔	"Get Down On It"	1981	10
➔	"Big Fun"	1982	21
➔	"Let's Go Dancin' (Ooh La La La)"	1982	6
➔	"Joanna"	1983	2
➔	"Tonight"	1984	13
➔	"Misled"	1984	10
➔	"Fresh"	1985	9
➔	"Cherish"	1985	2
➔	"Emergency"	1985	18
➔	"Victory"	1986	10
➔	"Stone Love"	1987	10
➔	"Peacemaker"	1987	58

Song	Year Released	Billboard Hot 100 Peak Position
"Holiday"	1987	43
"Rags To Riches"	1988	71

🔥 *My Favorite Kool & the Gang Songs*

❯ "Get Down On It" ❯ "Summer Madness" ❯ "Too Hot"

♥ *My Favorite Kool & the Gang Samples*

- "Summertime" by DJ Jazzy Jeff & the Fresh Prince sampled "Summer Madness"
- "I Got 5 On It" by Luniz feat. Mike Marshall sampled "Jungle Boogie"
- "Don't Sweat The Technique" by Eric B. & Rakim sampled "Give It Up"
- "Don't Walk Away" by Jade sampled "Jungle Jazz"

⊙ *My Take*

The Kool & the Gang song that resonates with me is "Get Down On It." My dad had the entire album and would play it nonstop on the stereo. I grew to love the song, the album, and the band. In fact, back in the mid-90s, when we all had pagers with voicemail/music before you punched in your number, "Get Down On It" was the song that greeted people before they were able to leave me a message or their number. I know many traditionalists objected to the addition of J.T. Taylor to the group, but history shows us that he propelled the group to heights they would not have reached without him. The rumor is that thanks go out to mutual acquaintance Ibrahim Bayoc, the band's road manager, for making that introduction.

Chapter 27

. . . .

THE OHIO PLAYERS

CIRCA 1970: Photo of Ohio Players. Photo by Michael Ochs Archives/Getty Images

THE OHIO PLAYERS WERE KNOWN ALMOST AS MUCH for their smash hits as they were for their sexually suggestive album covers.

The group formed in 1959 as the Ohio Untouchables. The leader of the

Untouchables was singer and guitarist Robert Ward; other early members included Marshall "Rock" Jones on bass, Clarence "Satch" Stachell on saxophone and guitar, Cornelius Johnson on drums, and Ralph "Pee Wee" Middlebrooks on trumpet and trombone.

After disagreements with Ward, the rest of the group eventually split with him and replaced their front man with Leroy "Sugarfoot" Bonner. They also added saxophonist Andrew Noland and drummer Greg Webster.

Singers Bobby Lee Fears and Dutch Robinson joined up, too, and the group renamed themselves the Ohio Players—a play on their new focus, both in music and romance. They became the house band for Compass Records before, in 1968, releasing their debut album, *Trespassin'*.

With Compass struggling, the Ohio Players moved to Capitol and released another album, *Observations in Time*.

By the 1970s, the Ohio Players were again facing a gut-check moment. The Players were all going in different directions.

They reemerged with still new members, among them vocalist and songwriter Walter "Junie" Morrison. And they had a new sound, one that would come to define classic hip-hop and G-funk songs from the 1980s and 1990s. That sound was refined on the album *Pain* and perfected on the follow-up, *Pleasure*, which featured the smash "Funky Worm." The song included Morrison's "granny" alter-ego, and, more significantly, a high-pitched synthesizer that was unique and different and instantly recognizable.

After the Ohio Players signed with Mercury, more lineup changes ensued—including Morrison signing with Parliament.

But for Mercury, everything—the musicality, range of instrumentals, and raw sexuality—came together as the Ohio Players found their greatest commercial success. Their 1974 album *Skin Tight* took them to a new level on the strength of songs like the title track and the classic "Fire." Pay attention to the lyrics and how they describe how the singer describes how the woman of their affection makes them feel.

The song, inlaid with the sound of a fire alarm, is fun and raunchy and a lot of fun to listen to, and it became the group's first number 1 hit.

Another smash followed with "Love Rollercoaster."

The band's album covers similarly featured suggestive names and imagery.

As the 1970s shifted to the 1980s, the Ohio Players' commercial peak had passed—but even amid many lineup changes and shifting musical tastes, the group remains popular and relevant, continuing to tour in recent years.

♕ GRAMMY NOMINATIONS: 1
♕ GRAMMY WINS: 0

CIRCA 1970: Photo of Ohio Players. Photo by Michael Ochs Archives/Getty Images

Billboard Hot 100 CHARTING SINGLES

Here is a list of the Ohio Players' *Billboard* Hot 100 hits in chronological order.

Song	Year Released	Billboard Hot 100 Peak Position
"Pain"	1972	61
"Funky Worm"	1973	15
"Fire"	1975	1
"Sweet Sticky Thing"	1976	33
"Love Rollercoaster"	1976	1
"Who'd She Coo?"	1976	18
"O-H-I-O"	1977	48
"Fopp"	1977	84

My Favorite Ohio Players Songs

"Love Rollercoaster"   "Fire"   "Skin Tight"

My Favorite Ohio Players Samples

- "Dopeman" by N.W.A sampled "Funky Worm"
- "Scenario (Remix)" by A Tribe Called Quest feat. Leaders of the New School and Kid Hood sampled "Ecstasy"
- "What's The 411?" by Mary J. Blige feat. Grand Puba sampled "Pride And Vanity"
- "Crumblin' Erb" by Outkast sampled "Sweet Sticky Thing"

⊙ *My Take*

My love for the Ohio Players came from hearing their samples on numerous hip-hop songs. Dr. Dre and other G-funk pioneers sampled numerous Ohio Players songs, which continues to cause their music to live onto this day. "Funky Worm" has been sampled in over 280 songs!

Chapter 28

· · · · · · ·

THE O'JAYS

CIRCA 1967: Photo of O'Jays (Photo by Michael Ochs Archives/Getty Images)

THE O'JAYS ARE BEST KNOWN FOR THE PHILLY soul sound of the 1970s, but their roots date back much earlier—and their impact stretches to the present.

The group first formed in 1958. At the time, the initial members—Eddie Levert, William Powell, Walter Williams, Bob Massey, and Bill Isles—were attending McKinley High School in Canton, Ohio, together.

They were first known as the Triumphs and played in local shows at YMCAs.

After working with a local songwriter to develop some songs, the Triumphs were off to New York to try to secure a record deal.

In 1959, the group—renamed the Mascots—signed with King Records. The quintet also connected with a disc jockey out of Cleveland, Eddie O'Jay, who in turn put them together with producer Don Davis and others.

Under O'Jay's tutelage, the group was renamed with the name that would stick: the O'Jays.

But even with a new moniker, it would take a full decade for the O'Jays to find their groove. Their harmonic love songs during the 1960s, such as "Lonely Drifter" with Imperial Records, were solid singles but failed to fully break through.

By the late 1960s, the O'Jays crossed paths with producers Kenny Gamble and Leon Huff and began recording songs for their Neptune label.

But when Neptune folded, the O'Jays faced an uncertain future. Group members Isles and Massey departed. Now a trio, the O'Jays fielded offers from a number of labels but chose to reteam with Gamble and Huff on their new Philadelphia International label. It was a smart gamble.

The producers pulled the O'Jays in a new direction, toward grittier, more socially conscious songs. Their first release on the label, "Back Stabbers," featured a lush, eerie, hypnotic beat that perfectly framed Levert, Powell, and Williams's harmonies. The song was just *different* with its distinctive chorus. The chorus describes how people who are backstabbers smile in your face while, behind the scenes, they are doing anything they can to speed up your demise. The way the O'Jays used the lyrics to succinctly describe what a back-stabber is was brilliant.

"Back Stabbers" became the O'Jays' first smash hit—it topped the R&B chart and reached number 3 on the *Billboard* Hot 100. And with it, Philly soul was born.

"We knew it was something special when [songwriters] Gene [McFadden] and John [Whitehead] taught it to us in a hotel room," Williams said years later. "That song took us from the chitlin circuit—which I had no qualms about because it kept us eating—to a whole other level. It was a big fat message that everyone could relate to or had experienced."

More hits followed, such as "Love Train," their first pop number 1 single, and "For the Love of Money," with Anthony Jackson's iconic bass line that repeats the word *money* several times.

The O'Jays found a balance of earworm hits and socially conscious lyrics, creating music with a message—in the case of "For the Love of Money," that money can corrupt.

Despite some lineup changes and personal setbacks, the O'Jays continued to release music and tour in the following decades. They were inducted into the Rock & Roll Hall of Fame in 2005.

The Rock & Roll Hall of Fame author Jerry Blavat noted the O'Jays as "the pinnacle of Seventies soul music. They were instrumental in popularizing Philly soul and the work of songwriting team Gamble and Huff. Their velvety, lush, yet funk-tinged sound establishes them as some of soul music's finest."

🏆 GRAMMY NOMINATIONS: 4
🏆 GRAMMY WINS: 0

CIRCA 1970: Photo of O'Jays. Photo by Michael Ochs Archives/Getty Images

Billboard Hot 100 CHARTING SINGLES

Here is a list of the O'Jays' *Billboard* Hot 100 hits in chronological order.

Song	Year Released	Billboard Hot 100 Peak Position
➜ "Lonely Drifter"	1963	93
➜ "Lipstick Traces (On a Cigarette)"	1965	48
➜ "Stand in for Love"	1965	81

Song	Year Released	Billboard Hot 100 Peak Position
"I'll Be Sweeter Tomorrow (Than I Was Today)"	1967	97
"Back Stabbers"	1972	3
"Love Train"	1973	1
"Put Your Hands Together"	1973	10
"For the Love of Money"	1974	9
"Give the People What They Want"	1975	45
"I Love Music"	1975	5
"Livin' for the Weekend"	1976	20
"Message In Our Music"	1976	40
"Darlin' Darlin' Baby (Sweet, Tender, Love)"	1976	54
"Family Reunion"	1976	18
"Sing a Happy Song"	1979	28
"Use Ta Be My Girl"	1978	4
"Cry Together"	1978	56
"She's Only a Woman"	1978	72
"Deeper (In Love With You)"	1979	48
"Brandy (I Really Miss You)"	1979	34
"Forever Mine"	1980	40
"Love You Direct"	1981	84

My Favorite the O'Jays Songs

➤ "I Love Music" ➤ "For the Love of Money" ➤ "Use Ta Be My Girl"

♥ *My Favorite the O'Jays Samples*

- ·· "Wish I Didn't Miss You" by Angie Stone sampled "Back Stabbers"
- ·· "For the Love of Money/Living for the City" by Troop and Levert feat. Queen Latifah sampled "For the Love of Money"
- ·· "Life Goes On" by 2Pac sampled "Brandy (I Really Miss You)"
- ·· "I'm Not a Player" by Big Pun sampled "Darlin' Darlin' Baby (Sweet, Tender, Love)"

⊙ *My Take*

What a decision to go with Gamble & Huff's new Philadelphia International label and be one of the originators of Philly soul, which is still celebrated today. Eddie Levert's son, Gerald Levert, was a major superstar as well. The first song I ever played during first ever DJ residency in Los Angeles was "I Love Music."

Chapter 29

. . . .

PARLIAMENT-FUNKADELIC
(P-FUNK)

Photo of Funkadelic; Studio, posed group, (Photo by Echoes/Redferns)

R&B OF THE '70S WAS LARGELY DEFINED BY smooth Philly soul—and George Clinton, recording as Parliament-Funkadelic, offered an antidote.

Clinton, with his sprawling network of musicians and sounds, changed music with his funk-fueled psychedelic style, inspiring artists as wide-ranging as the Red Hot Chili Peppers and Digital Underground.

Clinton started the Parliaments as a teen in New Jersey in 1955. The doo-wop group was based on Frankie Lymon & the Teenagers. Over the next decade, Clinton began working as a songwriter and producer, and the Parliaments recorded with Revilot Records.

According to Clinton's website, "The label ran into trouble and Clinton refused to record any new material. Instead of waiting for a settlement, Clinton decided to record the same band under a new name: Funkadelic."

After the label folded, their contracts were sold to Atlantic.

But Clinton was excited to explore his emerging sound, and he regained the rights to the "the Parliaments" name and signed the lineup to Invictus Records as *Parliament*.

Throughout the 1970s, Clinton amassed a roster of dozens of musicians—much like Motown had done—and recorded them as *Parliament* and *Funkadelic*.

"While Funkadelic pursued band-format psychedelic rock, Parliament engaged in a funk free-for-all, blending influences from the godfathers (James Brown and Sly Stone) with freaky costumes and themes inspired by '60s acid culture and science fiction," his website states.

The group experienced hits—among them "Flash Light" and "Aqua Boogie (A Psychoalphadiscobetabioaquadoloop)"—but they really stood out in albums and their endlessly inventive live shows.

As Clinton's website states, "In an era when Philly soul continued the slick sounds of establishment-approved R&B, Parliament/Funkadelic scared off more white listeners than it courted."

The collective reached its peak in 1978–79, followed by legal struggles and a rejection of disco and funk grooves.

But by the early 1990s, the rise of funk-inspired rap and funk rock reestablished the greatness of Clinton and his acts, and Parliament-Funkadelic was inducted into the Rock & Roll Hall of Fame in 1997.

Clinton brought funk to new places, and popular music was forever changed because of it.

♙ GRAMMY NOMINATIONS: 0

vLIVERPOOL, ENGLAND - MAY 1971: (L-R) Fuzzy Haskins, Tawl Ross, Bernie Worrell, Tiki Fulwood, Grady Thomas, George Clinton, Ray Davis, Calvin Simon and seated Eddie Hazel and Billy "Bass" Nelson of the funk band Parliament-Funkadelic pose for a portrait in May 1971 in Liverpool, England. (Photo by Michael Ochs Archives/Getty Images)

Billboard Hot 100 CHARTING SINGLES

Here is a list of Parliament-Funkadelic's *Billboard* Hot 100 hits
in chronological order.

Song	Year Released	Billboard Hot 100 Peak Position
"Up For The Down Stroke"	1974	63
"Chocolate City"	1975	91
"Tear The Roof Off The Sucker (Give Up The Funk)"	1976	15
"Flash Light"	1978	16
"Aqua Boogie (A Psychoalphadisco-betabioaquadoloop)"	1978	28
"One Nation Under a Groove"	1978	31
"(Not Just) Knee Deep"	1979	77

My Favorite P-Funk Songs

- "Flash Light" "Atomic Dog"
- "Tear The Roof Off The Sucker (Give Up The Funk)"

My Favorite P-Funk Samples

- "Let Me Ride" by Dr. Dre feat. Snoop Dogg, Jewell, and RC sampled "Mothership Connection (Star Child)"
- "The Humpty Dance" by Digital Underground sampled "Theme From The Black Hole" and "Let's Play House"
- "Foe Life" by Mack 10 sampled "Aqua Boogie (A Psychoalphad-iscobetabioaquadoloop)"

⊙ *My Take*

My true indoctrination to Parliament-Funkadelic came in college when many of the fraternities would step around campus to a bunch of their songs. The Parliament-Funkadelic catalog would be on high rotation at house parties and step shows. Also, it took George Clinton almost 20 years before he earned a Hot 100 charting hit. It is funny to think back at how, initially, Clinton patterned Parliament-Funkadelic off of Frankie Lymon & the Teenagers. What an evolution!

Chapter 30

· · · · · · ·

THE SPINNERS

Photo of DETROIT SPINNERS; Posed studio group portrait L-R: Henry Fambrough, Billy Henderson, John Edwards, Bobbie Smith, Pervis Jackson - post 1977 - (Photo by Echoes/Redferns)

THE SPINNERS BROUGHT HARMONY TO 1970S R&B AND recorded some of the decade's timeless hits, such as "I'll Be Around" and "Then Came You."

The group came out of Detroit—much like many other standout groups—during the late 1950s. The initial members (Bobbie Smith, George Dixon, Billy Henderson, Henry Fambrough, and Pervis Jackson) were classmates at Ferndale High School together and originally called themselves the Domingoes.

Writer and producer Harvey Fuqua discovered the group—soon named the Spinners—and took them under his wing. Their first charting single, for Fuqua's Tri-Phi label, was 1961's "That's What Girls Are Made For." Smith settled in as the Spinners' lead singer, and in time, Fuqua's brother-in-law, Berry Gordy, brought the Spinners to his Motown label.

The Spinners recorded a series of R&B hits in the mid-1960s, such as "I'll Always Love You" and "Truly Yours." With Motown's V.I.P. label, they worked with Stevie Wonder as their producer for "It's A Shame," which reached number 14 on the pop charts.

But the Spinners were frustrated—they weren't getting the support of other marquee Motown groups. So, at the encouragement of their friend Aretha Franklin, they signed with Atlantic.

And because their then-lead singer G. C. Cameron stayed with Motown, Phillipe Wynne took over lead vocal duties.

The addition of Wynne allowed the Spinners to complete their classic five-man lineup, which included Fambrough, Henderson, Jackson, and Smith. The velvet-voiced Wynne—paired with production from a young writer and arranger at Cameo Records, Thom Bell—took the Spinners to new heights behind top-10 singles like "I'll Be Around" and "Could It Be I'm Falling in Love."

As they toured with Dionne Warwick, they wound up recording a duet with her: "Then Came You." Beyond smooth harmonies, the Spinners also became known for their stage shows, which featured dance routines and comedy bits.

For the longtime Spinners members, the mid-1970s peak made all of their earlier struggles worth it.

"We always talked about how rough it was, but we hung in there thinking every year was gonna be our year," Jackson told a reporter in 1976. "To break up and quit would have defeated the whole purpose."

Even though the Spinners were going strong, Wynne departed in 1977 to pursue a solo career.

"In the following decades, the Spinners released eight more albums, including 2021's 'Round the Block and Back Again, gaining countless new fans on every continent drawn to the eternal joys of classic R&B. Icons such as Elton John, David Bowie, and Elvis Costello have sung their praises," noted the Rock & Roll Hall of Fame, which finally elected the Spinners in 2023 after they had previously been named finalists three times.

Fambrough, the only surviving original member at the time of the group's induction, was proud to see the group finally honored.

"Y'know, we made a pact with each other, back in the beginning; 'We're gonna make it or we're not gonna make it, but whatever we do we're gonna do it together,' " he told Billboard after the election was announced. "And when one of the guys would pass away, we would get somebody else to come in who was thinking like we thought and had the idea of the future that we wanted and just keep it going."

The Spinners just kept going—they've been around. They continue to tour and wow audiences with their timeless hits.

🏆 GRAMMY NOMINATIONS: 6
🏆 GRAMMY WINS: 0

CIRCA 1970: Photo of Spinners. Photo by Michael Ochs Archives/Getty Images

Billboard Hot 100 CHARTING SINGLES

Here is a list of the Spinners' *Billboard* Hot 100 hits in chronological order.

	Song	Year Released	Billboard Hot 100 Peak Position
➔	"That's What Girls Are Made For"	1961	27
➔	"I'll Always Love You"	1965	35
➔	"Truly Yours"	1966	16
➔	"It's A Shame"	1970	14

	Song	Year Released	Billboard Hot 100 Peak Position
➡	"I'll Be Around"	1972	3
➡	"Could It Be I'm Falling in Love"	1973	4
➡	"One of a Kind (Love Affair)"	1973	11
➡	"Ghetto Child"	1973	29
➡	"How Could I Let You Get Away"	1973	77
➡	"Mighty Love"	1974	20
➡	"Then Came You" (with Dionne Warwick)	1974	1
➡	"Living a Little, Laughing a Little"	1974	37
➡	"Love Don't Love Nobody"	1974	15
➡	"Then Came You" (with Dionne Warwick)	1974	1
➡	"They Just Can't Stop It (Games People Play)"	1975	5
➡	"Sadie"	1975	54
➡	"Love or Leave"	1976	36
➡	"The Rubberband Man"	1976	2
➡	"You Made a Promise to Me"	1977	80
➡	"You're Throwing a Good Love Away"	1977	86
➡	"I Don't Want to Lose You"	1980	52
➡	"Cupid/I've Loved You for a Long Time"	1980	4
➡	"Working My Way Back to You/Forgive Me, Girl"	1980	2

🔥 *My Favorite the Spinners Songs*

❯ "Could It Be I'm Falling in Love"   ❯ "It's A Shame"   ❯ "Sadie"

MY FAVORITE THE SPINNERS SAMPLES

•• "It's a Shame (My Sister)" by Monie Love feat. True Image sampled "It's A Shame"

•• "Dear Mama" by 2Pac sampled "Sadie"

•• "End of the Road" by Boyz II Men sampled "Love Don't Love Nobody"

⬇ *My Take*

If I were going to create a list of the top five most resilient R&B groups, the Spinners would be on the list.

Chapter 31

. . . .

THE STYLISTICS

Photo of Stylistics. (Photo by Echoes/Redferns)

THE STYLISTICS REPRESENT PURE PHILLY SOUL. THEIR FALSETTO-GUID-ED love songs are a blend of old and new, a bridge between R&B's early days and future.

The group formed in 1968 in Philadelphia from two other groups, the Monarchs and the Percussions. The founding members of the Stylistics included Russell Thompkins Jr., Airrion Love, James Smith, Herb Murrell, and James Dunn.

The group practiced and honed its sound until it got signed by the Sebring label, recording the single "You're A Big Girl Now."

The Stylistics later signed in 1970 with Avco Records and released the song; it was a minor hit behind Tompkins's tenor voice.

With Avco, the group began working with producer Thom Bell and Bell's writing partner, Linda Creed. Their first single with Bell and Creed was 1971's "Stop, Look, Listen," followed by "You Are Everything," the group's first top 10 hit.

And then came a signature 1970s ballad, "Betcha By Golly, Wow," a song that just gets stuck in your head the first time you hear it.

The hit established the Stylistics domestically and overseas, and other top-10 singles poured out, like "I'm Stone In Love With You" and "Break Up To Make Up."

The peak of their success came with "You Make Me Feel Brand New" in 1974, a pure dose of positivity during a pessimistic time.

The emergence of disco—and a shift to Van McCoy, instead of Bell, as producer—coincided with a dip in the Stylistics' sales. But there have always been fans wherever the Stylistics go, whether domestically or across the world, and the group has continued to tour in recent years.

🏆 GRAMMY NOMINATIONS: 1
🏆 GRAMMY WINS: 0

American soul group The Stylistics wearing BBC Radio 1 t-shirts, UK, 23rd March 1977; they are (L-R) Russell Thompkins, Airrion Love, Herb Murrell, James Smith, James Dunn. (Photo by Evening Standard/Hulton Archive/Getty Images)

Billboard Hot 100 CHARTING SINGLES

Here is a list of the Stylistics' *Billboard* Hot 100 hits in chronological order.

Song	Year Released	Billboard Hot 100 Peak Position
"You're A Big Girl Now"	1971	73
"Stop, Look, Listen (To Your Heart)"	1971	39
"You Are Everything"	1971	9
"Betcha By Golly, Wow"	1972	3

	Song	Year Released	Billboard Hot 100 Peak Position
➤	"People Make The World Go Round"	1972	25
➤	"I'm Stone In Love With You"	1972	10
➤	"Break Up To Make Up"	1973	5
➤	"You'll Never Get To Heaven (If You Break My Heart)"	1973	23
➤	"Rockin' Roll Baby"	1973	14
➤	"Sing Baby Sing"	1973	14
➤	"Let's Put It All Together"	1974	18
➤	"You Make Me Feel Brand New"	1974	2
➤	"Heavy Fallin' Out"	1974	70
➤	"Can't Give You Anything (But My Love)"	1975	51
➤	"Na-Na Is the Saddest Word"	1976	52
➤	"Funky Weekend"	1976	92

🔥 *My Favorite the Stylistics Songs*

❯ "Break Up To Make Up" ❯ "You Make Me Feel Brand New"
❯ "You Are Everything"

♥ *My Favorite the Stylistics Samples*

- •• "Everything" by Mary J. Blige sampled "You Are Everything"
- •• "Gangstas Make The World Go Round" by Westside Connection sampled "People Make The World Go Round"
- •• "Never Too Late" by Wiz Khalifa sampled "Stop, Look, Listen (To Your Heart)"

⊙ My Take

The Philly soul is strong with this group. They knew how to sing ballads, and I am in love with the sample ("You Are Everything") that Mary J. Blige used for her hit "Everything." Check out some of their performances on Soul Train via YouTube, and you will see how well they performed on stage.

Chapter 32

. . . .

HONORABLE MENTION—1970S

THE CHI-LITES

The Chi-Lites were a standout Windy City soul group that, in the early 1970s, took the music world by storm.

Initially named the Hi-Lites when they formed in 1959, the Chi-Lites became known for their smooth, soulful ballads.

They broke through in the early part of the 1970s while recording for Brunswick Records and were behind hits like "Have You Seen Her" and "Oh Girl." The singles were written by lead singer Eugene Record and his wife, Barbara Acklin.

As columnist Juan Rodriguez wrote of "Oh Girl" in the *Montreal Star* in 1972, the song "sounds like nothing on earth except the Chi-Lites, although it sounds like a lot of things in between, such as television theme music, funky git-tar in the background, rhapsodizing strings, quasi-Floyd Cramer piano, that ol' harmonica in the wings and the harmonies and oohs and ahhs."

The Chi-Lites' impact on popular music endured in the decades that followed—from using their recording techniques for Michael Jackson's *Off the Wall* record to being sampled in Beyoncé and Jay-Z's "Crazy in Love."

🏆 GRAMMY NOMINATIONS: 0

Billboard Hot 100 CHARTING SINGLES

Here is a list of the Chi-Lites' *Billboard* Hot 100 hits in chronological order.

	Song	Year Released	Billboard Hot 100 Peak Position
➜	"Give It Away"	1969	88
➜	"Let Me Be the Man My Daddy Was"	1969	94
➜	"Are You My Woman? (Tell Me So)"	1970	72
➜	"I Like Your Lovin' (Do You Like Mine)"	1970	72
➜	"(For God's Sake) Give More Power to the People"	1971	26
➜	"We Are Neighbors"	1971	70
➜	"I Want to Pay You Back (For Loving Me)"	1971	95
➜	"Have You Seen Her"	1971	3
➜	"Oh Girl"	1972	1

	Song	Year Released	Billboard Hot 100 Peak Position
➔	"The Coldest Days of My Life (Part 1)"	1972	47
➔	" A Lonely Man/The Man & the Woman (The Boy & the Girl)"	1972	57
➔	"We Need Order"	1972	61
➔	"A Letter to Myself"	1973	33
➔	"My Heart Just Keeps Breakin"	1973	92
➔	"Stoned Out of My Mind"	1973	30
➔	"I Found Sunshine"	1973	47
➔	"Homely Girl"	1974	54
➔	"There Will Never Be Any Peace (Until God Is Seated at the Conference Table)"	1974	63
➔	"You Got to Be the One"	1974	83
➔	"Toby"/"That's How Long"	1974	78
➔	"It's Time for Love"	1975	94

⊙ *My Take*

First, the working title to this book (*Have You Seen Her? Examining the disappearance of Black R&B Groups*), came from the Chi-Lites hit song "Have You Seen Her." The title has since changed, but for the longest time I used that song as the book title. Their hit "Oh Girl" is one of my top 10 favorite love songs of all time. Pure perfection.

THE DELFONICS

The Delfonics, like many of the 1970s' leading R&B groups, hailed from Philadelphia. They left an impact on the music world with their smooth harmonies and heartfelt ballads.

They started out as the Orphonics, a group of teens with a lot of dreams. They practiced and performed at local shows.

In 1966, they were connected with Thom Bell. Behind lead singer William Hart, they found their first success with 1968's "La-La-Means I Love You" for the Philly Groove label. Other early hits included "Ready or Not Here I Come (Can't Hide from Love)."

But nothing could match their 1970 single "Didn't I (Blow Your Mind This Time)," which netted a Grammy and helped to define the Philly soul sound.

The Delfonics would gain a new generation of fans with the release of the 1997 Quentin Tarantino movie *Jackie Brown*, which featured the group's biggest hits on its soundtrack.

🏆 GRAMMY NOMINATIONS: 1
🏆 GRAMMY WINS: 1

✹ Best R&B Performance by a Duo or Group, Vocal or Instrumental: "Didn't I (Blow Your Mind This Time)"

Billboard Hot 100 CHARTING SINGLES

Here is a list of the Delfonics' *Billboard* Hot 100 hits in chronological order.

Song	Year Released	Billboard Hot 100 Peak Position
"La-La Means I Love You"	1968	4
"I'm Sorry"	1968	42
"He Don't Really Love You" (re-release)	1968	92
"Break Your Promise"	1968	35
"Ready or Not Here I Come (Can't Hide from Love)"	1968	35
"Somebody Loves You"	1968	72
"Funny Feeling"	1969	94
"You Got Yours and I'll Get Mine"	1969	40
"Didn't I (Blow Your Mind This Time)"	1970	10
"Trying to Make a Fool of Me"	1970	40
"When You Get Right Down to It"	1970	53
"Hey! Love"	1971	52
"Over and Over"	1971	58
"Walk Right Up to the Sun"	1971	81
"Tell Me This Is a Dream"	1972	86
"I Don't Want To Make You Wait"	1973	91

⊙ *My Take*

"Didn't I (Blow Your Mind This Time)" is another classic love song, which is how I discovered the Delfonics while listening to the Quiet Storm on WHUR (96.3) in the DMV. My education about this group came from learning about them on that show and via Soul Train.

THE EMOTIONS

Turn on the radio, and you're bound to hear a song or sample connected to the Emotions, one of music's all-time great girl groups.

"Ain't No Half-Steppin' " by Big Daddy Kane. Mariah Carey's "Dreamlover." Paul Russell's "Lil Boo Thang." Snoop Dogg, Kanye, Queen Latifah, 50 Cent…they've all sampled the Emotions.

The Emotions originated in Chicago in the 1960s and consisted of three sisters born into a musical family: Sheila, Wanda, and Jeanette Hutchinson. At first, the sisters performed gospel as the Hutchinson Sunbeams.

In the late 1960s, they signed with Stax Records and were added to Stax's Volt imprint, which allowed them to work with powerhouse producers Isaac Hayes and David Porter. But it wasn't until the Emotions joined forces with Earth, Wind & Fire's Maurice White that they found breakthrough success.

Success would come with the release of the album *Flowers* for Columbia Records in 1976. The title track became their first top 20 pop hit. Their follow-up album, *Rejoice*, spawned their signature song, "Best of My Love."

But through all of their career ups and downs, the Emotions showcased sharp, funky beats and oozed musicality with their powerful, harmonious vocals. The Windy City siblings inspired countless artists who came after them and set a standard for girl groups.

🏆 GRAMMY NOMINATIONS: 2
🏆 GRAMMY WINS: 1

✹ Best R&B Vocal Performance by a Duo, Group or Chorus: "Best of My Love"

Billboard Hot 100 CHARTING SINGLES

Here is a list of the Emotions' *Billboard* Hot 100 hits in chronological order.

Song	Year Released	Billboard Hot 100 Peak Position
❯ "So I Can Love You"	1969	39
❯ "Show Me How"	1971	52
❯ "I Could Never Be Happy"	1972	93
❯ "Put a Little Love Away"	1974	73
❯ "Flowers"	1976	87
❯ "I Don't Wanna Lose Your Love"	1976	51
❯ "Don't Ask My Neighbors"	1977	44
❯ "Best of My Love"	1977	1
❯ "Boogie Wonderland" (with Earth, Wind & Fire)	1979	6

⬇ *My Take*

This was the group that I would hear on campus and see all of the sororities step to. "Best of My Love" in particular was in heavy rotation at the parties and step shows. "Don't Ask My Neighbor" is also a favorite of mine. Another member of the Stax Records family initially helped them get their start. This fact continues to show the impact that Stax Records had within the world of R&B.

HAROLD MELVIN & THE BLUE NOTES

Harold Melvin & the Blue Notes were an American soul and R&B vocal group formed in Philadelphia, Pennsylvania, in the late 1950s. Led by Harold Melvin, the lead singer, the group became known for their smooth harmonies, captivating performances, and emotionally charged ballads.

The group's story begins with Melvin, who had a passion for singing and sought to form a vocal group. In the late 1950s, he joined forces with fellow Philadelphia musicians Bernard Wilson, Roosevelt Brodie, Jesse Gillis Jr., and Franklin Peaker Jr. Together, they formed a group initially known as the Charlemagnes. However, after a lineup change and the addition of lead vocalist Teddy Pendergrass in 1970, they became Harold Melvin & the Blue Notes.

The name "the Blue Notes" is believed to have been inspired by a famous brand of school notebooks called Blue Notebooks Melvin reportedly liked the sound of the name and felt it had a certain appeal and uniqueness. The addition of his name, Harold Melvin, in front of "the Blue Notes" helped to establish him as the front man and leader of the group.

It's worth noting that after their initial formation, Harold Melvin & the Blue Notes later became most known for their collaborations with the legendary soul singer Teddy Pendergrass, who joined the group as their lead vocalist. Together, they achieved great success and produced several notable hits.

Harold Melvin & the Blue Notes caught the attention of Kenneth Gamble and Leon Huff, the renowned Philadelphia-based songwriting and production duo, through their performances in the Philadelphia music scene. Gamble and Huff were already established in the music industry and had founded their record label, Philadelphia International Records.

In the late 1960s, Harold Melvin & the Blue Notes performed at various venues in Philadelphia, including clubs and talent showcases. Their powerful vocals and energetic stage presence caught the ear of Kenneth Gamble and Leon Huff, who recognized their talent and potential. Impressed by their performances, Gamble and Huff decided to sign the group to Philadelphia International Records.

Under the guidance of Gamble and Huff, Harold Melvin & the Blue Notes refined their sound and released their breakthrough album, *I Miss You*, in 1972. The album introduced their signature blend of smooth soul and R&B, with heartfelt ballads that showcased Pendergrass's powerful vocals. The title track, "I Miss You," became a significant hit, reaching the top 10 on the *Billboard* R&B chart and establishing the group's presence on the national music scene.

In 1973, the group released their second album, *Black & Blue*, which further solidified their success. The album featured the hit single "The Love I Lost," a disco-influenced track that became a chart-topping success. "The Love I Lost" reached number 1 on the *Billboard* R&B chart and number 7 on the *Billboard* Hot 100, cementing Harold Melvin & the Blue Notes as one of the leading soul groups of the era.

Their next album, *To Be True* (1975), continued their streak of success. It featured the iconic ballad "If You Don't Know Me by Now," which became their biggest hit. The song reached number 1 on both the *Billboard* R&B chart and the *Billboard* Hot 100, and it remains a timeless classic, known for its heartfelt lyrics and Pendergrass's soul-stirring vocals.

The group's song "Wake Up Everybody" was inspired by the social and political climate of the time. Released in 1975, the song addresses important
issues such as social inequality, injustice, and the need for unity and collective
action. The inspiration behind the song reflects the broader social conscious-
ness and activism prevalent during the 1970s. It aligns with the civil rights
movement, the fight for equality, and the desire for social progress. "Wake Up
Everybody" became an anthem for those seeking social change and a powerful
reminder of the collective responsibility to address social issues and uplift
communities in need.

In 1975, Teddy Pendergrass, the group's lead vocalist and focal point, decided
to pursue a solo career. Despite this setback, Harold Melvin & the Blue Notes
continued with new lead vocalist David Ebo, and they released several albums
in the late 1970s and early 1980s. While they achieved a different level of
commercial success than they had in their earlier years, they maintained a
dedicated fan base and continued to deliver soulful performances.

Pendergrass's decision to embark on a solo career stemmed from a combination of factors, including his artistic aspirations, personal growth, and desire
for greater creative control. As the lead vocalist of Harold Melvin & the Blue
Notes, Pendergrass had already gained significant recognition and success.
However, he felt the need to explore his artistic potential and pursue his
musical vision on an individual level.

Pendergrass's solo career proved immensely successful, with his powerful
vocals and soulful performances garnering critical acclaim and a dedicated
fanbase. He released several hit albums and singles, solidifying his status as a
prominent figure in R&B and soul music. Pendergrass's decision to go solo
allowed him to fully showcase his talents, expand his artistic horizons, and
establish himself as a solo artist in his own right.

The legacy of Harold Melvin & the Blue Notes lies not only in their chart-topping hits but also in their influence on the soul and R&B genre. They paved the way for Philadelphia soul, a distinct sound characterized by lush arrangements, smooth harmonies, and heartfelt lyrics. Their music captured the emotions of love, heartbreak, and resilience, resonating with audiences worldwide.

Tragically, Harold Melvin passed away in 1997, but the impact of his group's music endures. Their soulful ballads and powerful vocals continue to be celebrated, and numerous artists have covered their songs over the years. Harold Melvin & the Blue Notes left an indelible mark on the music industry, and their contributions to soul and R&B music remain timeless and cherished by fans old and new.

♕ GRAMMY NOMINATIONS: 1
♕ GRAMMY WINS: 0

Billboard Hot 100 CHARTING SINGLES

Here is a list of Harold Melvin & the Blue Notes' *Billboard* Hot 100 hits in chronological order.

	Song	Year Released	Billboard Hot 100 Peak Position
➔	"I Miss You"	1972	58
➔	"If You Don't Know Me by Now"	1972	3
➔	"Yesterday I Had the Blues"	1973	63
➔	"The Love I Lost"	1973	7

	Song	Year Released	Billboard Hot 100 Peak Position
➤	"Satisfaction Guaranteed (Or Take Your Love Back)"	1974	58
➤	"Where Are All My Friends"	1974	80
➤	"Bad Luck"	1975	15
➤	"Hope That We Can Be Together Soon" (with Sharon Paige)	1975	42
➤	"Wake Up Everybody"	1975	12
➤	"Tell the World How I Feel About 'Cha Baby"	1975	94
➤	"Reaching for The World"	1977	74

⊙ *My Take*

Through the research for this book, I discovered that Teddy Pendergrass and Harold Melvin are actually two different people. I did not know that initially. A long while ago, I found Harold Melvin & the Blue Notes through Teddy Pendergrass and his discography. My question is how far this group could have gone if Pendergrass had not left. This is another Philly soul group that continues to show how much talent came from Philadelphia! Oh, and the song "If You Don't Know Me by Now" is a supreme work of art.

HEATWAVE

Heatwave was a British-American funk and disco group formed in the mid-1970s. They gained significant success during the disco era with their infectious grooves, smooth harmonies, and energetic live performances.

The group was founded by brothers Johnnie Wilder Jr. and Keith Wilder in Dayton, Ohio, in 1975. They recruited an array of talented musicians, including Rod Temperton, Roy Carter, Mario Mantese, Eric Johns, and Ernest Berger. Each member brought unique musical abilities and influences, resulting in a dynamic and distinctive sound.

Heatwave's origin story can be traced back to the late 1960s, when Johnnie Wilder Jr. met Rod Temperton while both were studying at the Croydon College of Art in London. They bonded over their shared passion for music and began collaborating on songs. After a few years, Wilder returned to the United States, and the idea of forming a band took shape.

In 1976, Heatwave signed with the GTO record label and released their debut album, *Too Hot to Handle*. The album immediately caught the attention of music lovers with its fusion of funk, disco, and R&B elements. It showcased the band's versatility and introduced their smooth harmonies and infectious rhythms, as well as Temperton's exceptional songwriting skills.

The album's lead single, "Boogie Nights," became Heatwave's breakthrough hit. With its catchy hooks and danceable groove, the song climbed the charts, reaching number 2 on the *Billboard* Hot 100. It was followed by another successful single, "Always and Forever," which became one of Heatwave's signature songs. The romantic ballad showcased the group's ability to deliver heartfelt and soulful performances, and it reached number 18 on the *Billboard* Hot 100.

The vibrant disco and funk music scene of the 1970s inspired "Boogie Nights." The song captures the spirit and energy of the disco era with its infectious grooves and lively atmosphere. It was written as an anthem for the nightlife and party culture that was prevalent during that time.

Building on their initial success, Heatwave released their second album, *Cen-*

tral Heating, in 1978. The album featured the hit single "The Groove Line," which further solidified their presence in the disco and funk scene. The song peaked at number 7 on the *Billboard* Hot 100 and showcased the band's ability to create infectious dance-floor anthems.

Tragedy struck the group in 1979 when Johnnie Wilder Jr. was paralyzed from the neck down in a car accident. Despite his injuries, Wilder remained an integral part of Heatwave, providing vocals and inspiration from his wheelchair. The band continued to release albums and perform live, showcasing their resilience and dedication to their craft.

Heatwave's success continued with their third album, *Hot Property*, released in 1979. It featured the hit single "Gangsters of the Groove," which reached number 21 on the *Billboard* R&B chart. The album showcased their evolving sound, incorporating elements of jazz and funk and demonstrating their ability to adapt to changing musical trends.

In the early 1980s, Heatwave faced challenges as disco's popularity waned. They released their fourth studio album, *Candles*, in 1981, but it didn't achieve the same level of success as their earlier releases.

🏆 GRAMMY NOMINATIONS: 2
🏆 GRAMMY WINS: 0

Billboard Hot 100 CHARTING SINGLES

Here is a list of Heatwave's *Billboard* Hot 100 hits in chronological order.

Song	Year Released	Billboard Hot 100 Peak Position
● "Boogie Nights"	1977	2
● "Always and Forever"	1978	18
● "The Groove Line"	1978	7

● *My Take*

I discovered Heatwave through the group Whistle's remake of "Always and Forever." Another favorite song on the same Whistle album is "Still My Girl."

THE MAIN INGREDIENT

The Main Ingredient was an American soul group formed in Harlem, New York, in the early 1960s. With their smooth harmonies and heartfelt performances, as well as a string of hit singles, they established themselves as one of the prominent soul acts of the era.

The group was originally formed as the Poets in 1964 by lead singer Donald McPherson and backup singers Luther Simmons Jr. and Tony Silvester. They initially performed in local clubs and venues, honing their vocal abilities and stage presence. In 1966, they caught the attention of producer and songwriter Bert Keyes, who signed them to his record label, Keymen Records. It was during that time that they changed their name to the Main Ingredient.

In 1969, the Main Ingredient signed with RCA Records, which provided them with a platform to showcase their talent to a wider audience. They released their debut album, *L. T.D. (Love, Togetherness & Devotion)*, that same year. While the album didn't achieve significant commercial success, it set the stage for their subsequent breakthrough.

The turning point for the Main Ingredient came with the addition of lead vocalist Cuba Gooding Sr. in 1971, following the tragic passing of Donald McPherson due to leukemia. Gooding's soulful and expressive voice added a new dimension to the group's sound and helped solidify their place in the soul music scene.

In 1972, the Main Ingredient released the album *Bitter Sweet*, which featured their first major hit single, "Everybody Plays the Fool." The song became an instant success, reaching number 3 on the *Billboard* Hot 100 and number 2 on the *Billboard* R&B chart. With its heartfelt lyrics and soulful delivery, "Everybody Plays the Fool" resonated with audiences and became an enduring soul classic.

Building on their newfound success, the Main Ingredient continued to release a string of hits. In 1973, their album *Afrodisiac* spawned the hit singles "You've Been My Inspiration" and "Just Don't Want To Be Lonely." The latter became their second biggest hit, reaching number 10 on the *Billboard* Hot 100 and number 3 on the *Billboard* R&B chart.

Throughout the 1970s, the Main Ingredient consistently delivered chart-topping R&B singles, including "Happiness Is Just Around The Bend" and "Rolling Down a Mountainside." They showcased their versatility by blending elements of soul, R&B, and pop, appealing to a broad range of listeners.

Despite their success, the Main Ingredient experienced some lineup changes over the years. Tony Silvester left the group in 1971 to pursue a solo career and was replaced by Carl Tompkins. Cuba Gooding Sr. also briefly left the group in 1977, but he returned soon after.

In the 1980s, the Main Ingredient faced some challenges as the musical landscape shifted. They continued to release music but struggled to achieve the same level of commercial success. However, their impact on soul music remained significant, and their earlier hits continued to resonate with audiences.

Sadly, in 1999, Cuba Gooding Sr. passed away, marking the end of an era for the group.

♔ GRAMMY NOMINATIONS: 0

Billboard Hot 100 CHARTING SINGLES

Here is a list of the Main Ingredient's *Billboard* Hot 100 hits in chronological order.

	Song	Year Released	Billboard Hot 100 Peak Position
➡	"You've Been My Inspiration"	1970	64
➡	"I'm Better Off Without You" (rerecording)	1970	91
➡	"I'm So Proud"	1970	49
➡	"Spinning Around (I Must Be Falling In Love)"	1971	52
➡	"Black Seeds Keep on Growing"	1971	97
➡	"Everybody Plays the Fool"	1972	3

	Song	Year Released	Billboard Hot 100 Peak Position
➔	"You've Got to Take It (If You Want It)"	1972	46
➔	"Just Don't Want To Be Lonely"	1974	10
➔	"Happiness Is Just Around The Bend"	1974	35
➔	"California My Way"	1974	75
➔	"Rolling Down a Mountain-side"	1975	92

⊘ *My Take*

Like many of you, I discovered the Main Ingredient through their classic song "Everybody Plays the Fool." And for me, it was when I heard Aaron Neville sing the remake that I learned that he was not the original artist.

1980's

From Top Left to Bottom left in clockwise order:
The Gap Band, The Whispers, Klymaxx, and DeBarge

Part Four
1980S

THE 1980S PROVED TO BE AN INTERESTING DECADE with numerous technological advances and a changing global political world. Reaganomics, "Just Say No," the Soviet Union collapsing, and the rise of AIDS were top headlines during these 10 years. Sandra Day O'Connor became the first woman on the United States Supreme Court. We had the *Challenger* disaster, the fall of the Berlin Wall, and the debut of a show we grew to love called *The Oprah Winfrey Show*. And in what might be the most influential advance of the decade, the Internet was created in early 1983.

Sports continued to have a huge impact on culture and life in the United States in the 1980s. The country experienced the Miracle on Ice in 1980, the Super Bowl Shuffle in 1985, the Celtics vs. Lakers rivalry (the entire decade) in the NBA, the emergence of the San Francisco 49ers in the NFL starting with "The Catch" in 1982 from the first Black Super Bowl–winning QB in 1988 (shout-out to Doug Williams and my favorite Washington NFL team!), the 1984 Olympics, and Michael Jordan's debut with the Chicago Bulls in 1984 (with his Air Jordans)! And we can't forget a young Mike Tyson taking the boxing world by storm, starting with his victory over Trevor Berbick in 1986.

Within music, Michael Jackson dominated the 1980s. *Thriller* was released and become the most successful album of all time. The videos that premiered on MTV helped to push Michael Jackson to a new stratosphere of stardom. Madonna and Prince were right behind him in terms of levels of stardom and successful albums.

Synthesizers became commonplace in all genres of music. Black musicians had to fight to get their songs played on MTV (just ask Rick James about "Super Freak"). Hip-hop music emerged as something that would not just be a fad, as "The Breaks" by Kurtis Blow peaked at number 87 on the *Billboard* Hot 100 charts. Disco disappeared quickly, and numerous pop and rock starts claimed the spotlight.

The '80s are commonly referred to as one of the best decades of music in history.

Cassette tapes were the primary way the public consumed music, with vinyl right behind. Early in the decade, people thought that cassette tapes (via mixtapes) were killing the music industry. Their thoughts were way off! The launch of MTV on August 1, 1983, also shifted the industry to include image at the same level of importance as the music—hence the popular saying "video killed the radio star."

Finally, the compact disc (or CD) was born, which brought superior audio quality and an unprecedented level of control for the user. While they were considered a device only for the wealthy for half of the decade, prices of CD players began to decline over time and, by the end of the decade, CD sales outpaced vinyl sales.

Additional technology that came to the forefront in the 1980s included the personal computer, Walkman (to play cassette tapes on the go), cable television (Black Entertainment Television—BET—was launched in 1980), VCR, and cell phone. This shift in how we communicated and consumed content would only be the beginning.

Oh…and in the distance…hip-hop music continued to gain momentum and attention worldwide.

This was an interesting decade, as the number of R&B groups' top 20 hits on the *Billboard* charts declined when compared to that in the 1970s. Record sales stayed strong, though, with numerous bands earning gold and platinum albums/singles. No R&B groups from the 1980s earned Grammys. New Edition dominated the charts in the 1980s and was one of the groups that proved to be a "bridge" to the 1990s era, where we saw white groups like *NSYNC, Backstreet Boys, and 98 Degrees capitalize on the New Edition formula of success.

There was also the blending of FM radio formats, which gave some R&B hits the crossover opportunity to be played on white radio stations. Finally, Frankie Beverly & Maze earned nine gold records throughout their career, which is the largest number within this entire book.

Chapter 33

. . . .

ATLANTIC STARR

(L-R) David Lewis, Jonathan Lewis, John Phillips, Wayne Lewis and Sharon Bryant (seated front) of the R&B band Atlantic Starr pose for a group portrait in circa 1983 in Los Angeles, California. (Photo by Ron Wolfson/Michael Ochs Archives/Getty Images)

ATLANTIC STARR WASN'T A FLASHY GROUP, BUT THEY overcame internal turmoil to release some of the 1980s' enduring ballads.

The group's origins trace to Greenburgh, New York, where they formed in the mid-1970s. The initial lineup included lead vocalist Sharon Bryant, brothers Wayne, David, and Jonathan Lewis, and musicians Cliff Archer, Porter Carroll, Joseph Phillips, Damon Rentie, and William Sudderth.

The group initially called themselves Newban, but when they signed with A&M Records in 1978, they were forced to change their name and chose Atlantic Starr as a nod to their East Coast roots.

Their first album, 1978's self-titled debut, was a modest success.

It wasn't until *Radiant*, released in 1981, that Atlantic Starr found its soulful groove behind singles "When Love Calls" and the lush "Send for Me." "Send for Me" harkened back to some of the best R&B of the 1970s, such as Lionel Richie and the Commodores—fitting, since Commodores' producer James Anthony Carmichael aided the group on the album.

Atlantic Starr was coming into its own. As Chris Rizik wrote on SoulTracks, "*Radiant* marked a change in the group's style to a smoother brand of funk/soul and also showed the development of Wayne and David Lewis as songwriters."

From that arrangement grew frictions that threatened to bring an end to Atlantic Starr.

"Everybody wanted to do what David and I were doing," Wayne said in a 1986 interview with the *Los Angeles Times*. "We're the main writers and we work hand-in-hand with the producers. All of a sudden everybody had their own ideas about concepts and directions. There was a tug-of-war in all directions."

The infighting came to a head during the recording of the 1983 album *Yours Forever*. It drove away Carmichael, who was producing Richie's uber successful solo work. And it drove away five members of the group—all but the Lewis brothers and Phillips departed. Amid the upheaval, the group was also dropped by A&M.

To replace Bryant, Atlantic Starr brought on new lead singer Barbara Weathers.

They embraced a softer sound for their 1985 album *As the Band Turns*. Their sound was poppier. And funkier. And faster. And it connected to audiences in a way the group's music hadn't previously.

Their song "Secret Lovers," a duet between Weathers and Lewis, became their first crossover hit, and it provided a model for the group's efforts moving forward.

So when Atlantic Starr signed with Warner Brothers in 1987, they were ready with "Always," a wedding and school dance staple that saw their pop leanings coming fully into focus. It reached the top of the pop and R&B charts.

But Atlantic Starr could never escape internal conflict. Weathers quit the group in 1988, leading to "a revolving door of female leads over the next decade and a continued degradation of the group's sound and fan base," as Rizik wrote.

Atlantic Starr continued forward but could never return to the commercial peak of the mid-1980s. Even so, they continue to tour today.

♫ GRAMMY NOMINATIONS: 0

(L-R) Jonathan Lewis, Wayne Lewis, Barbara Weather, Joseph Phillips, and David Lewis of the R and B band Atlantic Starr pose for a portrait in circa 1985. (Photo by Michael Ochs Archives/ Getty Images)

Billboard **Hot 100** CHARTING SINGLES

Here is a list of Atlantic Starr's *Billboard* Hot 100 hits in chronological order.

Song	Year Released	Billboard Hot 100 Peak Position
→ "Circles"	1982	38
→ "Touch a Four Leaf Clover"	1983	87
→ "Freak-A-Ristic"	1985	90
→ "Secret Lovers"	1985	3

	Song	Year Released	Billboard Hot 100 Peak Position
❯	"If Your Heart Isn't In it"	1986	60
❯	"Always"	1987	1
❯	"One Lover at a Time"	1987	58
❯	"Love Crazy"	1991	75
❯	"Masterpiece"	1992	3
❯	"I'll Remember You"	1994	55

My Favorite Atlantic Starr Songs

❯ "Secret Lovers" ❯ "When Love Calls" ❯ "Circles" ❯ "Always"

My Favorite Atlantic Starr Samples

- •• "Nobody Does It Better" by Nate Dogg feat. Warren G sampled "Let's Get Closer"

- •• "Love in This Club," Part II by Usher feat. Beyoncé and Lil Wayne sampled "Secret Lovers"

- •• "The M.I.C." by MF DOOM sampled "All In The Name Of Love"

- •• "Willing & Waiting" by Mary J. Blige sampled "When Love Calls"

⊙ My Take

It is a shame that internal conflicts tore this group apart. They had the potential for long-standing success across the 1980s and 1990s. "Secret Lovers" is one of the best love songs every made with simple, yet deep lyrics.

Chapter 34

. . . .

CAMEO

CIRCA 1970: Photo of Cameo. Photo by Michael Ochs Archives/Getty Images

HOW DO YOU EVEN START TO DEFINE CAMEO?

The funk and R&B group—which found its greatest successes in the mid-1980s behind hits like "Word Up!" and "Candy"—doesn't quite sound like anything before or after it. As Cameo leader and founder Larry Blackmon said in 2016, "Every time I hear 'Word Up!,' it's like the first day I heard it… You can play 'Word Up!' anyplace anywhere, and someone is going to be grooving and bobbing their head."

Or, as he said in 1987, "Call Cameo's music what you want to call it. The fact of the matter is that it's some of the most innovative stuff going on, and everybody else is trying to sound like it, wants to look like it and wants to be it."

Blackmon came to view Cameo's sound as "Black rock 'n' roll."

The group emerged in the mid-1970s, first as a 12-piece band known as the New York City Players—large groups had been in vogue due to outfits like Parliament-Funkadelic and Sly & the Family Stone. They signed with Chocolate City Records in 1976.

After a name change, Cameo's first success came in 1977 with their debut album, *Cardiac Arrest,* and the dance hit "Rigor Mortis." Blackmon and Tomi Jenkins shared lead vocal duties. There was an edge, and lots of musicality, to the group.

Cameo had a special sound, and they consistently landed singles on the R&B charts. It helped that they had premiere musicians performing with the group, such as bassist Aaron Mills.

They pushed all sorts of boundaries, wearing spandex and embracing gender-bending androgyny

But by 1981, Blackmon—burned out from the cycle of touring and releasing new music, and the expenses of such a large band—stripped down the group to five members: Blackmon, Jenkins, Nathan Leftenant, Charlie Singleton, and Gregory Johnson.

Blackmon also moved south and founded Atlanta Artists, a sublabel of Mercury Records.

Cameo continued releasing successful albums—and continued touring. Trips to England allowed Blackmon to tap into the era's New Wave influences, helping to set Cameo apart from other contemporary R&B and funk groups.

In London, a fan who met the band used the expression "word up."

And so it was that "Word Up!" became the lead single off the group's 13th album by the same name. The song became a statement—a call for people to hit the dance floor. It also redefined the group's style; the music video for the song was the first video appearance of Blackmon's high-top fade haircut and the red codpiece over his pants.

"Word Up!" topped the *Billboard* dance chart and reached the top 10 of the pop chart.

As Jenkins told the website StarTracks in 2009, "When we created 'Word Up!' these cats didn't want to release that record. They said it wasn't good, it's not going to sell, it's too different and this English guy in London said, 'This record is a smash. If you guys don't release this song, you're crazy.' They did. Of course, the rest is history."

Other singles from the album included the infectious "Candy" and "Back And Forth."

The album was Cameo's commercial and artistic peak. In 1987, Cameo was nominated for a Grammy for Best R&B Performance for "Word Up!"—though the award would go to Prince for "Kiss." Follow-up releases like "Machismo" were solid but failed to capture audience's attention in the same way. The music landscape was shifting.

By the 1990s, Cameo would see new resurgence through pop, rap, and hip-hop artists sampling their music—including Mariah Carey in "Loverboy"—and Mills would carry Cameo's connection further to the next generation by playing bass on a string of hits by the popular group Outkast.

The group took an unofficial hiatus for more than a decade before reemerging in recent years, releasing the single "El Passo" in 2019. Cameo continues to tour behind Blackmon, Anthony Lockett, Mills, and Jeff Nelson, while other former members have splintered to tour as "The Original Cameo Family."

Together or apart, Cameo's members have created lots of music to make you want to groove and bop your head—and nearly 40 years later, it still feels new and original.

🏆 **GRAMMY NOMINATIONS: 1**
🏆 **GRAMMY WINS: 0**

American funk band Cameo (Charlie Singleton, Larry Blackmon, and Tomi Jenkins) in the press room of the 1987 Soul Train Music Awards, held at the Santa Monica Civic Auditorium in Santa Monica, California, United States, 23rd March 1987. (Photo by Vinnie Zuffante/Getty Images)

Billboard Hot 100 CHARTING SINGLES

Here is a list of Cameo's *Billboard* Hot 100 hits in
chronological order.

Song	Year Released	Billboard Hot 100 Peak Position
"She's Strange"	1984	47
"Candy"	1986	21
"Word Up!"	1986	6
"Back And Forth"	1986	50
"You Make Me Work"	1988	85
"Loverboy" (with Mariah Carey)	2001	2

My Favorite Cameo Songs

"Candy"   "Word Up!"   "Single Life"

My Favorite Cameo Samples

- "All Bout U" by 2Pac, Dru Down, and Hussein Fatal feat. Nate Dogg, Snoop Dogg, and Yaki Kadafi sampled "Candy"
- "The Party Continues" by Jermaine Dupri feat. Usher and Da Brat sampled "She's Strange"
- "Hey Ladies" by Beastie Boys sampled "Shake Your Pants"

My Take

Once again, here is a group that had to stay resilient and true to their musical sound. They waited over 10 years before achieving any commercial suc-

cess. They had to prove to the label that the song "Word Up!" was worthy of releasing, which is crazy, looking back. It is one of their biggest hits and a timeless song. On a funny note, the sync placement of the song "Candy" in the movie "The Best Man" was brilliant. Check it out on YouTube.

Chapter 35

....

DEBARGE

R and B group DeBarge (top left James DeBarge, top right El DeBarge, middle Bunny DeBarge, bottom left Randy DeBarge and bottom right Mark DeBarge) pose for a portrait in August 1983 in Los Angeles, California. (Photo by Michael Ochs Archives/Getty Images)

ORIGINATING IN GRAND RAPIDS, MICHIGAN, DEBARGE CAME INTO its
own in the mid-1980s, putting out one hit after another.

The group—brothers Eldra (or "El"), James, Randy, and Mark, and sister
Bunny DeBarge—formed in the late 1970s and started singing gospel. Two
of the oldest DeBarge siblings, Tommy and Bobby, had already moved to Los
Angeles as part of the band Switch, and after Switch was signed to Motown,
the sibling group auditioned and was signed to the label as well.

DeBarge released its first album in 1981; the release stalled on the charts.

The following year, its follow-up album, *All This Love*, established the group's
sound behind El's countertenor vocals, whose voice carried flecks of desire
and sensitivity and longing. As *Rolling Stone* wrote in naming his voice one of
the 200 best in music history, "The ribbons of notes he lets loose during the
finish of the group's 'All This Love' are like caramel."

El's voice, paired with the siblings' production, got you moving and made
you want to dance, whether fast or slow. The group's breakout hits were
crossovers, "I Like It" and "All This Love," which El DeBarge had written for
Marvin Gaye, his longtime idol.

DeBarge fully came into its own with *In a Special Way*, which brought sleeker,
slicker production and the siblings sharing lead vocal duties. The album's
singles included "Love Me In A Special Way" and the number 1 R&B hit
"Time Will Reveal."

But the album's most enduring songs weren't singles at all—they were the
El-guided "Stay With Me," which pleads with a lover to stick around, and
the Bunny-anchored closing track, "A Dream," which aims to turn fantasy to
reality. Listen to 1990s hip-hop, and you'll immediately recognize the beats
for both of the songs. "Stay With Me" was sampled in the Notorious B.I.G.'s

"One More Chance" remix, while "A Dream" was sampled for 2Pac's hit single "I Ain't Mad At Cha."

The group's successes caused Luther Vandross to choose it to open for him on his "Busy Body Tour." But amid the growing success, the group was starting to fracture.

Things were spiraling.

And Motown leaned more and more heavily on other producers and songwriters to work with El to complete the group's next album, including the title track by an up-and-coming songwriter named Diane Warren: "Rhythm Of The Night."

It's the perfect mood-shifting song, calling on the listener to wash their frustrations away. And it was a massive crossover hit, reaching number 3 on the pop charts and topping the R&B charts.

But the song's upbeat, carefree nature belied the group's internal struggles. El and Bunny would pursue solo careers, while DeBarge trudged along, releasing one more studio album before addictions and drug arrests led the group to disband.

Despite the struggles of DeBarge's members, the music remains timeless. It was an iconic 1980s group whose outsized impact inspired and influenced music by other artists like Mary J. Blige, Ashanti, Blackstreet, and Nelly and whose music continues to pour from radio stations in various forms, today.

🏆 GRAMMY NOMINATIONS: 1
🏆 GRAMMY WINS: 0

JANUARY 01: Photo of DeBarge (Photo by Michael Ochs Archives/Getty Images)

Billboard Hot 100 CHARTING SINGLES

Here is a list of DeBarge's *Billboard* Hot 100 hits in chronological order.

	Song	Year Released	Billboard Hot 100 Peak Position
➔	"I Like It"	1982	31
➔	"All This Love"	1983	17
➔	"Time Will Reveal"	1983	18
➔	"Love Me In A Special Way"	1984	45
➔	"Rhythm Of The Night"	1985	3
➔	"Who's Holding Donna Now"	1985	6
➔	"You Wear It Well"	1985	46
➔	"The Heart Is Not So Smart"	1985	75

🔥 *My Favorite DeBarge Songs*

❯ "Time Will Reveal" ❯ "All This Love" ❯ "I Like It"

♥ *My Favorite DeBarge Samples*

- ·· "I Ain't Mad At Cha" by 2Pac feat. Danny Boy sampled "A Dream"

- ·· "One More Chance" by the Notorious B.I.G. sampled "All This Love"

- ·· "Ride Wit Me" by Nelly feat. City Spud sampled "I Like It"

⬇ *My Take*

I think DeBarge isn't talked about enough as a legendary R&B group. The run of hits the group had in the beginning of its career is very impressive. "A Dream" and "Stay With Me" not being singles is criminal in my opinion, and it goes to show how deep the group's early catalog was. The Switch connection is also notable—clearly, the family was supremely talented. And *Rolling Stone* voting El DeBarge's voice as one of the top 200 voices of all time is crazy (and cool!).

→

Chapter 36

. . . .

FRANKIE BEVERLY & MAZE

Photo of Maze; Featuring Frankie Beverley (Photo by Gems/Redferns)

FRANKIE BEVERLY WAS NEVER QUITE COMFORTABLE WITH THE spotlight—which probably kept his music from garnering more attention.

"If you make yourself too available, you'll be eaten alive, swallowed up by that big media monster," he said in a 1981 interview.

Beverly always wanted his music to do the talking for him—and listening to Frankie Beverly & Maze's output, it's easy to recognize how influential he's been for generations of R&B fans.

Frankie Beverly & Maze's beginnings date to Philadelphia in the late 1960s with his band Raw Soul—he assembled a talented group of musicians that included his brother Ron. But Beverly, and his group, never quite fit into the Philly soul mold, and he wound up moving to the Bay Area in the early 1970s. They caught the attention of Marvin Gaye, who chose the group to open for him.

Newly named "Maze," the group wound up signing with Capitol Records. Their debut album was released in 1977 and went gold.

Frankie Beverly & Maze—fueled by Beverly's upbeat, sophisticated, and sensual brand of R&B—found a devoted fan base with solid songs like "Happy Feelin's." They continued building that following with their albums *Golden Time of Day* in 1978, *Inspiration* in 1979, and *Joy and Pain* in 1980, which spawned the iconic, oft-covered title track. The following year saw them release a live album that included another timeless song, "Before I Let Go."

Beverly wrote "Before I Let Go" at the end of a relationship. It was about things he wanted to accomplish before the ending came.

"It was a situation I had to get out of, but I was in love. It came out of me pretty good, too. Even the music, it was all a gift from God," he told *Billboard*.

But it wasn't until 1985—and the hit "Can't Stop the Love"—that Frankie Beverly & Maze secured their first number 1 R&B hit with "Back In Stride."

They reached the top of the R&B charts again in 1989 with "Can't Get Over You."

Frankie Beverly & Maze garnered a new wave of fans in 2019 when Beyoncé covered "Before I Let Go" for her 2019 film *Homecoming*. Her version also included an interpolation of "Candy" by Cameo.

Beverly—who had first met Beyoncé when she was a teenager—called the cover "one of the high points of my life."

"I feel bigger than ever! I feel like I have a huge smash out there. It's definitely a blessing. Other people have done my songs, but the way she did this was in a class of its own," he added.

🏆 GRAMMY NOMINATIONS: 0

Frankie Beverly and the Maze perform at the Summer Soul Concert series at Newark Symphony Hall on July 12, 2009, in Newark, New Jersey. (Photo by Jemal Countess/Getty Images)

Billboard **Hot 100** CHARTING SINGLES

Due to the fact that Frankie Beverly & Maze have had minimal *Billboard* Hot 100 hits, I chose to include a list of some of their notable R&B *Billboard* hits as well. Here is a list of Frankie Beverly & Maze's *Billboard* Hot 100 hits in chronological order, as well as their R&B hits.

	Song	Year Released	Billboard Hot 100 Peak Position	Billboard R&B Chart Peak Position
➤	"While I'm Alone"	1977	89	21
➤	"Feel That You're Feeling"	1979	67	7
➤	"Before I Let Go"	1981		13
➤	"Running Away"	1982		7
➤	"Love Is the Key"	1982	80	5
➤	"Back In Stride"	1983	88	1
➤	"Can't Get Over You"	1985		1
➤	"Silky Soul"	1993		4
➤	"Laid Back Girl"	1978		15
➤	"Southern Girl"	1980		9
➤	"Never Let You Down"	1983		26
➤	"The Morning After"	1985		19

🔥 *My Favorite Frankie Beverly & Maze Songs*

➤ "Before I Let Go" ➤ "Southern Girl" ➤ "Joy And Pain"

♥ *My Favorite Frankie Beverly & Maze Samples*

- •• "California" by Colonel Loud feat. T.I., Young Dolph, and Ricco Barrino sampled "We Are One"
- •• "Joy and Pain" by Rob Base & DJ E-Z Rock feat. Omar Chandler sampled "Joy And Pain"
- •• "Too Long" by Daft Punk sampled "Running Away"

⊙ *My Take*

This group is an African American treasure that continues to give back (see Beyoncé covering "Before I Let Go"). I did not know the impact and love that Frankie Beverly & Maze had until I was a freshman at a party in the WUST at Howard University and the DJ dropped "Before I Let Go" in the middle of the party. The way everyone in the crowd went off shocked me completely, and now it makes sense. My dad would rock this album constantly at home, and when we finally got a tape deck in our car (late), that song was on all the time. "Before I Let Go" is an anthem for the African American community.

Frankie Beverly & Maze have numerous top 10 *Billboard* U.S. R&B hits, but no top 40 *Billboard* Hot 100 hits. This is very surprising, but at the same time, it's *not* surprising since Frankie Beverly prefers to keep a low profile. Their highest-charting hit was "Feel That You're Feeling," which hit number 67 on the Hot 100 chart in 1978! Seven of their eight studio albums hit gold status, but none (to date) have hit platinum status. That blows my mind!

Chapter 37

. . . .

THE GAP BAND

CIRCA 1980: (L-R) Charlie Wilson, Ronnie Wilson and Robert Wilson of the funk group "Gap Band" pose for a portrait in circa 1980. (Photo by Michael Ochs Archives/Getty Images)

THE GAP BAND WAS FOUNDED BY THREE BROTHERS—CHARLIE, Ronnie, and Robert Wilson—from Tulsa, Oklahoma.

Their name carries a message, and not about the age gaps between the brothers. Instead, it references a tragic 1921 massacre in which a white mob attacked and killed Black people in the city's Greenwood District near where the brothers grew up.

"We decided to call ourselves the Greenwood, Archer, and Pine Street Band and [grabbed] hold of that because we all knew what had happened on Greenwood in 1921, the race riots. It was rich, Black entrepreneurs who didn't want for anything. They had hospitals, they had motels, they had banks, they had everything you ever want. And to burn them out, I knew it was going to go out all over the world, and we would have to talk about that and where the name came from," Charlie Wilson said.

The brothers were raised in a musical family, and growing up, they honed their musical skills in the church. Their father was a church bishop and their mother was the organist.

"We sang and sang. Every time the church doors were open, we had to be there singing," Charlie Wilson recalled in a 1983 interview. "We learned our music from our mother. We all play everything."

The Gap Band began playing locally and generating a regional following. But it wasn't until the brothers connected with superproducer Leon Russell that they finally got their break. They wound up doing background instrumentals for Russell's *Stop All That Jazz* album in 1974. That year, the Gap Band also released their first album, *Magicians Holiday*.

Through the rest of the decade and into the 1980s, the Gap Band explored their eclectic sound, one that pulled from a massive range of influences.

Charlie called their music "sophisticated funk." Having such a wide range of styles and influences, including rock, soul, and P-funk, made it difficult for the group to find their identity—their sound was constantly evolving.

"The Gap Band is filling the spaces between the musical forms, filling the holes, the gaps," Ronnie Wilson said in 1983. As it turned out, the group's name did come to represent something musical in addition to its deeper meaning.

The Gap Band's earworm tactics were on display with their 1980 single "I Don't Believe You Want To Get Up And Dance," with its repeated chants of "Oops, upside your head." The song was later sampled by Snoop Dogg and provided the lyrical flow for Marc Ronson and Bruno Mars's hit single "Uptown Funk."

The Gap Band often incorporated sound effects into their songs, such as the tire screeching and engine revving in the motor-themed "Burn Rubber On Me (Why You Wanna Hurt Me)."

But no Gap Band single would have the lasting impact of their 1982 single "You Dropped A Bomb On Me." Atop a funky synth beat that imitates the sound of a bomb being dropped, the brothers sang about a girl who altered her man's world only to turn around and dump him.

While the band released a string of other successful albums throughout the 1980s, the decade saw the group drifting further from their commercial peak (undone in part due to spiraling drug addictions) and Charlie Wilson pursuing more and more solo projects.

Charlie Wilson hit rock bottom in the mid-1990s and went to rehab to address his drug problem. He was able to get clean—and stay clean.

The Gap Band continued forward before formally announced their retire-

ment in 2010. That year, Robert Wilson died of a heart attack at the age of
53. Ronnie Wilson died in 2021.

Charlie is now known as "Uncle Charlie" to a new generation of musicians
and music fans. He's collaborated with Snoop Dogg, Pharrell Williams,
Kanye West, and a who's who of other popular artists, an elder statesman
who continues to carry forward a musical legacy forged in Tulsa between
three brothers.

🏆 GRAMMY NOMINATIONS: 1
🏆 GRAMMY WINS: 0

Clockwise from top left: Robert Wilson, Ronnie Wilson, Charles Wilson, O'Dell Stokes, Tommy
Lokey, Roscoe Smith, Chris Clayton of the funk group "Gap Band" pose for a portrait in circa
1980. (Photo by Michael Ochs Archives/Getty Images)

Billboard Hot 100 CHARTING SINGLES

Here is a list of the Gap Band's *Billboard* Hot 100 hits in chronological order.

	Song	Year Released	Billboard Hot 100 Peak Position
→	"Burn Rubber On Me (Why You Wanna Hurt Me)"	1980	84
→	"Yearning For Your Love"	1981	60
→	"Early In The Morning"	1982	24
→	"You Dropped A Bomb On Me"	1982	31
→	"Outstanding"	1982	51

🔥 *My Favorite the Gap Band Songs*

❯ "Yearning For Your Love" ❯ "Outstanding"
❯ "Early In The Morning"

♥ *My Favorite the Gap Band Samples*

•• "Life's a Bitch" by Nas feat. AZ and Olu Dara sampled "Yearning For Your Love"

•• "Uptown Funk" by Mark Ronson feat. Bruno Mars sampled "I Don't Believe You Want To Get Up And Dance (Oops, Up Side Your Head)"

•• "Straight Outta Compton" by N.W.A sampled "Burn Rubber On Me (Why You Wanna Hurt Me)"

⊙ *My Take*

I view Charlie Wilson as the Gap Band living on today and in the future. He can still sing with the best of them. Credit to the brothers for naming the group after their hometown of Tulsa and the 1921 massacre that occurred there. More people need to know that story.

I read Charlie Wilson's autobiography, and I love his story of resilience and coming back from a serious drug addiction. I wonder what other music the group could have created if they didn't drift apart in the late '80s and early '90s.

"Yearning For Your Love" is as pure as a love song can be. "Outstanding" is a staple that you will always hear throughout the day at cookouts.

Chapter 38

....

LISA LISA & CULT JAM

NEW YORK - JULY 1985: Lisa 'Lisa Lisa' Velez of Lisa Lisa and Cult Jam poses for a portrait in July 1985 in New York City, New York. (Photo by Michael Ochs Archives/Getty Images)

LISA LISA & CULT JAM BLENDED POP, DANCE, and R&B elements to become one of the top acts of the mid-1980s.

The group's foundation was formed at a hangout called the Fun House, a
place frequented by breakdancers and rappers. It was where Madonna had
been discovered, and 16-year-old New York native Lisa Velez had similar ambitions.

Velez was the youngest of 10 children, and she would sneak to the Fun
House after dark.

There, she met Mike Hughes, a percussionist who played with the collective
Full Force. When considering what kind of group they wanted to establish,
Full Force looked to Motown for inspiration, considering the parallels be-
tween the emerging New Edition and the Jackson 5.

"In essence, since there was a 'new edition' of the Jackson 5, they'd create a
new edition of the Supremes," *Billboard* wrote.

Velez adopted the nickname "Lisa Lisa," and she and Hughes, along with
Hughes's friend, guitarist Alex "Spanador" Moseley, were nicknamed Lisa
Lisa & Cult Jam. They released their first single, "I Wonder If I Take You
Home," in 1984.

Velez didn't have a powerhouse voice, and that was the point. "They wanted
a little-girl, innocent voice," she said in a 1987 interview. But her voice was
strong enough to carry a string of R&B hits like the club song "Can You Feel
The Beat" and the ballad "All Cried Out."

Their first album went platinum, setting the stage for their follow-up, *Spanish
Fly*, in 1987. Two songs—"Head to Toe" and "Lost In Emotion"—reached
number 1 on the pop charts. The songs featured Motown influences.

"Motown hits were dance songs built around big four-four beats, and 'Lost In Emotion' keeps that insistence. It's also full of fun little flourishes like the bloopy synth-drums and the slap-bass breakdown," Tom Breihan wrote for *Stereogum*. "Full Force could make '60s structures work in an '80s dance-pop setting. They made it sound easy."

The group released one more album before breaking up in 1991. Velez continues to perform, both as a musician and actress, and paved the way for later Latino performers like Selena and Jennifer Lopez.

Near the start of the group's success, Velez was asked about her hopes for the group. "I have this idea about being a legend," she said. "The way I'm thinking is, I intend to keep working as hard as I can to get up there. I intend to make more music for people to know my voice and who I am." She's certainly done that.

♔ GRAMMY NOMINATIONS: 0

Singers Cheryl 'Pepsii' Riley (Cheryl Bridget Riley), Paul Anthony (Paul Anthony George)and Bowlegged Lou (Lucien George, Jr.) of Full Force and musician Mike Hughes of Lisa Lisa & Cult Jam (rear), and Alex "Spanador" Moseley and Lisa Lisa (Lisa Velez) of Lisa Lisa & Cult Jam poses for photos during the "Jack The Rapper" music convention at the Atlanta Hilton hotel in Atlanta, Georgia, in August 1991. (Photo By Raymond Boyd/Getty Images)

Billboard Hot 100 CHARTING SINGLES

Here is a list of Lisa Lisa & Cult Jam's *Billboard* Hot 100 hits in chronological order.

	Song	Year Released	Billboard Hot 100 Peak Position
➡	"I Wonder If I Take You Home"	1985	34
➡	"Can You Feel The Beat"	1985	69
➡	"All Cried Out" (with Full Force)	1986	8
➡	"Head to Toe"	1987	1
➡	"Lost In Emotion"	1987	1
➡	"Someone To Love Me For Me"	1987	78
➡	"Little Jackie Wants To Be A Star"	1988	29
➡	"Let the Beat Hit 'Em"	1991	37
➡	"Forever"	1991	95

My Favorite Lisa Lisa & Cult Jam Songs

➤ "I Wonder If I Take You Home" ➤ "All Cried Out"
➤ "Someone To Love Me For Me"

My Favorite Lisa Lisa & Cult Jam Samples

•• "I Need You Tonight" by Junior M.A.F.I.A. feat. Aaliyah sampled "I Wonder If I Take You Home"

•• "Move Ya Body" by Nina Sky feat. Jabba sampled "Can You Feel The Beat"

•• "All Cried Out" by Allure feat. 112 sampled "All Cried Out"

⊙ *My Take*

Lisa Lisa & Cult Jam is a rare group that was able to blend R&B music and freestyle music, which allowed them to grow their audience exponentially. "I Wonder If I Take You Home" is a perfect example of the R&B and freestyle crossover. "All Cried Out" has supreme lyrics and music production. What a song!

Lisa Lisa & Cult Jam (L-R Mike Hughes at the mic Alex "Spanador" Moseley in bike outfit and Lisa "Lisa Lisa" Velez) perform in a park circa 1987 in New York City, New York. (Photo by Michael Ochs Archives/Getty Images)

Chapter 39

·······

NEW EDITION

Johnny Gill, Ricky Bell, Ronnie Devoe, Ralph Tresvant, Bobby Brown, and Michael Bivins at the 1990 MTV Video Music Awards. (Photo by Jeff Kravitz/FilmMagic)

NEW EDITION WAS INITIALLY SEEN AS A 1980S version of the Jackson 5— but the Boston-based group quickly came into their own and later achieved massive solo success.

The group's members hailed from a housing project in Boston's Roxbury section. The quintet was composed of Bobby Brown, Ricky Bell, Michael Bivins, Ronald DeVoe, and Ralph Tresvant, and they founded the group in 1981. They were all between the ages of 12 and 14 at the time.

They got their break at a talent show, competing against dozens of other performers.

They performed a medley of Jackson 5 songs and came in second place. Music producer Maurice Starr, who sponsored the show, saw something special in New Edition, and he took them under his wing, helping them record an album.

Their debut album, *Candy Girl*, for the independent Streetwise Records, was anchored by the hit single of the same name. The song reached the top of the R&B chart. The song's lyrics were sugary sweet, and Starr's production helped it stand apart from other bubblegum pop.

"The kids our age really didn't have anyone to look up to, to idolize," Tresvant said in a 1985 interview. "The girls didn't have a group that they could go screaming after. They had a lot of actors, but they didn't really have any singers their age that they could say, 'I want to marry him someday.' So we came at the right time."

Follow-up singles "Is This the End" and "Popcorn Girl" solidified the group's success. But money—or a lack thereof—soured things, as it often does. Starr only signed the group to a single album deal, and amid a lawsuit with Starr over earnings, New Edition signed a contract with MCA through Jump & Shoot Productions.

The MCA contract allowed New Edition to record with a who's who of producers, including Vincent Brantley and Rick Timas, Michael Sembello and

Richard Rudolph, Ray Parker Jr., Peter Bunetta, and Rick Chudacoff.

New Edition's self-titled sophomore album was released in September of 1984 and sent them into a new stratosphere. "Cool It Now," a call from a guy's friends to take things slow with his love for a girl, became a top five pop hit, while "Mr. Telephone Man"—written by Ray Parker Jr.—reached the top of the R&B chart.

They were teen stars—drawing bigger and bigger crowds of screaming female fans.

But while their career was taking off, New Edition also found themselves confronting the business side of the industry when they learned they weren't actually signed to MCA Records; they'd have to buy themselves out of the production deal.

After New Edition released their third album, 1985's *All for Love*, Brown left the group—he departed to begin his successful solo career.

Johnny Gill joined New Edition in 1987 and shared lead vocal duties with Tresvant. The lineup, with the help of famed producers Jimmy Jam and Terry Lewis, took a step toward more mature music with their album *Heart Break*. New Edition's bubblegum sound had been replaced by a more grown-up, confident sound.

And the album resonated, selling more than two million copies on the strength of five hit singles, the biggest of which was "If It Isn't Love."

But with Brown reaching solo superstardom with "My Prerogative," the rest of New Edition's members felt the pull to pursue separate projects. Tresvant and Gill released successful solo albums, while the group's other members formed a trio, and Bell Biv DeVoe was born. Their smash song "Poison" was an instant classic and helped to define the 1990s' new jack swing style.

All six members of New Edition reunited in the mid-1990s to record an album, *Home Again*, that topped the *Billboard* charts. But during the ensuing tour, old tensions flared and the members went their separate ways.

The members of New Edition continue to collaborate in various assortments, and a Las Vegas residency was scheduled for 2024. The accolades were long overdue. New Edition set a standard for boy bands, successfully crossed from bubblegum to adult music, and shaped decades of hip-hop and R&B music.

Where other boy bands like New Kids on the Block and *NSYNC featured shorter peak windows and fewer breakout performers, New Edition has endured.

"None of them can compete with New Edition," Bell told the *Los Angeles Times* in 2022. "We have the best of R&B, the best of hip-hop, the best of pop…all of that combined in one group."

🏆 GRAMMY NOMINATIONS: 1
🏆 GRAMMY WINS: 0

Portrait of the members of American R&B group New Edition, 1980s.
(Photo by Michael Ochs Archives/Getty Images)

Billboard Hot 100 CHARTING SINGLES

Here is a list of New Edition's *Billboard* Hot 100 hits in chronological order.

	Song	Year Released	Billboard Hot 100 Peak Position
➔	"Candy Girl"	1983	46
➔	"Is This the End"	1983	85
➔	"Cool It Now"	1984	4
➔	"Mr. Telephone Man"	1984	12
➔	"Lost In Love"	1985	35
➔	"Count Me Out"	1985	51
➔	"A Little Bit Of Love (Is All It Takes)"	1986	38
➔	"With You All The Way"	1986	51
➔	"Earth Angel (Will You Be Mine)"	1986	21
➔	"Can You Stand The Rain"	1988	44
➔	"If It Isn't Love"	1988	7
➔	"You're Not My Kind Of Girl"	1988	95
➔	"Hit Me Off"	1996	3
➔	"I'm Still In Love With You"	1996	7
➔	"One More Day"	1997	61
➔	"Hot 2 Nite"	2004	87

🔥 *My Favorite New Edition Songs*

- ❯ "Candy Girl" ❯ "Can You Stand The Rain"
- ❯ "You're Not My Kind Of Girl"
- ❯ "A Little Bit Of Love (Is All It Takes)"

♥ *My Favorite New Edition Samples*

- •• "Like You" by Bow Wow feat. Ciara sampled "I'm Leaving You Again"

- •• "In My Feelings" by Kehlani sampled "If It Isn't Love"

- •• "Iesha" by Another Bad Creation sampled "Cool It Now"

⬇ *My Take*

This is my favorite group of all time. I grew up with their songs as the soundtrack to my life. I would listen to their tapes (and then CDs) nightly as I was going to bed. Many a slow-jam mixtape would have at least one of their songs on it. As you might recall from the introduction, I remember sitting in my room and waiting for "Candy Girl" to come on the radio so I could record it. This was the first song I ever heard from New Edition. Many of us thought "Candy Girl" was the Jackson 5 when it first came out, which was an honest mistake back in the day. When "N.E. Heart Break" came out when I was a freshman in high school, that was what I listened to on my Walkman walking to and from school. One of the first concerts I almost went to was the New Edition concert at the DC Convention Center for Budweiser Summerfest. My dad took me down to the concert, and we were going to buy some scalped tickets until I got scared and said, "Let's go home."

Of course, I am biased, but how do they *not* have a Grammy Award yet—and how do they have only one nomination? I don't understand.

From left to right New Edition band members Ronnie DeVoe, Michael Bivins, Ricky Bell, Bobby Brown, Johnny Gill, and Ralph Tresvant attend the 21st Annual American Music Awards at Shrine Auditorium in Los Angeles, California, 7th February 1994. (Photo by Vinnie Zuffante/ Getty Images)

Chapter 40

·······

READY FOR THE WORLD

Portrait of American R&B band Ready for the World, left to right, Gordon Strozier, John Eaton, Gregory Potts, Melvin Riley, Willie Triplett, and Gerald Valentine at the U.I.C. Pavilion (University of Illinois - Chicago) in Chicago, Illinois, November 10, 1985. (Photo by Paul Natkin/Getty Images)

YOU'D BE FORGIVEN IF, WHEN YOU HEARD THE 1985 chart-topper "Oh Sheila," you thought for a second you were listening to Prince.

It wasn't the Purple One—the song was actually released by Ready for the World, a teen group that broke out during the mid-1980s.

The group hailed from Flint, Michigan, and included vocalist Melvin Riley, keyboardist Gregory Potts, guitarist John Eaton, bassist Gerald Valentine, drummer Willie Triplett, and keyboardist/synthesizer programmer Gordon Strozier. Riley and Strozier cofounded the group while they were both students at Northern High School, and they recruited the other members through various bands and talent shows.

Members practiced and honed their sound before cutting a demo tape. They gave the tape to a local radio promoter, Charles Johnson, known as the Electrifying Mojo, who gave them airplay and connected them with others.

Pretty soon, Ready for the World was signing a contract with MCA Records.

The lead single, "Tonight," charted on the *Billboard* R&B chart, as did the follow-up "Deep Inside Your Love."

Their third single, "Oh Sheila," didn't just reach the pop chart, it made it all the way to number 1. A mix of Prince confusion or mimicry, fueled in part by the song's name, their opening at concerts for Kool & the Gang and Luther Vandross, and the uniqueness of the song—including Riley speaking in a British accent to start the song—took it to the top of the charts.

"I like that kind of accent, so I thought I'd use that sound," Riley said in 1985.

The album sold well—it would go platinum—but the 18 months between the release of their debut album and follow-up, 1986's *Long Time Coming*, made it too easy for listeners to move on from the group.

The lead single from their second album, the Riley-penned "Love You Down," reached the top of the R&B chart and became a top 10 pop hit.

Ready for the World released additional albums here and there for the next few decades, but subsequent albums never reached the same level of success as their first two.

Their music remains perfect for a classic R&B soundtrack. Kanye West and Jamie Foxx recognized that, name-dropping the group in their smash single "Slow Jamz."

Ready for the World knew how to set the party off right, indeed—with the British accent and Prince comparisons to boot.

♗ GRAMMY NOMINATIONS: 0

Singers and musicians Gordon Strozier, Willie Triplett, Melvin Riley, Gregory Potts, Gerald Valentine and John Eaton from Ready for the World poses for photos backstage at the U.I.C. Pavilion in Chicago, Illinois, in June 1985. (Photo By Raymond Boyd/Getty Images)

Billboard Hot 100 CHARTING SINGLES

Here is a list of Ready for the World's *Billboard* Hot 100 hits in chronological order.

	Song	Year Released	Billboard Hot 100 Peak Position
➤	"Oh Sheila"	1985	1
➤	"Digital Display"	1985	21
➤	"Love You Down"	1986	9

◔ *My Favorite Ready for the World Songs*

❯ "Love You Down" ❯ "Deep Inside Your Love" ❯ "Tonight"

♥ *My Favorite Ready for the World Samples*

- •• "Let Me" by Usher sampled "Love You Down"
- •• "Don't Stop" by Girl Talk sampled "Oh Sheila"
- •• "Girl Tonite" by Twista feat. Trey Songz sampled "Tonight"

⊙ *My Take*

I was also one of the people who confused Ready for the World with Prince at first. I consider "Love You Down" as one of my top five love songs of all time. Slow, simple lyrics and excellent production let this song enter the "timeless" category. "Deep Inside Your Love" was a great follow-up to "Love You Down" that went in with even more intense and salacious lyrics.

Chapter 41

. . . .

THE S.O.S. BAND

Photo of S.O.S. BAND (Photo by GAB Archive/Redferns)

THE S.O.S. BAND, AS THEIR BIGGEST HIT URGED, took their time and did it right.

The group—their name stood for *Sounds of Success*—came out of Atlanta.

Keyboardist/vocalist Jason Bryant, saxophonists Billy Ellis and Willie "Sonny" Killebrew, guitarist Bruno Speight, bassist John Alexander Simpson, drummer James Earl Jones III, and Davis started playing together in 1977 at an Atlanta nightclub as Santa Monica.

After their manager sent a demo to Clarence Avant at Tabu Records, the group was signed. They began working with songwriter/producer Sigidi Abdullah, who wound up suggesting the band's new name.

But it took three years for the S.O.S. Band to break through. It wasn't until 1980 that they began seeing success, when they released a massive dance and R&B hit in "Take Your Time (Do It Right)," which rose to number 3 on the *Billboard* pop chart and topped the R&B chart for five weeks.

As lead singer Mary Davis said in a 1983 interview, "I think it proves the old saying that good things come to those who wait."

The song, behind its big bass and percussion, suggestive lyrics, and Davis's growling vocals, was the perfect blend of disco and R&B.

"Take Your Time" was a hit domestically and overseas, especially in New Zealand, and it drove sales of their self-titled album, which sold 800,000 copies. After its release, the band also added trumpeter and vocalist Abdul Ra'oof.

But subsequent albums, though solid, didn't connect with listeners the same way.

Working with top-flight producers—Leon Sylvers III, as well as Jimmy Jam and Terry Lewis (best known for their work with Janet Jackson)—helped the S.O.S. Band round out their sound with hits like "High Hopes," which charted in 1982.

They followed that up with their second gold album, *On the Rise*, in 1983. It contained the hit singles "Just Be Good To Me" and "Tell Me If You Still Care."

The steady string of hit R&B albums and songs continued, many to the beat of a Roland TR-808 drum machine.

As the 1980s wore down, the S.O.S. Band saw departures—primarily Davis, who left to pursue a solo career—and diminished sales.

In the mid-1990s, Davis and Ra'oof constructed a new S.O.S Band with the same funk of its predecessor, and they continued consistently touring in the years that followed.

But in the 2020s, when Davis retired due to health issues, the S.O.S. Band brought on new singers to fill her shoes. They continue to tour and to introduce their funky, soulful music to new generations of fans.

🏆 GRAMMY NOMINATIONS: 0

Billboard Hot 100 CHARTING SINGLES

Here is a list of the S.O.S. Band's *Billboard* Hot 100 hits in chronological order.

Song	Year Released	Billboard Hot 100 Peak Position
"Take Your Time (Do It Right)"	1980	3
"Just Be Good To Me"	1983	55
"Tell Me If You Still Care"	1983	65

Song	Year Released	Billboard Hot 100 Peak Position
➡ "Just The Way You Like It"	1984	64
➡ "The Finest" (with Alexander O'Neal)	1986	44

🔥 My Favorite the S.O.S. Band Songs

➤ "Just Be Good To Me"   ➤ "Weekend Girl"
➤ "Take Your Time (Do It Right)"

💜 My Favorite the S.O.S. Band Samples

- "Always Be My Baby (Mr. Dupri Mix)" by Mariah Carey feat. Da Brat and Xscape sampled "Tell Me If You Still Care"

- "Ascension (Don't Ever Wonder) (The Tribute Cut)" by Maxwell sampled "No One's Gonna Love You"

- "Come & Go" by 50 Cent feat. Dr. Dre sampled "Just Be Good To Me"

⊙ My Take

I thought it was interesting that the S.O.S. Band was one of the first bands to get their start in Atlanta before the city was on the map. "Take Your Time (Do It Right)" still works in opening DJ sets and in lounges. Timeless tune right there. My dad would rock "Just Be Good To Me" on repeat Saturday mornings in the basement. In a time when lyrics weren't so direct, the lyrics in "Weekend Girl" win every time!

Chapter 42

·······

THE WHISPERS

(L-R) R and B singers Marcus Hutson, Nicholas Caldwell, Wallace "Scotty" Scott, Leaveil
Degree, and Walter Scott of the R and B band The Whispers pose for a portrait in circa 1980.
(Photo by Michael Ochs Archives/Getty Images)

THE WHISPERS HUNG IN THERE AFTER HITTING A career downturn—and
struck gold twice.

Their first timeless track, the smooth, upbeat "And the Beat Goes On," was released 15 years after the group's members first began singing together as students at Jordan High School in Watts, California.

Throughout the 1970s, the Whispers—originally made up of twin brothers Wallace "Scotty" and Walter Scott, along with Gordy Harmon (later replaced by Leaveil Degree), Marcus Hutson, and Nicholas Caldwell—recorded a steady stream of harmonious R&B hits.

However, their talent and dedication caught the attention of *Soul Train* television show creator and host Don Cornelius.

Cornelius saw potential in the Whispers and invited them to perform on *Soul Train*, a popular platform for showcasing African American musical talent. Their appearances on *Soul Train* exposed them to a broader audience and helped increase their visibility in the music industry.

Through their exposure on *Soul Train*, the Whispers attracted the attention of Dick Griffey, a talent promoter and executive at Soul Train Records. Impressed by their performances, Griffey signed the group to his newly formed record label, Solar Records, in the mid-1970s.

Finally, once they signed with Solar Records and began working with producer Leon Sylvers, the Whispers broke through. "And the Beat Goes On," which topped the soul chart in 1979, captures a powerful sentiment—staying positive after losing out on love. It doesn't wallow and doesn't entertain the thought of being sad, which sets it apart from typical R&B hits. And it has a beat that makes you want to dance.

The lyrics are about how their love is everlasting just like, as the song title states, the beat goes on. There are parallels in these lyrics and the Whispers' career because this group continued to push forward despite setbacks.

With their hit, the Whispers were introduced to a lot more listeners—many of whom saw them as a new act. Walter Scott, in a 1980 interview, noted how the lines between R&B and pop were becoming increasingly blurred. "R&B is a little bit different than it used to be," he said. "It's not as hard driving now. It's smooth, almost middle of the road, with a beat everybody can shake their head to. It's easy listening R&B."

The beat went on for the Whispers. They'd release a record and tour, rinse and repeat, over and over, but by the mid-1980s, they were back to being overlooked. They hadn't scored another massive hit. The Whispers were a whisper on the charts.

But the group still had lots of support. As they were considering new material to record, one song from the duo of Antonio "L.A." Reid and Kenneth "Babyface" Edmonds stood out to them. The members of the Deele—and soon-to-be music royalty—were Whispers fans.

"As soon as the guys came to us, we said, 'Yeah, that's it. That's us,' " Wallace Scott said in 1987.

That song, "Rock Steady," was the Whispers' second smash hit, reaching the top 10 on the *Billboard* pop chart and topping the R&B chart. It crossed over in every direction—pop, R&B, adult contemporary, rock, dance...and it cemented the Whispers' legacy status.

They've continued to release new music and tour in recent decades—but even as members have passed away, the triumvirate of Walter Scott, Wallace "Scotty" Scott, and Leaveil Degree have continued on as the Whispers.

In addition to inductions to countless music halls of fame, in recent years, the Whispers have begun rerecording their catalog of music in an effort to own their sound recordings. Those efforts started with their two biggest hits, "And the Beat Goes On" and "Rock Steady."

As the group members stated on the group's website, "Inspired and encouraged by artists such as Taylor Swift and Kelly Clarkson who recently brought the rerecording issue to the forefront, and Anita Baker's struggles to acquire ownership of her masters, the Whispers' goal is to own the sound recordings of their life's work."

🏆 GRAMMY NOMINATIONS: 1
🏆 GRAMMY WINS: 0

(L-R) R and B singers Leaveil Degree, Walter Scott, Marcus Hutson, Wallace "Scotty" Scott and Nicholas Caldwell of the R and B band The Whispers pose for a portrait in circa 1976. (Photo by Michael Ochs Archives/Getty Images)

Billboard Hot 100 CHARTING SINGLES

Here is a list of the Whispers' *Billboard* Hot 100 hits in chronological order.

Song	Year Released	Billboard Hot 100 Peak Position
"Seems Like I Gotta Do Wrong"	1970	50
"Your Love Is So Doggone Good"	1971	93
"Somebody Loves You"	1972	94
"A Mother for My Children"	1973	92
"One for the Money (Part 1)"	1976	88
"Make It with You"	1977	94
"And the Beat Goes On"	1980	19
"Lady"	1980	28
"It's a Love Thing"	1981	28
"Tonight"	1983	84
"Rock Steady"	1987	7
"Innocent"	1990	55

My Favorite the Whispers Songs

- "It's a Love Thing" - "And the Beat Goes On"
- "Keep On Lovin' Me"

My Favorite the Whispers Samples

- "Miami" by Will Smith sampled "And the Beat Goes On"

•• "Look My Way" by Kylie Minogue sampled "Rock Steady"

•• "So Gone" by Monica sampled "You Are Number One"

⊙ *My Take*

It is not commonly known that the Whispers released their debut single, "It Only Hurts for a Little While" in 1964. It took 16 years after that for them to get their first *Billboard* Hot 100 top 20 song with "And the Beat Goes On" in 1980! For that reason, I view them as the top group in my top five most resilient R&B groups. That amount of time to continue to perform, to switch labels, producers, and sound before finding their space, is admirable. In the current era of music, I cannot imagine a group being given 16 years to work on their craft and continue to release music.

Chapter 43

....

HONORABLE
MENTION—1980S

GUY

Guy is an influential R&B group that emerged in the late 1980s. The group was formed in Harlem, New York, by singer-songwriter Teddy Riley, who is considered one of the pioneers of the new jack swing genre. Riley teamed up with brothers Aaron Hall and Damion Hall to create the trio.

When Riley and the Hall brothers formed the group, they adopted Riley's nickname as their band name, thus becoming known as Guy. The name not only served as a representation of Riley's musical identity but also became synonymous with their collective vision and musical style.

Guy's self-titled debut album was released in 1988 and became a huge success, introducing the world to its unique blend of R&B, hip-hop, and new jack swing. The album spawned several hit singles, including "Groove Me," "Teddy's Jam," and "I Like." These songs showcased Guy's infectious grooves and catchy melodies and Riley's innovative production style.

In the mid-1990s, the members of Guy decided to pursue solo projects, leading to a hiatus for the group. Riley went on to produce for various artists and became a sought-after producer in the R&B and hip-hop industries. Aaron Hall released a successful solo album, while Damion Hall also pursued a solo career but did not reach the same heights as his former group members.

The impact of Guy's music is still felt today, as they are recognized as one of the pioneering groups in the new jack swing genre. Their innovative sound and catchy hits have left a lasting influence on R&B and hip-hop music.

🏆 GRAMMY NOMINATIONS: 0

Billboard Hot 100 CHARTING SINGLES

Here is a list of Guy's *Billboard* Hot 100 hits
SSin chronological order.

	Song	Year Released	Billboard Hot 100 Peak Position
➔	"I Like"	1989	70
➔	"My Fantasy"	1989	62
➔	"Wanna Get With U"	1990	50
➔	"Let's Chill"	1991	41
➔	"Dancin' "	1999	19

My Take

Guy's song "I Like" is currently my cell phone ringtone. Do you know about the hidden words in the song "Piece of My Love"? I also recently discovered that Charlie Wilson wrote what is arguably Guy's biggest hit, "Let's Chill." I discovered this while hearing him in concert in Las Vegas in 2022. Check out his version on the streaming platform of your choice.

KLYMAXX

The women of Klymaxx are R&B royalty. They are fun, serious, sultry, and super talented.

And they guided their own production at a time when other female groups were stuck working with male producers and writers.

Klymaxx was the creation of drummer and vocalist Bernadette Cooper. Other original members included Lorena "Lungs" Porter Shelby, Cheryl Cooley on guitar, Robbin Grider on keyboards and guitar, and Lynn Malsby on keyboard. Joyce "Fenderella" Irby joined the group soon after.

The group's first album, *Never Underestimate the Power of a Woman*, was released in 1981. The members didn't have much creative control.

Its second album saw the group members working with producers Jimmy Jam and Terry Lewis, who urged them to take more creative control.

"They were the only people telling us, 'You guys have what it takes. You guys should do your own stuff,' " Fenderella told the *Cincinnati Post* in 1986.

So they did.

Klymaxx was given the creative control to produce their third album, *Meeting in the Ladies Room*, and the group members wrote some of the songs, including "The Men All Pause" and "I Miss You," the latter of which shot up the charts, peaking at number 5 on the *Billboard* Hot 100.

While the group's classic lineup broke up in 1989, and despite lingering legal confrontations over credits and usage of the group's name, Klymaxx remains a pioneering female group and one of the 1980s' iconic R&B acts.

♫ GRAMMY NOMINATIONS: 0

Billboard Hot 100 CHARTING SINGLES

Here is a list of Klymaxx's *Billboard* Hot 100 hits in chronological order.

	Song	Year Released	Billboard Hot 100 Peak Position
➡	"Meeting In The Ladies Room"	1985	59
➡	"I Miss You"	1986	5
➡	"The Men All Pause" (re-release)	1986	80
➡	"Man Size Love"	1986	15
➡	"I'd Still Say Yes"	1987	18

⬇ *My Take*

An all-female band playing the instruments and writing the music was a rarity when Klymaxx hit its stride. It also bridged the gap between R&B and free-style music, which was very cool. Due to those reasons and many more, I have plenty of love and respect for Klymaxx. Once the group stopped performing as much, Irby would still search for artists and found the R&B singer Lloyd while living in Atlanta. And the song "I Miss You" is a classic ballad that still works today.

SHALAMAR

Shalamar began as a creation of Soul Train Records—dancers Jody Watley and Jeffrey Daniel, along with singer Howard Hewett, comprised the group's best-known lineup.

The group found recording success in the late 1970s, including the hit single "The Second Time Around," but it wasn't until Hewett joined the group— previous vocalist Gerald Brown had left over money grumblings—that things clicked into place. Their dance skills brought them extra attention, especially Daniel's body-popping on the BBC program *Top of the Pops*.

Watley and Daniel left Shalamar in 1983 and were replaced by Micki Free and Delisa Davis.

Shalamar achieved its first Grammy nomination with the song "Dead Give-away." The group was embracing more of a new-wave/synth-pop sound.

The group found soundtrack success with "Dancing in the Sheets" from the *Footloose* soundtrack, and the *Beverly Hills Cop* soundtrack won a Grammy in 1985.

After Hewett left the group, Shalamar released a few more albums before splitting up.

🏆 GRAMMY NOMINATIONS: 0

Billboard Hot 100 CHARTING SINGLES

Here is a list of Shalamar's *Billboard* Hot 100 hits
in chronological order.

Song	Year Released	Billboard Hot 100 Peak Position
"Uptown Festival (Part 1)"	1977	25
"Take That to the Bank"	1978	79
"The Second Time Around"	1979	8
"Full of Fire"	1980	55
"Make That Move"	1980	60
"A Night to Remember"	1982	44
"Dead Giveaway"	1983	22
"Dancing in the Sheets"	1984	17
"Amnesia"	1984	73

⊙ *My Take*

I'm a big Jody Watley fan, so it makes sense to me that the group's dancing skills first got them attention from record labels. If you look at Watley's videos from her solo career, you can see the signs. Sidenote: Watley also released one of my favorite songs of all time, "Friends" with Eric B and Rakim.

This is another group that, if they had stayed together, could have had a long run of hits. The recipe was there.

ZAPP & ROGER

Zapp & Roger was best known for exploring funk's electronic side—and its talk-box effect and loud, funky beats made them a favorite for sampling on hip-hop and rap tracks.

The group emerged from Dayton, Ohio, in the late 1970s. Zapp & Roger was founded by Roger Troutman, and many of his siblings appeared in the group.

After serving as protégés to George Clinton and Bootsy Collins of P-Funk, the members of Zapp & Roger released their debut album in 1980. It featured the single "More Bounce to the Ounce," which climbed to number 2 on the R&B charts and was later sampled by the Notorious B.I.G. ("Going Back to Cali") and Ice Cube ("Friday").

Its next album, *Zapp II*, included the hit "Dance Floor," with a repetitive chant that was interpolated for 2Pac's "California Love" (Roger and Larry Troutman were among those listed as songwriters on the Grammy-nominated track).

The group released a succession of albums through the mid-1980s, and its hit tracks included 1985's "Computer Love."

Roger focused more and more attention on his solo career.

During the 1990s, Roger experienced a career resurgence—amid the height of hip-hop and rap, he guested on classic albums like Snoop Dogg's "Doggy-style" and remained an in-demand producer.

But in April 1999, Roger was fatally shot outside of his recording studio. He was 47 years old. His brother Larry was found dead nearby from a self-inflicted gunshot wound. The tragic murder-suicide stunned the music world.

Members of the Troutman family continue to perform, carrying forward a musical legacy of trendsetting funk.

🏆 GRAMMY NOMINATIONS: 0

Billboard Hot 100 CHARTING SINGLES

Here is a list of Zapp & Roger's *Billboard* Hot 100 hits in chronological order.

	Song	Year Released	Billboard Hot 100 Peak Position
➡	"More Bounce to the Ounce"	1980	86
➡	"Mega Medley"	1993	54
➡	"Slow and Easy"	1993	43

⬇ *My Take*

Zapp & Roger was one of the first groups I was exposed to through my dad. I had the 45 of the single "Computer Love" and another one of "More Bounce to the Ounce." A special shout-out to Shirley Murdock and Charlie Wilson for appearing on "Computer Love" and adding amazing background vocals. Zapp and Roger opened up for Teena Marie in 1996, which still ranks as the favorite concert I have ever attended in person!

1990's

From Top Left to Bottom left in clockwise order:
Blackstreet, Total, Jodeci and Mint Condition.

Part Five
1990S

THE 1990S USHERED IN RAPID CHANGE AND EVOLUTION across the world. Nelson Mandela became president of South Africa after being in prison for 27 years. After the Rodney King verdict, the Los Angeles riots occurred. The OJ trial took center stage in 1995. The company we now know as Amazon was launched, and the movie *Titanic* became the first film to make more than $1 billion worldwide. We lived through the Persian Gulf War, *Friends* started its long run on television, and Princess Diana passed away tragically in 1997. Oh…and in 1998, Google was founded.

Michael Jordan took over the basketball world, winning six titles during this decade. The Dream Team in 1992 solidified American dominance in basketball, winning games by an average of 43.8 points a game. George Foreman became the oldest heavyweight champion in history by winning the title in 1994. We can't forget Cal Ripken Jr. becoming the true Iron Man by passing Lou Gehrig's record for consecutive games played in 1995 (I am an Orioles fan, so this makes me happy!). The city of Atlanta hosted the Olympics in 1996 (I was living and working there during that time). Tiger Woods won his first major championship, stunning everyone at the Masters in 1997. A young tennis player by the name of Serena Williams started her run to the top of the tennis world by winning the U.S. Open as a 17-year-old in 1999.

Examining the musical landscape brings us to the release of the classic album *The Chronic* by Dr. Dre. The Spice Girls were taking the world by storm with their debut album. Gangsta rap became a prominent subgenre, and an East Coast–West Coast rivalry dominated hip-hop news. Unfortunately, this rivalry led to the untimely deaths of the Notorious B.I.G. and 2Pac. The rise of the boy bands introduced us to the Backstreet Boys, *NSYNC, and 98 Degrees. A popular R&B girl group, Destiny's Child, started to gain momentum, and both Britney Spears and Christina Aguilera dominated the charts.

As much as a text message seems commonplace now, it was unique and brand new in 1992 when the first SMS was sent. Digital video discs (DVDs) were launched in 1995 with significant storage capacity and a much clearer picture and sound than their predecessors. A small South Korean company developed the MP3 player in 1998. This device had approximately 64 MB of memory, which was enough to hold only 18 songs. This was the precursor to the iPod, which would be launched in 2001. Finally, the World Wide Web was launched with the Mosaic web browser, which made the internet accessible to everyone in 1993. I remember using the web browser in AOL to track my sports scores and results after class at Howard University. And wait…on the horizon…Napster, the original file-sharing music platform, was launched in 1999. *Uh-oh…*

This era is commonly referred to as the golden era of R&B music and it was a time when Black R&B groups dominated the popular charts. This was the only decade in the history of the music industry where two R&B groups earned Diamond status (10 million+ sales) of an album—Boyz II Men (*II*) and TLC (*CrazySexyCool*)! These two groups earned numerous *Billboard* Top 20 hits and platinum albums/singles. Will we ever see this again? The domination of the *Billboard* Hot 100 charts was like the perfect storm of all the work of the groups from decades before. Boyz II Men and TLC led the efforts, but there were plenty other groups that contributed to the astronomical numbers coming from this specific segment of R&B music.

Outside of the R&B groups, you had R&B singers such as Mary J. Blige, Mariah Carey, Janet Jackson, Whitney Houston, and R. Kelly dominating the airwaves, movie screens, and television screens with hit after hit. Numerous *Billboard* records were broken, and the money from record sales was flowing at a high rate. Complementing these legendary R&B singers were younger singers coming in toward the end of the decade, with Brandy, Monica, and Usher leading the way. Wherever you looked, there were R&B artists winning awards, topping the charts, and playing on radio stations around the world.

Many famous R&B groups were born from previous iterations. Bell Biv DeVoe was born from New Edition. Boyz II Men was discovered by a member of Bell Biv DeVoe. Blackstreet was born from Guy. K-Ci and JoJo came from Jodeci. Lucy Pearl was born from Tony! Toni! Toné! and En Vogue. L.S.G. came about via a member of Levert and New Edition. The connections are endless. We also began to see hip-hop and R&B collaborations in this decade, as Total, SWV, and 112 had numerous hits with this formula.

It is important to note that an important law that would affect the landscape of R&B groups was passed in the 1990s. The passing of the Telecommunications Act of 1996 was the first major overhaul of telecommunications law in approximately 62 years. The goal of the new law was to let anyone enter any communications business and let any communications business compete in any market against each other. Within the music industry, radio stations became more consolidated and more homogenized. Pretty quickly, you could travel to Philadelphia, Atlanta, or Los Angeles and hear similar songs dominate popular radio. Gone was the local flavor of each city, which would include up-and-coming R&B groups. The squeeze from radio (and eventually the *Billboard* charts) was beginning.

Chapter 44

. . . .

BELL BIV DEVOE (BBD)

Bell Biv DeVoe (Photo by Jeff Kravitz/FilmMagic)

FROM THE WIND DOWN OF NEW EDITION CAME one of the 1990s' iconic groups, Bell Biv DeVoe.

BBD—featuring Ricky Bell, Michael Bivins, and Ronnie DeVoe—brought the new jack swing movement to the forefront with its debut album and smash hit of the same name, *Poison*. The group was born during New Edition's hiatus in 1989 at the suggestion of producers Jimmy Jam and Terry Lewis.

"Me, Mike and Ron became close through being in the back," Ricky Bell said in 1990. "We were always stuck together as far as business or whatever."

The Boston-born triumvirate formed a new group and got to work recording new music. But instead of re-creating the youthful New Edition sound, the members of BBD took their sound in a new, more adult, direction.

It helped that BBD was working with powerhouse producers like Eric Sadler, Hank Shocklee, and Keith Shocklee of "The Bomb Squad," the team behind groups like Public Enemy. And it helped that the group had songs written for them like "Poison" by Elliot Straite, also known as Dr. Freeze. "Poison" was inspired by Straite's ex-girlfriend.

"I didn't know that record was going to be that big," Straite said in a 2009 interview. "It was a little song I wrote on the train, a revenge song about a woman. They picked it up and they loved it."

So did everyone who heard it. From the new-jack beat to the belt-out-loud chorus, the song got stuck in your mind as soon as you heard it.

Notably, BBD shouted out its New Edition members near the end of the song. Even amid this new venture, they were still connected to their previous groupmates.

The song rocketed up the *Billboard* charts, topping out at number 3 on the Hot 100.

The sexually charged single "Do Me!" followed, and it also reached number 3 on the pop chart. The singles helped the album go on to sell more than four million copies. The album was also nominated for a Soul Train award.

Following a remix album, BBD returned to the studio to release *Hootie Mack* in 1993.

Subsequent albums include *BBD* in 2001 and *Three Stripes* in 2017.

The members of BBD have regularly toured with one another and with New Edition—and more than 30 years later, "Poison" remains a favorite.

♔ GRAMMY NOMINATIONS: 0

(L-R) Musicians Michael Bivins, Ronnie DeVoe, and Ricky Bell of the group Bell Biv DeVoe attend the 20th Annual Urbanworld Film Festival, *The New Edition Story* Screening at AMC Empire 25 theater on September 24, 2016, in New York City. (Photo by Mike Coppola/Getty Images)

Billboard Hot 100 CHARTING SINGLES

Here is a list of BBD's *Billboard* Hot 100 hits
in chronological order.

Song	Year Released	Billboard Hot 100 Peak Position
"Poison"	1990	3
"Do Me!"	1990	3
"B.B.D. (I Thought It Was Me)?"	1990	26
"When Will I See You Smile Again?"	1990	63
"The Best Things in Life Are Free" (with Luther Vandross, Janet Jackson, and Ralph Tresvant)	1992	10
"Gangsta"	1993	21
"Something In Your Eyes"	1993	38

My Favorite BBD Songs

- "When Will I See You Smile Again?"
- "B.B.D. (I Thought It Was Me)?"
- "Something In Your Eyes"

My Favorite BBD Samples

- "Tell Me" by Bow Wow sampled "When Will I See You Smile Again?"
- "Here I Am" by Rick Ross feat. Nelly and Avery Storm sampled "Do Me!"
- "Hit Me Off" by New Edition sampled "Do Me!"

◔ *My Take*

"Poison" still remains a classic song that is more popular globally than any New Edition song. That is crazy to me, but it shows the beauty of timing. It is very rare for a group to have an offshoot of another group *and* experience the level of success that BBD had. That is a testament to BBD's work ethic and ability to embrace new ideas and producers. Props to the group. And…I still know all the words to "When Will I See You Smile Again?"

Chapter 45

. . . .

BLACKSTREET

CIRCA 1990: Photo of Blackstreet. Photo by Al Pereira/Michael Ochs Archives/Getty Images

NO DIGGITY.

Blackstreet rose out of the ashes from another leading R&B group—Teddy Riley's Guy—and overcame turmoil and lineup changes to find massive success in the mid-1990s.

Riley was listless during the early 1990s. The new jack swing prodigy split Guy and produced Wreckx-n-Effect's "Rump Shaker," but he was looking for something more, a new outlet.

The original lineup for Blackstreet included Riley, Chauncey "Black" Hannibal, Joseph "Street" Stonestreet, and Levi Little. Hannibal and Stonestreet's nicknames were brought together to form the group's name. The name remained even after Stonestreet departed soon after the group's formation; he was replaced by Dave Hollister.

The group's first single, "Baby Be Mine," appeared on the soundtrack for the Chris Rock movie *CB4*. Its self-titled debut followed, and it included the song "Before I Let You Go," which reached the top 10 of the *Billboard* Hot 100 chart.

But Riley wasn't done tinkering. After a falling out with Hollister and Little, he brought on Eric Williams and Mark Middleton.

He also sharpened the group members' focuses to steer them away from earlier songs like "Booti Call," an ode to the hookup.

For Riley, Blackstreet served as a role model and needed to steer clear of temptation.

"I've seen too many black artists destroyed by drink, drugs and violence to make music which celebrates that lifestyle," he said in 1997. "I look at artists who live a crazy and dangerous life and I know who's gonna be around longest. I've seen what happens. I know to glamorize it is to lie."

All of those elements coalesced with *Another Level*, released in 1996. The album featured lots of elements—soul, R&B, gospel, new jack, and even a cover of the Beatles' "Can't Buy Me Love," along with an overlooked song that used a sample from Bill Withers's classic song "Grandma's Hands." The members of Blackstreet didn't know what to think of the song, and Riley had offered the track to others, but they passed.

The members' reticence caused Riley to sing the first verse of "No Diggity" himself. And he called on Dr. Dre and Brooklyn emcee Queen Pen for some help.

The song unseated the overplayed "Macarena" atop the *Billboard* Hot 100, nabbed a Grammy, and would go on to become one of the enduring R&B songs of all time. As *Billboard* wrote in 2023 when naming "No Diggity" one of the top 500 pop songs of all time, "No song sounded like it at the time, and no song has re-captured its full effect since."

The success of "No Diggity" and "Another Level," which went four times platinum, led to guest spots on Jay-Z's "The City Is Mine" and a team-up with Mya and Mase for "Take Me There," which was included on the soundtrack for the *Rugrats* movie.

The group released subsequent albums in 1999 and 2003 before embarking on solo projects.

Some of Blackstreet's past members reunited in 2014, and the group continues to perform today.

R&B royalty? No doubt.

🏆 GRAMMY NOMINATIONS: 1
🏆 GRAMMY WINS: 1
🏆 Best R&B Performance by a Duo or Group with Vocal: "No Diggity"

Blackstreet (L-R) Levi Little, Chauncey Hannibal, Teddy Riley, Terrell Phillips pose for a portrait circa 1997 in Los Angeles, California. (Photo by Aaron Rapoport/Corbis/Getty Images)

Billboard Hot 100 CHARTING SINGLES

Here is a list of Blackstreet's *Billboard* Hot 100 hits in chronological order.

Song	Year Released	Billboard Hot 100 Peak Position
"Booti Call"	1994	34
"Before I Let You Go"	1994	7
"Tonight's the Night" (with SWV)	1995	80
"Joy"	1995	43
"No Diggity" (with Dr. Dre)	1996	1
"Fix" (with Ol' Dirty Bastard, Slash, and Fishbone)	1997	58

Song	Year Released	Billboard Hot 100 Peak Position
"Take Me There" (with Mya, Mase, and Blinky Blink)	1998	14
"The City Is Mine" (with Jay-Z)	1998	52
"I Get Lonely" (remix) (with Janet Jackson)	1998	3
"Girlfriend/Boyfriend" (with Janet Jackson, Ja Rule & Eve)	1999	47

My Favorite Blackstreet Songs

- "Get Me Home" (with Foxy Brown)
- "Before I Let You Go"
- "Joy"

My Favorite Blackstreet Samples

- "Toss It Up" by Makaveli (2Pac) feat. K-Ci & JoJo, Danny Boy, and Aaron Hall sampled "No Diggity"

- "Oh I" by the Game feat. Jeremih, Young Thug, and Sevyn Streeter sampled "Get Me Home"

My Take

Initially, I thought of adding Guy into this segment, but I chose to keep them separate as to not diminish the impact of either group. The fact that no one wanted "No Diggity" and then it became a classic song is wild. Teddy Riley knew, and he stuck to his belief in the song. Props to him. When I am DJing out at party or event and I can fit in "Get Me Home," I put it on and it still works!

Chapter 46

·······

BOYZ II MEN

CIRCA 1990: Photo of Boyz II Men. From left to right: Shawn Stockman, Wanya Morris, Michael McCary, and Nathan Morris. Photo by Al Pereira/Michael Ochs Archives/Getty Images

IF NEW EDITION FOUND A NEW LEVEL FOR R&B boy bands, Boyz II Men perfected it.

It's fitting, then, that the group's name came from a New Edition track, and its first manager happened to be former New Edition (and later, Bell Biv DeVoe) member Michael Bivins.

During the mid-1990s, you couldn't escape Boyz II Men's smash hits like "I'll Make Love to You" and "End of the Road." And why would you want to? The chart-topping group found the perfect balance of four-part harmonies and slick production and covered the whole spectrum from sexual energy and confidence to vulnerability.

Boyz II Men blended Motown, Philly soul, and new jack swing into earworm hits that stuck with you.

The group was formed in the mid-1980s at the Philadelphia High School for Creative and Performing Arts. Early members of the group—initially called Unique Attraction—included Nathan Morris and Marc Nelson. Wanyá Morris and Shawn Stockman would join later. Their classmates included Ahmir "Questlove" Thompson, the music polymath of the Roots.

The group began performing at events, talent shows, and mall food courts. The group members wanted to get noticed—or at least get a fair shot at getting their break. So they snuck backstage at a concert hosted by Power 99 (WUSL-FM) and encountered Bivins.

"We weren't looking for a record deal, we just wanted somebody in the industry to hear us, and give us their opinion," Morris told the *Philadelphia Inquirer* in 1994.

Bivins was impressed by the group and became Boyz II Men's first manager, helping the group get a record deal and guiding the group members through the release of their first album, *Cooleyhighharmony*. The album—which was produced by Dallas Austin—hit all of the high notes and was anchored by the single "Motownphilly," a reference to the group's Motown and Philly soul influences. The song served as the group's introduction to the music world—a biographical journey and hint at what was to come. The song resembled a stew of influences, from doo-wop to new jack swing.

The lyrics reminisce about being back in school dreaming about being in a group that made it big. The lyrics continue to share how the group would start singing in the hallways of school and how it sounded smooth. From there…the group was born!

As "Motownphilly" promised, the group was the perfect blend of hard and soft. And with its next single, the a cappella hit "It's So Hard To Say Goodbye To Yesterday," the members explored the tender side of love and heartbreak, showcasing their range with the tearful hit. The song reached number 2 on the *Billboard* Hot 100 and topped the R&B chart.

Other singles emerged from the album—"Uhh Ahh" and "Please Don't Go"—and in early 1992, the group built on its emerging fame by touring on MC Hammer's 2 Legit 2 Quit tour. That year, it was given a song that would send it to another stratosphere.

"End of the Road," which was written by Kenneth "Babyface" Edmonds, Antonio "L.A." Reid, and Daryl Simmons, appeared on the soundtrack for the Eddie Murphy movie *Boomerang*. And through Boyz II Men's smooth harmonies and sharing of vocal duties, as well as McCary's bass interlude, the song became a timeless hit.

It reached the top of the *Billboard* charts in August 1992, and it stayed there for a then-record 13 weeks.

After the dust settled, it was time for the group to record new material. That new material was released on 1994's *II*, under the tutelage of Babyface (Bivins and the group amicably went their separate ways).

The album's lead single, "I'll Make Love to You," was released in July 1994. It didn't top the *Billboard* chart for 13 weeks—it topped it for 14. Other chart-topping hits included "On Bended Knee" and "Water Runs Dry."

II wound up selling more than 12 million copies, making it one of the most successful albums of all time.

Boyz II Men followed up in 1995 with an even bigger hit, "One Sweet Day" with Mariah Carey, which topped the *Billboard* Hot 100 for a then-record 16 weeks. The tearful ballad involves the death of a loved one. It was a theme that was close to Carey's heart, as well as the group's—Morris had been working up a similar song of his own.

Boyz II Men released their third studio album—*Evolution*—in 1997. It featured the singles "Four Seasons of Loneliness" and the Babyface-penned "A Song For Mama."

By the end of the decade, the group's momentum had slowed. Their commercial appeal was waning, and health issues were starting to crop up, most notably for McCary—he would leave the group in 2003 due to chronic back problems, later revealed to result from multiple sclerosis.

In the years since, Boyz II Men—now full-fledged adults—have continued to release material, with some commercial and award recognition. Their 2007 album *Motown: A Journey Through Hitsville USA* was nominated for two Grammy Awards and was a strong seller. The album also reinforced—through covers of the Temptations, Marvin Gaye, and Smokey Robinson—what made the group so special.

The three remaining members of the group continue to perform and appear in national commercials for brands like GEICO. They've also served a residency in Las Vegas, toured Asia, popped up in TV shows, and played many tours.

Through it all, they've held true to their credo—not too hard, not too soft.

⚜ GRAMMY NOMINATIONS: 15
⚜ GRAMMY WINS: 4

❋ Best R&B Performance by a Duo or Group with Vocal: "Cooleyhighharmony"

❋ Best R&B Performance by a Duo or Group with Vocal: "End of the Road"

❋ Best R&B Album: //

❋ Best R&B Performance by a Duo or Group with Vocal: "I'll Make Love to You"

American R&B group Boyz II Men (American singer Michael McCary, American singer Nathan Morris, American singer Wanyá Morris, American singer and songwriter Shawn Stockman) in the press room of the 35th Annual Grammy Awards, held at the Shrine Auditorium in Los Angeles, California, 24th February 1993. The band received the Best R&B Performance by a Duo or Group with Vocal award for their song "End of the Road." (Photo by Vinnie Zuffante/Getty Images)

Billboard Hot 100 CHARTING SINGLES

Here is a list of Boyz II Men's *Billboard* Hot 100 hits in chronological order.

Song	Year Released	Billboard Hot 100 Peak Position
→ "Motownphilly"	1991	3
→ "It's So Hard To Say Goodbye To Yesterday"	1991	2
→ "Uhh Ahh"	1991	16
→ "Please Don't Go"	1992	49
→ "End of the Road"	1992	1
→ "In The Still Of The Nite (I'll Remember)"	1993	3
→ "Let It Snow" (with Brian McKnight)	1993	32
→ "Thank You"	1994	21
→ "I'll Make Love to You"	1994	1
→ "On Bended Knee"	1994	1
→ "One Sweet Day" (with Mariah Carey)[8]	1995	1
→ "Water Runs Dry"	1995	2
→ "Vibin' "	1995	56
→ "I Remember"	1995	46

---

8   "One Sweet Day" by Mariah Carey and Boyz II Men is the longest-running number 1 song on the *Billboard* Hot 100 chart. It spent 16 consecutive weeks at the top of the chart from December 2, 1995, to March 16, 1996. This record was broken in 2019 with the song "Old Town Road" from Lil Nas X and Billy Ray Cyrus.

Song	Year Released	Billboard Hot 100 Peak Position
➡ "Hey Lover" (with LL Cool J)	1995	3
➡ "4 Seasons Of Loneliness"	1997	1
➡ "A Song For Mama"	1997	7
➡ "I Will Get There"	1999	32
➡ "Pass You By"	2000	25
➡ "Thank You In Advance"	2000	80

My Favorite Boyz II Men Songs

➤ "Your Love" ➤ "Uhh Ahh" ➤ "I Sit Away"

My Favorite Boyz II Men Samples

- "Countdown" by Beyoncé sampled "Uhh Ahh"
- "Gimme the Loot" by the Notorious B.I.G. sampled "It's So Hard To Say Goodbye To Yesterday"
- "Strictly Business, Pt 1 & 2" by Action Bronson and Statik Selektah sampled "Motownphilly"

My Take

First, it should be noted (and talked about frequently) that Boyz II Men is the only male Black R&B group in history (as of the writing of this book) to achieve Diamond status for an album (*II*). This is a historic accomplishment that is seemingly forgotten by all music historians. Boyz II Men also appears on my top five most resilient R&B group list because, from where they were at their peak (rumored to play in front of approximately 200,000 at a festival in Philadelphia) to where they are now (playing at shows in front of 3,000 people), they have stuck with it. The Las Vegas residency was a great rebirth for them, and I expect them to continue to have a positive renaissance as the years continue. When I think of my very first answering machine (yes, one of those devices) when I was a senior in high school getting recruited to play Division I soccer across the country, it brings up a Boyz II Men memory for me. I had the piano prelude to "Your Love" playing at the beginning of the message, and then my voice would come on. I got many compliments, and a coach recruiting me even commented on my taste!

Chapter 47

. . . .

EN VOGUE

Singers Dawn Robinson, Maxine Jones, Cindy Herron, and Terry Ellis of En Vogue poses for photos at WGCI-FM radio in Chicago, Illinois, in April 1990. (Photo By Raymond Boyd/Getty Images)

THE GIRL GROUPS OF YESTERYEAR TYPICALLY HAD A lead singer. Diana Ross and the Supremes. Veronica Bennett and the Ronettes. Shirley Owens and the Shirelles.

En Vogue spun that model on its head by relying on four lead singers—and their efforts led to some of the 1990s' fiercest, sultriest hits, like "Hold On" and "My Lovin' (You're Never Gonna Get It)."

The girl group was the creation of Oakland-based producers Denzil Foster and Thomas McElroy, who were interested in assembling a group that resembled the female R&B groups of the past.

But instead of re-creating the male-dominated model of the past, the producers wanted the singers to be involved in decision-making.

They held auditions and found singer-songwriter Dawn Robinson, dancer-singer Cindy Herron, vocalist Maxine Jones, and gospel-trained singer Terry Ellis.

As Jones recalled in 1991, "When I went in with the girls, my voice fit in with theirs—like we had the same tone qualities or something. It was amazing: Denny tried every possible combination of the four of us, and it seemed to work. Everything we did seemed to work."

The quartet began work on their debut album, *Born to Sing*, which was released in early 1990. The album spawned hits like "Hold On" and "You Don't Have to Worry." It bridged the gap between rap and R&B, between style and substance.

And just as quickly, En Vogue was on the road, touring with the likes of M.C. Hammer and appearing in a Diet Coke commercial directed by Spike Lee. The group, from its creation, understood the commercial side of the music world and capitalized.

A follow-up album, *Funky Divas*, followed in 1992 and brought the smash "My Lovin' (You're Never Gonna Get It)" to the world. The song samples

James Brown's "The Payback."

En Vogue also provided vocals for the Salt-N-Pepa smash hit "Whatta Man," a classic ode to men who are the epitome of respect.

The group's biggest international single, "Don't Let Go (Love)" came for the soundtrack for the movie *Set It Off* and captures the yearning surrounding someone wanting more out of a relationship.

The song was reflective of the tensions that were brewing underneath the surface of the group. Before En Vogue released its third album, Robinson chose to leave due to contractual negotiations. The remaining members carried forward as a triumvirate, releasing the album *EV3* in 1997 and *Masterpiece Theatre* in 2000.

Jones departed in 2001, and in her place, Amanda Cole, and later Rhona Bennett, were added.

En Vogue's original lineup has reconvened at various points, but lawsuits and stalled projects have cropped up in recent decades.

Today, En Vogue continues to perform behind a lineup of Ellis, Herron, and Bennett—fierce as ever and still sharing lead vocal duties.

♙ GRAMMY NOMINATIONS: 7
♙ GRAMMY WINS: 0

En Vogue backstage at B.B. King Blues Club & Grill on May 10, 2009, in New York City.
(Photo by Johnny Nunez/WireImage)

Billboard Hot 100 CHARTING SINGLES

Here is a list of En Vogue's *Billboard* Hot 100 hits
in chronological order.

	Song	Year Released	Billboard Hot 100 Peak Position
➔	"Hold On"	1990	2
➔	"Lies"	1990	38
➔	"You Don't Have to Worry"	1990	57
➔	"My Lovin' (You're Never Gonna Get It)"	1992	2
➔	"Giving Him Something He Can Feel"	1992	6
➔	"Free Your Mind"	1992	8

	Song	Year Released	Billboard Hot 100 Peak Position
➔	"Give It Up, Turn It Loose"	1992	15
➔	"Love Don't Love You"	1993	36
➔	"Runaway Love"	1993	51
➔	"Whatta Man" (Salt-N-Pepa with En Vogue)	1994	3
➔	"Don't Let Go (Love)"	1997	2
➔	"Whatever"	1997	16
➔	"Too Gone, Too Long"	1997	33
➔	"No Fool No More"	1997	57
➔	"Riddle"	1997	92

🔥 *My Favorite En Vogue Songs*

❯ "Part of Me" ❯ "Yesterday" ❯ "Hold On"

💜 *My Favorite En Vogue Samples*

- •• "Blue Magic" by Jay-Z feat. Pharrell Williams sampled "Hold On"
- •• "Thug Life" by 21 Savage sampled "Giving Him Something He Can Feel"
- •• "More Than" Friends by James Hype feat. Kelli-Leigh sampled "Don't Let Go (Love)"

⊙ *My Take*

To be introduced to a group for their first single, "Hold On," with the a cappella intro, is just brilliant. I wonder how many takes it took for them to get it down. I am upset that the music industry and group relations tore this group apart before they could have a bigger musical impact. No Grammys? No number 1 *Billboard* Hot 100 hits (they seemed to be stuck at number 2)? Crazy. Four powerhouses singing across the entire album is like a chef's kiss! I also love their remake of the classic song "Yesterday." Beautiful!

Members of the musical group En Vogue (from L): Dawn Robinson, Maxine Jones, Terry Ellis, and Cindy Herron hold their trophy 25 January 1993 at the American Music Awards in Los Angeles, CA. (Photo credit should read VINCE BUCCI/AFP via Getty Images)

Chapter 48

. . . .

JODECI

Singers DeVanté Swing (Donald Earle DeGrate, Jr.), JoJo (Joel Hailey), K-Ci (Cedric Renard Hailey), and Mr. Dalvin (Dalvin Ertimus DeGrate) of Jodeci poses for photos at Jimmy's Records in Chicago, Illinois, in October 1991. (Photo By Raymond Boyd/Getty Images)

JODECI WAS FORGED ON A FOUNDATION OF GOSPEL—BUT its members would veer in a very different direction, becoming masters of the slow jam.

The group remains revered and continues to inspire the world's biggest musicians.

Jodeci's members, two pairs of brothers, hail from Charlotte, North Carolina. *Jodeci* is an abbreviation of their names—*Jo* for Joel "JoJo" Hailey, *de* for brothers Dalvin and Donald DeGrate (Mr. Dalvin and DeVanté Swing), and *ci* for Cedric "K-Ci" Hailey.

The DeGrates and Haileys both performed with gospel groups established by their fathers—Little Cedric and the Hailey Singers, and the De-Grate Delegation.

But R&B pulled them in.

Like Sam Cooke and lots of other artists, the members of Jodeci came to that crossroads of gospel and secular music and passed through. But none, before or since, have made such a massive transition from gospel to *freaky*.

DeVanté Swing was the heart of Jodeci, the group's main songwriter and producer. The group recorded dozens of songs, honing its sound before driving, unannounced, to Uptown Records. Music legends Heavy D and Andre Harrell listened to their demo, and then the group was asked to perform—there was skepticism around the demo's high production quality.

Jodeci was signed and assigned to an Uptown intern named Sean "Puffy" Combs. He worked to define the group's style, outfitting them in hoodies, baseball caps, and Timberlands as a counterbalance to New Edition's polished image.

Jodeci released its first album, *Forever My Lady*, in May 1991. It contained versions of many of the songs the group had recorded before leaving North Carolina. Five singles were released from the album, including "Come and Talk to Me," which topped the R&B charts and reached number 11 on the

Billboard Hot 100.

The group's follow-up effort, *Diary of a Mad Band*, released in late 1993, received mixed reviews but solidified Jodeci's sound. Notably, it also featured appearances by two protégés of DeVanté Swing who would reshape music in the years ahead—Missy Elliott and Timbaland.

Jodeci's music was just *different*. The album's first single, "Cry For You," captures the emotions of someone lost without their love.

The hit "Feenin'," meanwhile, classified a woman as the highest feeling you can feel. As K-Ci sang, he described the woman taking his money, house, and cars in exchange for a moment with her as being with her was a true addiction.

The members of Jodeci were gaining a reputation as R&B bad boys. In the mid-1990s, DeVanté was dating Madonna, K-Ci was seeing Mary J. Blige, and Dalvin was with T-Boz of TLC. But there was an undercurrent of misogyny to Jodeci's sexual songs, an element Amy Linden explored in a 1994 *New York Times* article: "Jodeci cloaks its misogyny in thundering beats in an attempt to render the underlying message innocuous. Yet for all the larger-than-life sexual escapades on 'Diary of a Mad Band,' there's little emotion. Jodeci's idea of seduction is conquest at any cost," she wrote.

The criticisms didn't deter the group from taking freakiness to another level. Its third album, *The Show, the After Party, the Hotel*, was anchored by the single "Freek'n You." The sharply produced song wasn't very cryptic or vague; the singer simply describes waking up with a feeling of arousal, as the woman of his affection was on his mind as soon as his eyes opened.

By 1996, it had been too much of everything, and Jodeci needed a break. The members went in different directions—DeVanté produced other artists, Dalvin went on to release solo material, and K-Ci and JoJo decided to team up and take on pop radio with adult contemporary hits like "All My Life."

Their new focus was sappy, the stuff middle school dances were made for, but it was also music their mother could listen to, and there's something to be said for that.

Over the years, Jodeci has maintained mythical status among later music stars, especially Drake, who's referenced his love for the group on numerous occasions and even released a "Jodeci Freestyle."

The members of Jodeci reunited for the 2014 Soul Train awards, walking to the stage as smoke billowed and performing a medley of hits such as "Freek'n You." The audience sang along and danced—they knew every word.

Jodeci released an album the following year, and the group continued to appear in concert in the years that followed, ready to reclaim its throne among R&B royalty.

🏆 GRAMMY NOMINATIONS: 0

Singers K-Ci (Cedric Renard Hailey), DeVanté Swing (Donald Earle DeGrate, Jr.), Jo Jo (Joel Hailey), and Mr. Dalvin (Dalvin Ertimus DeGrate) of Jodeci poses for photos backstage after their performance at The Arena in St. Louis, Missouri, in June 1992. (Photo By Raymond Boyd/Getty Images)

Billboard Hot 100 CHARTING SINGLES

Here is a list of Jodeci's *Billboard* Hot 100 hits in chronological order.

Song	Year Released	Billboard Hot 100 Peak Position
"Forever My Lady"	1991	25
"Stay"	1992	41
"Come & Talk To Me"	1992	11
"I'm Still Waiting"	1992	85
"Cry For You"	1993	15
"Feenin' "	1994	25
"Love U 4 Life"	1995	31
"Freek'n You"	1995	14
"Get On Up"	1996	22

My Favorite Jodeci Songs

❯ "U And I"   ❯ "What About Us"   ❯ "Feenin' "

My Favorite Jodeci Samples

•• "How Bout Now" by Drake sampled "My Heart Belongs To U"

•• "You're Everything" by Bun B feat. Rick Ross, David Banner, and 8Ball & MJG sampled "Cry For You"

•• "The Impossible" by Mariah Carey sampled "Forever My Lady"

⊙ My Take

When I got the Jodeci CD *Forever My Lady* from the Wiz in College Park, Maryland, I would play the first five tracks (all slow jams) on repeat. It became my "falling asleep" soundtrack, even when, many nights, my dad would come up to my room in the attic and angrily turn off my stereo. You see, even on these slow jams, the bass was too thick, and he would hear it in his room right below mine. Wow! I am also very partial to the Spanish being spoken at the beginning of "U And I." What an intro! When *Diary of a Mad Band* came out while I was living in the Howard Towers (at Howard University), you could hear this CD on every floor at any time. It was a massive hit all throughout our school! I love the lyrics in "What About Us."

Chapter 49

. . . .

112

Singers Marvin "Slim" Scandrick, Michael "Mike" Keith, Quinnes "Q" Parker, and Daron Jones of 112 poses for photos atop Loft 1625 in Chicago, Illinois, in August 2003. (Photo By Raymond Boyd/Getty Images)

AT A TIME WHEN MUSIC WAS GETTING HARDER, 112 offered an antidote: sleek, smooth romantic harmonies.

The group originated in Atlanta in the early 1990s and consisted of four members who attended high school together: Quinnes "Q" Damond, Marvin "Slim" Scandrick, Michael Marcel, and Daron Tavaris. At first, they honed their sound on the local talent show circuit.

After being discovered by and working with producers Tim & Bob (Tim Kelley and Bob Robinson), the group—initially called Forte—entered the orbit of Sean "Puffy" Combs and Bad Boy Records, which signed the group.

With Bad Boy, they joined a powerhouse roster that included Christopher Wallace, the rapper known as the Notorious B.I.G.

As Damond told the *Atlanta Constitution* about Wallace in 1997, "He was the big brother of the Bad Boy family. And from Day 1 he embraced us. Like brothers, we would look out for each other."

Their self-titled debut album, released in 1996, featured the hits "Only You" and "Cupid" and established their brand of smooth jams. 112 also guested on tracks by other stars such as B.I.G., including his song "Sky's the Limit" off of his album *Life After Death*.

Sadly, 112's biggest single—an appearance on "I'll Be Missing You"—was released to honor Wallace after he was shot dead in 1997. The smash hit reached the top of the charts and later took home a Grammy for Best Rap Performance by a Duo or Group.

"We're where we've always dreamed of being," Marcel said in 1997. "We're out here making the kind of music that's true to our hearts. And when a lot of people are out there doing the derogatory thing—and selling lots of records—honestly, we were wondering whether such a romantic R&B record would work, but it has."

In 1998, 112 released their second album, *Room 112*, with a new batch of hits, including "Love Me" and the sultry "Anywhere."

Another major hit, "Peaches & Cream," followed on 2001's *Part III*. With "Peaches & Cream," 112 earned a Grammy nomination for Best R&B Duo or Group, losing to Destiny's Child and "Survivor."

By 2002, the group members recognized they weren't a priority for Bad Boy and decided to split from the label, jumping to Def Jam. Their next album— *Hot & Wet*—was delayed amid the negotiations between the labels.

Following 2005's *Pleasure & Pain*, the members of 112 took a break to pursue their solo careers.

112 has since reunited in the past decade and released new material, including the 2017 album *Q, Mike, Slim, Daron*.

♔ GRAMMY NOMINATIONS: 2
♔ GRAMMY WINS: 1
✹ Best Rap Performance by a Duo or Group: "I'll Be Missing You"

Portrait of members of R&B group 112 and American rappers Notorious B.I.G. (also known as
Biggie Smalls, born Christopher Wallace, 1972–1997) (second left) & Lil Kim (born Kimberly
Jones) (center fore) as they pose at an unspecified restaurant, New York, New York, circa
1996. The members of 112 include Marvin Scandrick (also known as Slim), Quinnes Parker,
Daron Jones, and Michael Keith. (Photo by Nitro/Getty Images)

Billboard Hot 100 CHARTING SINGLES

Here is a list of 112's *Billboard* Hot 100 hits
in chronological order.

Song	Year Released	Billboard Hot 100 Peak Position
"Only You" (with the Notorious B.I.G.)	1996	13
"Cupid"	1997	13
"Come See Me" (with Mr. Cheeks)	1997	33
"Love Me" (with Mase)	1998	17
"Anywhere" (with Lil Zane)	1999	15

Song	Year Released	Billboard Hot 100 Peak Position
➔ "Peaches & Cream"	2001	4
➔ "Dance With Me" (with Beanie Sigel)	2001	39
➔ "It's Over Now"	2001	6
➔ "Na Na Na Na" (with Super Cat)	2003	75
➔ "Hot & Wet" (with Ludacris)	2003	70
➔ "U Already Know" (with Foxy Brown)	2005	32

🔥 My Favorite 112 Songs

❯ "It's Over Now" ❯ "Only You" ❯ "Peaches & Cream"

💜 My Favorite 112 Samples

- "Mo Money Mo Problems" by the Notorious B.I.G. feat. Puff Daddy, Mase and Kelly Price sampled "Only You"
- "Change" by Arin Ray and Kehlani sampled "Only You"
- "Turn Me On" by Kevin Lyttle feat. MaddZart sampled "All My Love"

⊙ My Take

112 is a group from Atlanta that has done very well on their own and with multiple collaborations. I feel they were one of the best groups at partnering with hip-hop groups and bringing the singing element to the tracks. When DJing, one time I mixed out of "Only You" and a young lady came up to me and scolded me for mixing out before Biggie's verse. She had a point. I never mixed out early again!

(L-R) Quinnes "Q" Parker, Michael "Mike" Keith, Marvin "Slim" Scandrick, and Daron Jones of 112 attend the 2017 Soul Train Awards, presented by BET, at the Orleans Arena on November 5, 2017, in Las Vegas, Nevada. (Photo by Leon Bennett/Getty Images for BET)

Chapter 50

. . . .

SWV

NEW YORK - MARCH 1993: Coko (Cheryl Gamble), Lelee (Leanne Lyons) and Taj (Tamara Johnson) of the R and B group "SWV" aka Sisters with Voices (Photo by Al Pereira/Michael Ochs Archives/Getty Images)

S...DOUBLE-U...V!

The vocal trio Sisters with Voices—which included Cheryl (Coko) Gamble, Tamara (Taj) Johnson-George, and Leanne (Lelee) Lyons—became one of the most successful girl groups with a string of 1990s hits.

The trio hailed from New York City. Gamble and Lyons sang gospel before teaming up with Johnson-George, who brought a fresh energy as a rapper and emcee.

"I wanted to get into R&B because it has a different feel," Gamble told the *Los Angeles Times* in 1993. "I can sing about different subjects—and deliver some feminist messages."

SWV represented a female antidote to male groups like Guy, the original new jack swing group and Jodeci, a group that could get listeners in the mood to dance or make love. RCA's Kenny Ortiz was impressed by SWV's demo and signed them to a contract in 1991. The trio was paired with Brian Alexander Morgan to produce their debut album.

It's About Time burst onto the scene the following year. The members went from relative unknowns to breakout performers in short order.

SWV's first single was "Right Here," which was a solid hit on its own but broke into a new stratosphere months later after being mixed with Michael Jackson's "Human Nature." The members of SWV were skeptical of the remix, but it wound up topping the *Billboard* R&B chart and reaching number 2 on the Hot 100.

In between the original and the remix came a handful of other massive singles.

"I'm So Into You," with its hip-hop beats and sharp harmonies, reached the top 10 of the charts.

Their third single took SWV to a new level. It was a song Morgan had written about young love and his crush on singer Chanté Moore—a song he had initially wanted Charlie Wilson to sing, but that SWV made their own: "Weak."

Anchored by Gamble's lead vocals, with the other members supporting her and sparse instrumentals underneath, the song allowed the members' voices to really come through.

The song was simple and straightforward, talking about how the cause and cure for their illness was the person of their affection.

And it shot all the way to the top of the charts.

Soundtrack opportunities and a remix album followed, and SWV's follow-up album *New Beginning* was released in 1996. It contained the single "You're the One," one of SWV's biggest hits, and it saw the group shifting away from new jack swing to explore more traditional R&B. Another song off the album, "Use Your Heart," was among the first production credits for the Neptunes, the superproducer team of Pharrell Williams and Chad Hugo.

The album *Release Some Tension* was released in 1997—but despite the title, SWV were struggling to release the growing tension between each other. After they released a Christmas album, the group members took a long hiatus and explored solo options.

Gamble released some solo material before finding success with her gospel roots. Johnson-George starred in a reality show with her husband, NFL star Eddie George, and also appeared on *Survivor*.

Despite some team-ups, collaborations, and hints at new material, SWV didn't really reconvene until 2011, when they released the fittingly titled *I Missed Us*. The group later appeared on the reality TV series *SWV Reunited* and battled against fellow 1990s R&B girl group Xscape in a *Verzuz* webcast battle.

🏆 **GRAMMY NOMINATIONS: 3**
🏆 **GRAMMY WINS: 0**

Coko (Cheryl Gamble), Lelee (Leanne Lyons), and Taj (Tamara Johnson) of the R and B group SWV aka Sisters with Voices attend an event in March 1993 in New York. (Photo by Al Pereira/ Michael Ochs Archives/Getty Images)

Billboard Hot 100 CHARTING SINGLES

Here is a list of SWV's *Billboard* Hot 100 hits in chronological order.

	Song	Year Released	Billboard Hot 100 Peak Position
➡	"Right Here"	1992	92
➡	"I'm So Into You"	1993	6
➡	"Weak"	1993	1
➡	"Right Here (Human Nature Remix)"	1993	2
➡	"You're Always On My Mind"	1993	54
➡	"Anything"	1994	18

Song	Year Released	Billboard Hot 100 Peak Position
● "Freedom"	1995	45
● "Tonight's the Night" (with Blackstreet)	1995	80
● "You're the One"	1996	5
● "Use Your Heart"	1996	22
● "It's All About U"	1996	61
● "Can We" (with Missy Elliott)	1997	75
● "Someone"	1997	19
● "Rain"	1998	25

🔥 *My Favorite SWV Songs*

❯ "I'm So Into You" ❯ "When This Feeling" ❯ "Fine Time" ❯ "Love Is So Amazing"

💜 *My Favorite SWV Samples*

- •• "Pullin' Me Back" by Chingy feat. Tyrese sampled "Rain"
- •• "The Trip (Downtown)" by Wale sampled "Downtown"
- •• "Table" by Kehlani feat. Little Simz sampled "Use Your Heart"

⊙ *My Take*

I still proudly own SWV's debut CD, which is lime green and has so many hits. If you ever meet me in person, ask me to share my story about the song "Downtown" from the first album. I remember attending Freaknik in 1993, and whenever we would hear the song "I'm So Into You," it would bring me immense joy. I always wanted SWV to appear for a record signing at the

Howard University Wiz, but it never happened. In many circles, the "Right Here (Human Nature Remix)" is considered one of the best remixes of all time. I agree!

SEPTEMBER 01: Photo of SWV (Photo by Raymond Boyd/Michael Ochs Archives/Getty Images)

Chapter 51

. . . .

TLC

R&B group TLC (Tionne Watkins aka T-Boz; Lisa Lopes aka Left Eye; Rozonda Thomas aka Chilli) appear in a portrait taken on October 10, 1992, in New York City. (Photo by Al Pereira/ Michael Ochs Archives/Getty Images)

TIONNE WATKINS WAS WORKING AT AN ATLANTA BEAUTY salon when she heard that an all-girl group was being formed.

The group was initially called 2nd Nature and consisted of three members: Watkins, Lisa Lopes, and Crystal Jones. They swung an audition with pop singer Perri "Pebbles" Reid, who was getting into the production side of the business. The girls had promise—but they could use a new name.

Reid decided that an acronym for the group members' names—Tionne, Lisa, and Crystal—would draw in listeners, and TLC was born. But before the group took off, Crystal was replaced by Rozonda Thomas, who adapted the nickname "Chilli" to keep the name intact (Watkins became "T-Boz," while Lopes was nicknamed "Left Eye").

The trio signed a record deal with LaFace Records, which was cofounded by Pebbles's then-husband Antonio "L.A." Reid, and got to work with a who's who of producers. Reid. Kenneth "Babyface" Edmonds. Jermaine Dupri. Dallas Austin. Marley Marl. Daryl Simmons.

Oooooooohhh…On the TLC Tip was released in February 1992, bringing the group to the masses. The album would go on to sell millions of copies behind singles like the Grammy-nominated "Ain't 2 Proud 2 Beg," an ode to sexual confidence. The album's second single, the slow jam "Baby-Baby-Baby," performed even better, topping the *Billboard* R&B chart and rising to number 2 on the Hot 100 (behind Boyz II Men's "End of the Road").

The blend of Watkins's funk, Lopes's hip-hop, and Thomas's R&B influences brought TLC to the forefront of the "new jill swing" movement and helped carve a path for acts that followed, such as Destiny's Child and Blaque. TLC also stood out for the messages in its lyrics—they weren't afraid to tackle topics like addiction, safe sex, and female empowerment.

The group's image was just as original as its hit singles. TLC's members found a smart balance, settling on a look that Thomas later classified as "prissy tomboy." In the mid-1990s, that typically meant overalls with condoms pinned to them to promote safe sex.

But visibility and success also came with turmoil, especially when it came to Lopes's relationship with NFL player Andre Rison. In early 1994, following a fight, Lopes attempted to burn Rison's shoes in a bathtub and instead caused a major fire at his house. She spent part of the year attending alcohol rehab.

The rehab stint coincided with TLC recording its next album, and Lopes appeared for some recording sessions.

As with its first album, while recording their second album, TLC had the chance to work with top-flight producers, such as Austin, Babyface, Sean "Puffy" Combs, Jermaine Dupri, and the Atlanta collective Organized Noize.

This time around, TLC was more grown up, more sure of itself. And it was at its full artistic power.

The album's lead single, "Creep," dealt with a woman looking for affection elsewhere after her man wasn't showing her any. It wound up topping the *Billboard* charts and was one of the year's biggest singles.

It was followed by the sultry, simmering "Red Light Special," another top five hit.

The album's third hit became TLC's most famous song, "Waterfalls," which called on people to avoid self-destructive behaviors.

As Thomas reflected to the *Guardian* years later,

We definitely wanted to be role models. We felt like a lot of females didn't have other females pulling for them—so every song we put out was a girl-power song. We told it from a woman's point of view. Women liked that and men respected it.

AIDS is still out there. You still have bullying. You still have drugs. But you have to continue to bring awareness so that people can become more responsible and want to do the right things. You can never have too many records like Waterfalls.

Lopes's verse on the song—a message of resilience involving rainbows and not giving up on yourself—was especially impactful, particularly when considering the struggles she'd faced.

TLC wound up winning an MTV Video Music Award for video of the year for "Waterfalls," as well as a Grammy for "Creep" as *CrazySexyCool* went on to sell 12 million copies.

But even so, TLC, at the height of its commercial success, wound up filing for bankruptcy; the group argued its contracts were less than favorable. Tensions continued to brew ahead of recording the group's third album amid Thomas's relationship with Austin, their main producer.

The members of TLC began increasingly working on solo projects, such as Lopes's starting a production company and signing performers like fellow girl group Blaque.

Things were patched up in order to complete *FanMail*, which was released in early 1999. The album contained two more massive hits—"Unpretty" and "No Scrubs"—which sought to empower women to believe in themselves and leave their good-for-nothing men behind.

FanMail would be their final album released as a threesome. In April 2002, Lopes died in a car crash in Honduras. She was only 30 years old.

TLC continued forward as a duo, declining to replace Lopes—something that's carried forward to the present.

After a few more albums, and a hiatus, Watkins and Thomas reconvened and have been together ever since, inspiring women—and men—with their timely messages and infectious rhymes.

🏆 GRAMMY NOMINATIONS: 12
🏆 GRAMMY WINS: 4
* Best R&B Album: *CrazySexyCool*
* Best R&B Performance by a Duo or Group with Vocal: "Creep"
* Best R&B Album: *FanMail*
* Best R&B Performance by a Duo or Group with Vocal: "No Scrubs"

(L-R) American singer, songwriter, actress, author, and executive producer Tionne "T-Boz" Watkins, American rapper and singer Lisa "Left Eye" Lopes (1971–2002) and American singer, dancer, actress, television personality and model Rozonda "Chilli" Thomas, of the American R&B girl group TLC, speak at an Arista event circa October, 1994, in Los Angeles, California. (Photo by Lester Cohen/Getty Images)

Billboard Hot 100 CHARTING SINGLES

Here is a list of TLC's *Billboard* Hot 100 hits
in chronological order.

Song	Year Released	Billboard Hot 100 Peak Position
"Ain't 2 Proud 2 Beg"	1991	6
"Baby-Baby-Baby"	1992	2
"What About Your Friends"	1992	7
"Hat 2 da Back"	1992	30
"Get It Up"	1993	42
"Creep"	1994	1
"Red Light Special"	1995	2
"Waterfalls"	1995	1
"Diggin' On You"	1995	5
"No Scrubs"	1999	1
"Unpretty"	1999	1
"Dear Lie"	2000	51
"Girl Talk"	2002	28
"Damaged"	2003	53

My Favorite TLC Songs

"What About Your Friends"　"Red Light Special"　"Get It Up"

♥ *My Favorite TLC Samples*

- ·· "Shape of You" by Ed Sheeran sampled "No Scrubs"
- ·· "Ain't No Nigga" by Jay-Z feat. Foxy Brown sampled "Creep"
- ·· "You Can Get It All" by Bow Wow feat. Johntá Austin sampled "Baby-Baby-Baby"

⊙ *My Take*

TLC is the only all-female group, besides the Chicks, to earn Diamond status (over 10 million in album sales) in history! This is an amazing accomplishment that needs to be discussed more. TLC is the only African American female group to ever accomplish this. To do this while also filing for bankruptcy is another whole story. The run the group had was unheard of in a time when musical options were abundant. I would love to write a whole biography of TLC. Their story has so many lessons, peaks, and valleys. TLC would be on the city of Atlanta's Mount Rushmore of music groups. I love the simple and true lyrics for "What About Your Friends" and I think Morris Day would be proud of "Get It Up."

TLC performing at the MTV 20th Anniversary party, "MTV20: Live and Almost Legal" at Hammerstein Ballroom in New York City on 8/1/01. Photo by Scott Gries/ImageDirect

Chapter 52

. . . .

TONY! TONI! TONÉ!

Photo of Tony! Toni! Toné! Photo by Michael Ochs Archives/Getty Images

TONY! TONI! TONÉ! WAS PURE SOUL—AND PURE MUSICALITY.

Raphael Wiggins (later Raphael Saadiq), his brother D'Wayne Wiggins, and their cousin Timothy Christian Riley formed the group in Oakland in 1986 and were driven to make the type of music they listened to. Producers Denzil Foster and Thomas McElroy—who also developed En Vogue—helped the group get discovered.

Tony! Toni! Toné! represented a throwback, choosing substance and musicianship over flash and gimmicks.

The group members were especially drawn to live instrumentation and worked with a seasoned group of backing musicians. As Michael Goldberg wrote in a 1993 article for the *San Francisco Chronicle*, "Live, Tony Toni Toné's mastery of classical soul music can send chills up a listener's spine."

The group released its first album, *Who?*, in 1988 and its second, *The Revival*, in 1990.

The albums were well received and featured a series of top R&B songs, including "Feels Good," which was the group's first top 10 pop hit.

The group leaned further into its musical influences for the 1993 album *Sons of Soul* by paying homage to performers like Earth, Wind & Fire and Sly & the Family Stone. The members even moved their recording sessions to Trinidad to get the album into shape and produced the album themselves.

"We wanted to do it like they used to do it," D'Wayne said in 1993. "Guys would sit down with a guitar, drums and a keyboard and come up with something. But today, when most people write, it's like computer get-down. We just went back to home with our thing."

Sons of Soul marked the group's commercial peak. The double-platinum album produced five singles, including "If I Had No Loot," which is about fair-weather friends.

A *Billboard* reviewer called the album "a prismatic record from a maturing band."

But it was also a band in need of a break. Following the success of *Sons of Soul*, the members of Tony! Toni! Toné! decided to pursue solo projects and helped produce for other performers.

They reconvened for a final album, *House of Music*, released in 1996, before going their separate ways.

Members of Tony! Toni! Toné! came together to perform instrumentals on Alicia Keys's Grammy-nominated song "Diary," released as a single in 2004, and the lineup held a reunion tour in 2023 to mark the 30th anniversary of *Sons of Soul*.

♖ GRAMMY NOMINATIONS: 2
♖ GRAMMY WINS: 0

Portrait of the members of American R&B group Tony Toni Toné (styled as Tony! Toni! Toné!) as they pose with Gerardo, Tara Kemp, and Fab Five Freddie, backstage at the Marcus Amphitheater, Milwaukee, Wisconsin, July 3, 1991. Pictured are Timothy Christian Riley (left) and his cousins, brothers Raphael Saadiq (born Charles Wiggins) (third left) and D'wayne Wiggins (second right), all of the group Tony! Toni! Toné!, Gerardo (born Gerardo Mejía) (second left), Tara Kemp, third right), and Fab Five Freddy (born Fred Brathwaite). (Photo by Paul Natkin/Getty Images)

Billboard Hot 100 CHARTING SINGLES

Here is a list of Tony! Toni! Toné!'s *Billboard* Hot 100 hits in chronological order.

Song	Year Released	Billboard Hot 100 Peak Position
➡ "Little Walter"	1988	47
➡ "Feels Good"	1990	9
➡ "The Blues"	1990	46
➡ "It Never Rains (In Southern California)"	1990	34
➡ "Whatever You Want"	1991	48
➡ "If I Had No Loot"	1993	7
➡ "(Lay Your Head On My) Pillow"	1994	31
➡ "Anniversary"	1993	10
➡ "Leavin' "	1994	82
➡ "Thinking Of You"	1997	22

🔥 *My Favorite Tony! Toni! Toné! Songs*

➤ "Little Walter" ➤ "For The Love Of You" ➤ "Whatever You Want"

♥ *My Favorite Tony! Toni! Toné! Samples*

- •• "Only You" by 112 feat. the Notorious B.I.G. sampled "Feels Good"
- •• "To Live & Die in L.A." by Makaveli (2Pac) sampled "It Never Rains (In Southern California)"
- •• "Melodies From Heaven" by Kirk Franklin sampled "Anniversary"

⊙ My Take

The video for "Hey Little Walter" remains one of my favorite videos of all time. So clever and well done.

Portrait of the members of American R&B group Tony Toni Toné (styled as Tony! Toni! Toné!) as they pose backstage at the Marcus Amphitheater, Milwaukee, Wisconsin, July 3, 1991. Pictured are, from left, Timothy Christian Riley and his cousins, brothers Raphael Saadiq (born Charles Wiggins) and D'wayne Wiggins. (Photo by Paul Natkin/Getty Images)

Chapter 53

. . . .

XSCAPE

Singing group Xscape(LaTocha Scott, Tameka "Tiny" Cottle-Harris, Tamika Scott-Byas and Kandi Burruss), poses for photos at the LeMeridien Hotel in Chicago, Illinois, in September 1994. (Photo By Raymond Boyd/Michael Ochs Archives/Getty Images)

JERMAINE DUPRI WANTED TO DEVELOP A GIRL GROUP.

The producer had discovered Kris Kross and wrote their smash hit "Jump." And in 1993, he discovered Xscape after the group was brought to his birthday party.

"[A friend who] knew I was looking for acts brought them by my party to sing 'Happy Birthday' to me," Dupri told the *Atlanta Journal* in 1993. "And from a song as simple as that, I knew they had it going on. Other than En Vogue, there weren't any big girl groups out there. And I knew then I was going to work with them."

Xscape—which included high school friends Kandi Burruss, Tameka Cottle, Tamika Scott, and LaTocha Scott—released its debut, *Hummin' Comin' at 'Cha*, in October 1993. The album was full of hits. "Just Kickin' It" reached number 2 on the *Billboard* Hot 100 chart. Other singles included "Understanding" and "Love On My Mind."

The singers had vocal range, but they tried to present a down-low vibe in overalls and flannel shirts.

As Cottle explained it in a 1994 interview, the group's style was "street edge… just the girl next door. We're not too glamorous where you'd say, 'I'm scared to meet that person.' We're just regular normal people."

Xscape released its second album, *Off the Hook*, in 1995 and *Traces of My Lipstick* in 1998. Both went platinum.

But following the release of its third album, Xscape went on a hiatus.

The group members tried, over the years, to make a sustained comeback, efforts that didn't pick up until 2017. Three of the members—Cottle, LaTocha Scott, and Tamika Scott, minus Burruss, who was pursuing Broadway roles—formed XSCAP3 and released an EP, *Here for It*.

The group has also appeared in Bravo series and *Verzuz* battles.

After a dispute, LaTocha Scott wound up distancing herself, but the group's remaining three members—Burress, Cottle, and Tamika Scott—have continued forward and still tour.

♔ GRAMMY NOMINATIONS: 0

(L-R) Tiny, Tamika Scott, Kandi Burress, and LaTocha Scott of Xscape attend Eighth Annual Essence Awards on April 22, 1994, at the Paramount Theater in New York City. (Photo by Ron Galella, Ltd./Ron Galella Collection via Getty Images)

Billboard Hot 100 CHARTING SINGLES

Here is a list of Xscape's *Billboard* Hot 100 hits in chronological order.

Song	Year Released	Billboard Hot 100 Peak Position
"Just Kickin' It"	1993	2
"Understanding"	1993	8
"Love On My Mind"	1994	46

	Song	Year Released	Billboard Hot 100 Peak Position
➡	"Who Can I Run To"	1995	8
➡	"Feels So Good"	1995	32
➡	"Do You Want To/Can't Hang" (with MC Lyte)	1996	50
➡	"The Arms of the One Who Loves You"	1998	7
➡	"My Little Secret"	1998	9

🔥 My Favorite Xscape Songs

❯ "Understanding" ❯ "Is My Living In Vain"

❯ "Softest Place On Earth"

💜 My Favorite Xscape Samples

•• "Might Be" by Anderson.Paak sampled "Who Can I Run To"

•• "Give It 2 You" by Da Brat sampled "Just Kickin' It"

•• "Secret" by 21 Savage feat. Summer Walker sampled "My Little Secret"

⊙ My Take

I was turned on to Xscape by my roommate Chico Bryson in college. He knew the kind of music I loved, and he was right on target. Xscape had a strong run of five years from 1993 to 1998 and helped usher in Atlanta as a new place to respect in terms of music!

Tamika Scott, Kandi Burruss, LaTocha Scott, and Tameka "Tiny" Harris of Xscape attends 2019 Black Music Honors at Cobb Energy Performing Arts Centre on September 05, 2019, in Atlanta, Georgia. (Photo by Paras Griffin/Getty Images for Black Music Honors)

Chapter 54

. . . .

HONORABLE
MENTION—1990S

702

702 recorded one of the great sisterhood anthems in "Where My Girls At?"

The girl group—named after the area code of their hometown of Las Vegas—was discovered by Michael Bivins, who had a busy decade between performing in Bell Biv DeVoe and New Edition and discovering Boyz II Men. He became their manager and signed them to his Biv 10 Records label, a subsidiary of Motown.

The group initially consisted of sisters LeMisha, Orish, and Irish Grinstead, along with Amelia Childs, but 702 faced multiple lineup changes before establishing itself, with Amelia and Orish departing and Tiffany Villarreal joining for a stretch.

702 found its footing with a lineup of Kameelah Williams and LeMisha and

Irish Grinstead and released its debut album, *No Doubt*, and debut single "Steelo," which featured Missy Elliott, in 1996.

The group entered a new level of success with its self-titled second album and its breakout hit. "Where My Girls At?" peaked at number 4 on the *Billboard* Hot 100 chart, one spot behind "No Scrubs" by TLC, the group that had initially passed on the song.

So 702 made it its own, an ode to women supporting other women and not stealing each other's men.

After releasing the album *Star* in 2003, 702 disbanded in 2006. Tragedy followed. Orish died in 2008, while Irish died in 2023.

"That girl was as bright as the stars! She was not only beautiful on the outside, but also within. Sharing the stage with her was a joy I will cherish for the rest of my life!" LeMisha wrote online to honor her sister.

The remaining members of 702 have continued forward and continue to tour with other 1990s R&B artists like Faith Evans, Ashanti, and Ginuwine.

♜ GRAMMY NOMINATIONS: 0

Billboard Hot 100 CHARTING SINGLES

Here is a list of 702's *Billboard* Hot 100 hits in chronological order.

Song	Year Released	Billboard Hot 100 Peak Position
➜ "Steelo"	1996	32

	Song	Year Released	Billboard Hot 100 Peak Position
➜	"Get It Together"	1997	10
➜	"All I Want"	1997	35
➜	"Where My Girls At?"	1999	4

⊙ My Take

I used to own the cassette single for "Get It Together" and would play it almost every morning on my way to work in Chicago. That song is my favorite.

BLAQUE

Blaque had a fresh, unique sound and a strong sense of purpose. The girl group's name stands for "Believing in Life and Achieving a Quest for Unity in Everything."

In the late 1990s and early 2000s, Blaque—Natina Reed, Shamari Fears (later Shamani DeVoe), and Brandi Williams—achieved quite a lot. The group formed in Atlanta, and after an introduction to Lisa "Left Eye" Lopes of TLC, Blaque signed with Left Eye Productions.

Their debut self-titled album was released in May 1999, and it featured three singles—"808," "I Do," and "Bring It All to Me"—which propelled the album to platinum status. They also opened for *NSYNC and TLC.

Blaque seamlessly blended singing and rap, and they collaborated with many of the biggest acts of the 1990s.

The following year, the group appeared as cheerleaders in the movie *Bring It On*.

But by 2001, the group's momentum stalled. Columbia Records shelved their sophomore album, *Blaque Out!*, and their mentor, Lopes, died in a car crash the following year. The album was released years later.

A third album, *Torch*, was completed but put on the shelf for years.

Reed died in 2012 after being struck by a car.

DeVoe, in recent years, has appeared on Bravo's *The Real Housewives of Atlanta*. Her husband is a fellow R&B icon, Ronnie DeVoe of New Edition and Bell Biv DeVoe.

Torch was finally released in 2019 and served as a reminder of Blaque's originality and talent. The album includes collaborations with Timbaland and Missy Elliott and is as sharp as anything Blaque has released.

Williams and DeVoe occasionally appear in concerts together, carrying forward Blaque's impact to new fans. It's a shame that music's business side and bad luck kept Blaque from building on the momentum from their first album.

🏆 GRAMMY NOMINATIONS: 0

Billboard Hot 100 CHARTING SINGLES

Here is a list of Blaque's *Billboard* Hot 100 hits in chronological order.

Song	Year Released	Billboard Hot 100 Peak Position
"808" (featuring Missy Elliott)	1999	8
"Bring It All to Me" (with *NSYNC's JC Chasez)	1999	5

⊙ My Take

I wonder how this group could have grown if Lopes had not passed away. They had the formula to follow in TLCs footsteps, but everything stalled rather abruptly. "Bring It All to Me" is still a bop though.

MINT CONDITION

Mint Condition was inspired by a mix of different music styles—from Parliament-Funkadelic to jazz, hip-hop, and dance—and that eclectic palette made them one of the 1990s' most unique R&B groups.

As lead singer and drummer Stokley Williams said in 1991, "It's all a part of African American culture—put it in the pot, stir it up and it comes up like mint."

The group, which formed in Minneapolis, Minnesota, in the mid-1980s, originally included Williams, guitarist Homer O'Dell, keyboardist Larry Waddell, keyboardist and saxophonist Jeff Allen, keyboardist and guitarist Keri Lewis (he later married R&B singer Toni Braxton), and bassist Rick Kinchen.

Mint Condition found their groove playing in and around Minneapolis before being discovered by producers Jimmy Jam and Terry Lewis, and they were signed to Perspective Records.

Their first album, *Meant to Be Mint*, was released in 1991. That album included the crossover ballad "Breakin' My Heart (Pretty Brown Eyes)," which entered the top 10 of the pop charts and reached number 5 on the R&B chart.

They followed up that effort with their 1996 album *Definition of a Band*, which included the single "What Kind Of Man Would I Be." The song and the album were both nominated for Soul Train awards.

They released a greatest hits album and then *Life's Aquarium* in 1999 before taking a hiatus.

Mint Condition returned from their break in 2005 and has been making music off and on ever since.

Their 2015 Christmas album *Healing Season*, featuring tracks like "Santa Claus Goes Straight to the Ghetto," was nominated for a Grammy for best R&B album.

🏆 GRAMMY NOMINATIONS: 1
🏆 GRAMMY WINS: 0

Billboard Hot 100 CHARTING SINGLES

Here is a list of Mint Condition's *Billboard* Hot 100 hits in chronological order.

	Song	Year Released	Billboard Hot 100 Peak Position
➔	"Breakin' My Heart (Pretty Brown Eyes)"	1991	6
➔	"Forever In Your Eyes"	1992	81
➔	"U Send Me Swingin' "	1994	33
➔	"What Kind Of Man Would I Be"	1996	17
➔	"You Don't Have To Hurt No More"	1997	32
➔	"If You Love Me"	1999	30

● My Take

This group released one of my favorite slow jams of all time ("Pretty Brown Eyes"), and their musicality grew on me as I matured and observed how the music industry has become more cookie cutter. This group has continued to value instrumentation, live bands, and smart lyrics. As a result, their legend continues to grow.

TOTAL

Total was an American R&B girl group formed in 1994. The group originally consisted of members Kima Raynor, Keisha Spivey, and Pamela Long.

Raynor and Spivey were childhood friends who grew up together in Brooklyn, New York. They both had a passion for singing and performing. Long, on the other hand, was from East Orange, New Jersey, and was already involved in the local music scene.

The three members met while participating in various auditions and talent showcases in the New York City area. They recognized each other's talent and shared a common goal of pursuing careers in the music industry. Their chemistry was evident, and they decided to form a group.

Total's breakthrough came when they caught Combs's attention. Combs signed the group to Bad Boy Records, which was under the umbrella of Arista Records.

Under Combs's guidance and production, Total released its debut album, *Total*, in 1996. The album featured successful singles like "Can't You See" (featuring the Notorious B.I.G.) and "No One Else." It garnered commercial success and established Total as a rising R&B group.

Total continued to work with notable artists and producers within the Bad Boy Records roster, collaborating with acts like Mase, Foxy Brown, and Missy Elliott. The group released its second album, *Kima, Keisha, and Pam*, in 1998, which featured the hit single "Trippin'."

Throughout the group's career, Total released several well-known songs that became R&B classics. In addition to "Can't You See," some of its other notable tracks include "No One Else," "What About Us," "Kissin' You," and "Sittin' Home." These songs showcased the group's distinct sound, combining soulful vocals, catchy melodies, and contemporary R&B production.

🏆 GRAMMY NOMINATIONS: 0

Billboard Hot 100 CHARTING SINGLES

Here is a list of Total's *Billboard* Hot 100 hits in chronological order.

	Song	Year Released	Billboard Hot 100 Peak Position
➲	"Can't You See" (with the Notorious B.I.G.)	1995	13
➲	"No One Else" (with Da Brat)	1995	22
➲	"Kissin' You"	1996	12
➲	"Do You Think About Us?"	1996	61
➲	"When Boy Meets Girl"	1996	50
➲	"What About Us"	1997	16
➲	"Trippin' " (with Missy Elliott)	1998	7
➲	"Sitting Home"	1999	42

● *My Take*

Total brings back fond memories of classic hip-hop tracks with the group singing in the background. Total is the girl group from Bad Boy Records and has the hits to prove it. I still feel the group is a bit underrated!

TROOP

The R&B group Troop formed in the late 1980s through a combination of friendships and shared musical aspirations. The original members of the group were Steve Russell, Allen McNeil, Rodney Benford, John Harreld, and Reggie Warren.

The core members of Troop—Russell, McNeil, and Benford—grew up together in Pasadena, California. They were childhood friends who shared a common love for music and singing. Recognizing their musical talents, they decided to form a group.

Later, Harreld and Warren joined the group, completing the lineup. These additions enhanced the group's vocal abilities and dynamics.

Troop started performing locally, honing their skills and building a local following. They gained attention through their energetic live performances and tight harmonies, attracting the interest of record executives.

Troop was discovered by music producer and executive Vincent Davis.

Davis, the president of Atlantic Starr Enterprises, happened to witness a performance by Troop at a talent show in Pasadena, California. Impressed by their vocal abilities, stage presence, and potential, he recognized the opportunity to develop them as a successful R&B group.

Troop's association with Atlantic Records allowed them to work with various producers and release their self-titled debut album in 1988. The album featured the hit singles "Mamacita" and "My Heart" and helped establish Troop as a promising R&B act.

The group got their name, "Troop," from a combination of the words "Total Respect of Other People," as they wanted to promote positivity and unity through their music. They started out by performing at local talent shows and clubs, gaining recognition for their smooth harmonies and captivating stage presence.

Troop went on to release several successful albums throughout the 1990s, including *Attitude* (1989), *Deepa* (1992), and *Mayday* (1998). Some of their most well-known songs include "Spread My Wings," "All I Do Is Think of You," "Sweet November," and "I Will Always Love You." These songs showcased their smooth vocal harmonies and their ability to blend contemporary R&B with elements of new jack swing, which was popular at the time.

♔ GRAMMY NOMINATIONS: 0

Billboard Hot 100 CHARTING SINGLES

Here is a list of Troop's *Billboard* Hot 100 hits in chronological order.

	Song	Year Released	Billboard Hot 100 Peak Position
❯	"All I Do Is Think of You"	1990	47
❯	"Whatever It Takes (To Make You Stay)"	1992	63
❯	"Sweet November"	1992	58

⊙ *My Take*

I discovered Troop through their single "Spread My Wings." Then I heard "All I Do Is Think of You," and I thought they were the song's original performers. Thankfully, I watched the group being interviewed by Donnie Simpson on *Video Soul* and heard him mention that the Jackson 5 were the original artists. "I Will Always Love You," from Troop's second album, is also another personal favorite song.

2000's

From Top Left to Bottom left in clockwise order:
Jagged Edge, Outkast, 3LW and Danity Kane

Part Six
THE 2000S

IN SOME CIRCLES, THE 2000S' FIRST DECADE IS known as the decade of disruption. At the beginning of the decade, we experienced the September 11th attacks in the United States, which changed life as we knew it forever. This led to wars in Afghanistan and Iraq, which eventually caused a global financial crisis and eventually the Great Recession (which heavily impacted the music business). Hurricane Katrina destroyed much of the southern cities on the Gulf of Mexico, including New Orleans. In 2008, history was made as Barack Obama became the first African American to hold the office of president of the United States. It seems funny to discuss now, but at the beginning of the decade, we were all worried about the Y2K bug shutting down all of our systems across the world. The worry and fear were much ado about nothing!

We experienced the beginning of the New England Patriots dynasty, led by Tom Brady, during this decade. Usain Bolt and Michael Phelps put themselves on the map at the 2008 Olympics. Kobe and Shaq dominated the NBA, while the San Antonio Spurs also won plenty of titles. The Boston Red Sox broke an 86-year curse with a historic comeback against their rivals, the New York Yankees. And a special shout-out to my favorite college basketball team, the Maryland Terrapins, who won their first National Championship in 2002. Fear the Turtle!

The entertainment industry continued to evolve at a rapid pace. We saw the introduction of the iPod in 2001, as well as the emergence of reality TV (do you remember who won the first season of *American Idol*?). Streaming-to-watch television went mainstream with Netflix beginning the first video-on-demand service via the internet. Social media became addicting—Facebook launched in 2004 and would eventually become the world's largest social media platform (quickly relegating Myspace to a footnote in history books). We never looked at the word *like* the same way again.

In the music industry, Eminem released *The Marshall Mathers LP*, which became the fastest-selling rap album of all time. By the time the year 2000 was over, Napster had over 75 million users, and people enjoyed the ability to download music (for free) directly and start the practice of collecting individual songs and not albums. After angering a specific rock band known as Metallica, Napster was sued by the band and the RIAA (Recording Industry of America), which eventually severely diminished the platform to a skeleton of what its user base had been just one year prior. Many of us can remember the day we logged onto AOL into the chat rooms to get some music and saw no servers available. Next up were LimeWire and Kazaa, which took Napster's place for a short time. The rise of these platforms, combined with the success of the iPod, signaled that the MP3 was the future for music. iTunes, launched in 2001, also focused on the MP3 trend, and the high profits record companies saw from CDs were quickly vanishing.

The whole music industry mourned the loss of Michael Jackson in 2009, as he died from a lethal combination of sedatives and propofol. His shoes can never be filled in terms of the impact he had on the music industry.

This look at the 2000s decade and Black R&B groups is very limited on purpose. First, there are many questions about why Outkast is included in the list of groups from the 2000s. After intensive research, it was decided that due to the evolution of their music and style starting from the *Speakerboxxx/The Love Below* album that was primarily R&B, they would be included. There was a massive decline in R&B groups charting on the *Billboard* Hot 100 compared to the previous decades. Destiny's Child experienced great success until its formal disbandment in 2006. R&B groups quickly exited the *Billboard* charts for good at that time and were never (to date) seen as prominently across the entire industry. In conclusion, once the research data set reaches approximately 2004, the data proves the initial assumption that 2004 was the last year where R&B Groups were on the *Billboard* Hot 100 charts was correct. The number of *Billboard* Hot 100 hits by R&B groups went down to zero and has yet to return to the levels seen in the 1980s and 1990s.

Explanations as to why this occurred will be covered once we highlight these groups from the 2000s.

Chapter 55

. . . .

DANITY KANE

(L-R) Andrea Fimbres, Dawn Richard, Wanita "D. Woods" Woodgett Aubrey O'Day and Shannon Bex of the group Danity Kane pose backstage during MTV's *Total Request Live* at the MTV Times Square Studios on June 14, 2006, in New York City. (Photo by Peter Kramer/ Getty Images)

DANITY KANE WAS CREATED FOR TV BUT TURNED into something bigger.

The group was formed in 2005 and 2006 as part of the third MTV's *Making the Band* iteration, hosted by Sean "Puffy" Combs. The initial lineup included Aubrey O'Day, Dawn Richard, Shannon Bex, Wanita "D. Woods" Woodgett, and Aundrea Fimbres.

The series saw the group members working with vocal and dance coaches and learning how to sing together.

Following the series' second season, the group was signed to Bad Boy Records and was paired with producers like Timbaland and Rodney "Darkchild" Jerkins.

Danity Kane's self-titled debut, released in August 2006, sold well—on the way to going platinum—to top the *Billboard* 200. It was led by the single "Show Stopper."

It was a solid R&B album that had a built-in publicity machine behind it. As Rob Sheffield wrote for *Rolling Stone* in giving the album three stars, " 'Show Stopper' is already one cool radio hit—every summer needs an R&B anthem about driving around and looking good and feeling mean…Ride on, Danity Kane."

Danity Kane did ride on, and its 2008 sophomore album, *Welcome to the Dollhouse*, cemented the group in the record books as the first female group to debut their first two albums atop the charts.

Amid the second album's release, Combs removed O'Day and Woodgett from the group.

O'Day, Bex, and Richard reunited in 2014, but after infighting, Danity Kane disbanded ahead of the release of their album *DK3*.

An EP, *Strawberry Milk*, was released in 2020, but in recent years, the group has remained on hiatus.

🏆 GRAMMY NOMINATIONS: 0

Danity Kane visits MTV's TRL at the MTV studios in Times Square on August 19, 2008, in New York City. (Photo by Andrew H. Walker/Getty Images)

Billboard Hot 100 CHARTING SINGLES

Here is a list of Danity Kane's *Billboard* Hot 100 hits in chronological order.

Song	Year Released	Billboard Hot 100 Peak Position
"Show Stopper"	2006	8
"Ride for You"	2006	78
"Damaged"	2008	10

⚭ *My Favorite Danity Kane Songs*

❯ "Damaged"   ❯ "Show Stopper"

♥ *My Favorite Danity Kane Sample*

•• "The Wizard of Ahhhs" by Todrick Hall and Pentatonix sampled "Damaged"

⊙ *My Take*

Danity Kane had potential, but the group could not stay together long enough to build on the success of previous albums. This shows just how hard it is to "force" a group together and then have them stay with each other.

Chapter 56

. . . .

DESTINY'S CHILD

American pop group Destiny's Child, 2001; they are Kelly Rowland, Beyoncé Knowles, and Michelle Williams. (Photo by Tim Roney/Getty Images)

ED MCMAHON TOOK THE MICROPHONE AND INTRODUCED THE next performer on *Star Search* in 1993.

It was another music act hoping to make it big. They were "a young group from Houston…the hip-hop rapping Girl's Tyme."

Girl's Tyme was hopeful about their chances—they'd been practicing their dance moves. This was the moment when they were going to take the leap to superstardom.

But when the winner was announced, Girl's Tyme lost to a rock group called Skeleton Crew. The loss became a defining moment for two members of Girl's Tyme, Beyoncé Knowles and Kelly Rowland, who would go on to form Destiny's Child on Beyoncé's path to redefining pop superstardom.

Following the *Star Search* defeat, Beyoncé's father, Mathew Knowles, began managing the group, which would settle on Destiny's Child as its name and a lineup of Beyoncé on lead vocals, Rowland as number two, and LaTavia Roberson and LeToya Luckett as backup vocalists.

"Everybody else was outside playing, and we were working. But we still played," Rowland said in a 1998 interview.

Destiny's Child signed with Columbia Records in 1997; its self-titled debut album was released early the next year. Their first single, "No, No, No," reached the top of the *Billboard* Hot R&B/Hip-Hop chart. Their song "Killing Time" was also featured on the *Men in Black* soundtrack.

Fame—which had eluded Beyoncé years earlier—had finally come.

"It's a trip, but it's a blessing," the 16-year-old said in 1998. "We appreciate everything, and we do understand that all of this can be taken away the next day," she added. "You can be No. 1 and then the next week, nothing."

Where the group's first album was promising but didn't set Destiny's Child apart, its second album—1999's *The Writing's on the Wall*—was a revelation. The group worked with a range of successful producers—such as Kevin "She'kspere" Briggs, Missy Elliott, and Rodney Jerkins—and the album focused on a "Commandment of Relationships."

The album produced four singles, including "Bills, Bills, Bills," which was penned with help from Briggs and Xscape's Kandi Burruss. The lyrics were fun and innovative, playfully called out slacker boyfriends.

Another hit, "Say My Name," also topped the *Billboard* Hot 100.

But despite the album's success, the group was ensnared in controversy after Luckett and Roberson—frustrated over their proportion of the group's earnings—were dumped from the group and replaced by Farrah Franklin and Michelle Williams. While Franklin didn't last long, Williams became a permanent member.

The new lineup's first recording together, "Independent Women Part 1" for the *Charlie's Angels* soundtrack, spent nearly three months on top of the *Billboard* Hot 100. Even with the swirling legal issues, people didn't much seem to care, and Destiny's Child hadn't missed a beat.

Beyoncé assumed more control during the creation of the group's next album, *Survivor.*

The title track, with lyrics that spoke of doubts publicly shared by former band members, ended up being fuel for the success of future albums. The lyrics also spoke to the group moving past its controversial lineup change; the lyrics resurfaced later in court in a legal battle with Luckett and Roberson over a nondisparagement clause.

A follow-up single, "Bootylicious," was another smash, an ode to sexy, curvy women.

But in the wake of the album's release and the ensuing publicity cycle, and after dropping a Christmas album, the remaining members of Destiny's Child decided to pursue individual projects. Williams became a successful gospel singer, releasing the chart-topping single "Heart to Yours." Rowland paired with Nelly on the Grammy-winning single "Dilemma" and released her album *Simply Deep*. And Beyoncé starred in *Austin Powers in Goldmember* and pursued solo projects of her own, such as the single "Crazy in Love."

The previous members of the group found individual success too. Luckett and Roberson initially started a new project of their own, Anjel, that fell through. Luckett carved out a successful music career for herself, releasing a chart-topping album in 2006 behind the hit song "Torn." Roberson, meanwhile, has participated in various stage plays, music projects, and reality TV shows while starting a family.

Destiny's Child's remaining three members came back together to release the album *Destiny Fulfilled* in 2004, but the group's disbandment came soon after.

While Destiny's Child hasn't reconvened since, the remaining three members continue to appear in each other's projects and support each other.

♔ GRAMMY NOMINATIONS: 9
♔ GRAMMY WINS: 2

- ✸ Best R&B Performance by a Duo or Group with Vocal: "Say My Name"
- ✸ Best R&B Performance by a Duo or Group with Vocal: "Survivor"

Destiny's Child performs at halftime of the New York Giants v. New York Jets game on August 20, 1998, at Giants Stadium in East Rutherford, New Jersey. (l to r: LeToya Luckett; Kelly Rowland; Beyoncé Knowles; LaTavia Roberson) (Photo by Al Pereira/Michael Ochs Archives).

Billboard Hot 100 CHARTING SINGLES

Here is a list of Destiny's Child's *Billboard* Hot 100 hits in chronological order.

	Song	Year Released	Billboard Hot 100 Peak Position
➔	"No, No, No Part 2" (with Wyclef Jean)	1997	3
➔	"Bills, Bills, Bills"	1999	1
➔	"Bug a Boo"	1999	33
➔	"Say My Name"	2000	1
➔	"Jumpin', Jumpin' "	2000	3
➔	"Independent Women, Part 1"	2000	1
➔	"Survivor"	2000	2

Song	Year Released	Billboard Hot 100 Peak Position
"Bootylicious"	2001	1
"Emotion"	2001	10
"Days of Christmas"	2001	2
"Lose My Breath"	2004	3
"Soldier"(with T.I. & Lil Wayne)	2004	3
"Girl"	2005	23
"Cater 2 U"	2005	14
"Check On It"	2005	1

My Favorite Destiny's Child Songs

"Say My Name" "She Can't Love You" "Lose My Breath"

My Favorite Destiny's Child Samples

- "Playing Games" by Summer Walker sampled "Say My Name"
- "Talk Of The Town" by Jack Harlow sampled "Lose My Breath"
- "You" by Lloyd feat. Lil Wayne sampled "Soldier"

My Take

Once all of the members of Destiny's Child decided to pursue individual project in the mid-2000s, it was the beginning of the end for all R&B groups in terms of success and appearances on the *Billboard* Hot 100 charts. The drop-off is significant and almost instantaneous. I feel that another entire book could be written on the years after Beyoncé went solo.

"Say My Name" is a timeless song. I have fond memories of driving through Miami blasting this CD from my Honda Accord. I feel it is ironic that Destiny's Child's last single as a group went to number 1 in the charts. I could imagine that if the group chose to release a reunion album later in life, it would do extremely well.

American R&B group Destiny's Child (American singer, songwriter and actress Kelly Rowland, American singer, songwriter and actress Beyoncé Knowles, American singer and actress LeToya Luckett, and American singer and songwriter LaTavia Roberson) attend the 1998 Soul Train Music Awards, held at the Shrine Auditorium in Los Angeles, California, 27th February 1998. (Photo by Vinnie Zuffante/Getty Images)

Chapter 57

. . . .

DRU HILL

American R&B group Dru Hill (American singer James "Woody Rock" Green, American singer Mark "Sisqó" Andrews, American singer Tamir "Nokio' Ruffin, and American singer Larry "Jazz" Anthony) attend the 9th *Billboard* Music Awards, held at the MGM Grand Garden Arena in Las Vegas, Nevada, 7th December 1998. (Photo by Vinnie Zuffante/Getty Images)

DRU HILL'S ORIGIN STORY IS SUGARY SWEET.

The Baltimore, Maryland, natives worked at a candy shop, the Fudgery, and were known to sing while working. The on-the-job experience helped the group's members—Mark "Sisqó" Andrews, James "Woody" Green, Larry "Jazz" Anthony, and Tamir "Nokio" Ruffin—hone their harmonies.

The candy shop jobs didn't last too long. Dru Hill—their name is a shortened reference to the nearby Druid Hill Park—was founded in 1992.

The group got noticed the old-fashioned way, by wowing the crowd at the Apollo Theater's amateur night. Their debut album followed in 1996—it went platinum behind hits like "In My Bed," which tells the story of a clueless partner being cheated on, and "Never Make A Promise," about a partner staying true to their word.

Following its successful start, the group was in heavy demand for soundtrack appearances—*Soul Food*, *Def Jam's How to Be a Player*, and *Rush Hour*—and began working with other artists, such as Mya.

This all built momentum for the group's second album, the Asian- and Bruce Lee-influenced *Enter the Dru*. The members of Dru Hill were credited as executive producers and wrote many of the album's songs.

The effort—behind singles like "How Deep Is Your Love" and "These Are The Times"—sold more than two million copies. It increasingly showcased Andrews's powerful voice.

But soon after the release, and following mergers and acquisitions involving their label, Green (Woody Rock) wound up leaving Dru Hill to pursue a solo career in gospel, and the other group members pursued solo projects.

The most notable of those efforts were Andrews's, released as Sisqó: "Thong Song," which was a smash hit devoted to the cheeky undergarment, and the chart-topping follow-up "Incomplete."

Dru Hill reconvened in the years that followed and released *Dru World Order* in 2002, but the group was later dropped by their label, Def Soul.

The group has continued releasing new material over the years, and while the lineup has evolved, the core group, minus Woody, remains intact.

♬ GRAMMY NOMINATIONS: 0

Dru Hill at the 30th Annual AMAs held at the Shrine Auditorium in Los Angeles, CA, January 13, 2003. Photo by Kevin Winter/ABC/Getty Images

Billboard Hot 100 CHARTING SINGLES

Here is a list of Dru Hill's *Billboard* Hot 100 hits in chronological order.

Song	Year Released	Billboard Hot 100 Peak Position
"Tell Me"	1996	18

	Song	Year Released	Billboard Hot 100 Peak Position
➡	"In My Bed"	1997	4
➡	"Never Make A Promise"	1997	7
➡	"We're Not Making Love No More"	1997	13
➡	"How Deep Is Your Love"	1998	3
➡	"These Are The Times"	1999	21
➡	"You Are Everything" with Ja Rule	1999	84
➡	"Beauty"	1999	79
➡	"I Should Be..."	2002	25
➡	"I Love You"	2002	77

🔥 *My Favorite Dru Hill Songs*

> ❯ "Beauty" ❯ "These Are The Times"
> ❯ "The Beautiful Ones" with Mariah Carey

💜 *My Favorite Dru Hill Samples*

- •• "Better" by Estelle sampled "Tell Me"
- •• "Thong Song" by Sisqó sampled "Real Freak"
- •• "SAVE YOURSELF" by Snoh Aalegra sampled "Beauty"

⬇ My Take

Dru Hill had a strong run in the late 1990s and early 2000s. Their origin story is one of the coolest ones I discovered while researching this book. Too bad the Fudgery is now closed. I'm glad Dru Hill still tours, and I secretly wish that they would release new material—including an album—in the next few years.

Chapter 58

. . . .

JAGGED EDGE

The musical group Jagged Edge poses for photographers at the 15th Annual Soul Train Awards February 28, 2001, at the Shrine Auditorium in Los Angeles, CA. (Photo by Chris Weeks/Liaison)

JAGGED EDGE IS JAGGED IN NAME ONLY—THEIR RHYMES are smooth as silk.

Want a club hit? A tear-drenched piano ballad? An ode to monogamy? Jagged Edge delivered all of them with heart and skill.

During their commercial peak, you couldn't go to a party without hearing their music.

The Atlanta quartet formed in the mid-1990s and features Richard Wingo, Kyle Norman, and identical twin brothers Brian and Brandon Casey. Xscape's Kandi Burruss recommended the group to producer Jermaine Dupri, and he signed them to his So So Def imprint.

As Norman said in a 1999 interview, "We got a church vibe, an R&B vibe and a hip-hop vibe." He referred to the group's formula as "good R&B ballads and up-tempo beats."

Jagged Edge's first album, *A Jagged Era*, was a modest success, but they didn't break through until 1999's *J.E. Heartbreak* and the hit single "Let's Get Married," which helped the album go double platinum.

The song's lyrics capture the protagonist's vulnerability—he's pouring out his heart and putting himself out there. He simply wants to get married.

The album also produced the hit singles "He Can't Love U" and "Promise."

The party anthem "Where the Party At" with Nelly marked Jagged Edge's commercial peak—it topped the R&B charts and reached number 3 on the *Billboard* Hot 100. The song was nominated for a Grammy and provided a canvas to showcase both Jagged Edge's range and Dupri's hitmaking prowess.

The album *Hard* was released in 2003, while *Jagged Edge* was released in 2006.

New albums have followed every few years.

Where many 1990s and early 2000s groups broke up and went their separate ways, Jagged Edge never have. They've remained together, still creating their unique blend of ballads and up-tempo tracks.

🏆 **GRAMMY NOMINATIONS: 1**
🏆 **GRAMMY WINS: 0**

(L to R) Kyle Norman, Brandon and Brian Casey and Richard Wingo of Jagged Edge attend the 29th Annual American Music Awards at the Shrine Auditorium January 9, 2002, in Los Angeles, CA. (Photo by Vince Bucci/Getty Images)

Billboard Hot 100 CHARTING SINGLES

Here is a list of Jagged Edge's *Billboard* Hot 100 hits in chronological order.

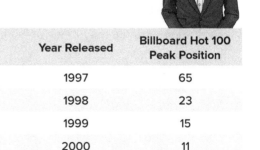

Song	Year Released	Billboard Hot 100 Peak Position
"The Way That You Talk"	1997	65
"I Gotta Be"	1998	23
"He Can't Love U"	1999	15
"Let's Get Married"	2000	11
"Promise"	2000	9

Song	Year Released	Billboard Hot 100 Peak Position
"Where the Party At" (with Nelly)	2001	3
"Goodbye"	2001	58
"Walked Outta Heaven"	2003	6
"What's It Like"	2004	85
"Good Luck Charm"	2006	73

🔥 *My Favorite Jagged Edge Songs*

❯ "I Gotta Be" ❯ "Walked Outta Heaven" ❯ "Goodbye"

🖤 *My Favorite Jagged Edge Samples*

•• "Hotel Room Service" by Pitbull (2009) sampled "Nasty Girl"

•• "Walked Out" by Tory Lanez sampled "Walked Outta Heaven"

⊙ My Take

I remember going to a training session in Newport News, Virginia, and hearing the song "I Gotta Be" on the local radio for the first time. I was like "OMG…this song is everything," and I pondered why I had not heard the song yet on the local radio in Chicago. The song ended up being my favorite song by Jagged Edge, and it still stays in my rotation. "Gotta Be" is a timeless wedding song in my opinion. Another strong group coming from Atlanta!

Chapter 59

. . . .

OUTKAST

Big Boi and André 3000 of OutKast on the set of their video shoot for a song which will be featured in the movie Scooby-Doo. 4/28/02. Los Angeles, CA. photo by Kevin Winter/ ImageDirect

OUTKAST WAS OUT OF THIS WORLD.

The eclectic hip-hop group, which consisted of Antwan "Big Boi" Patton and André "André 3000" Benjamin formed in 1992 while they attended Atlanta's Tri-Cities High School together.

They fell in with Organized Noize, the Atlanta-based production company that worked with performers like TLC, and were close with Goodie Mob, which included CeeLo Green.

They signed with the label that would become LaFace Records in 1992, and after appearing on a TLC remix, they released their first single, "Player's Ball," in November 1993. The Christmas-themed song spoke of a heaven for Black men full of smoke, drink, and women.

Their album *Southernplayalisticadillacmuzik* followed a few months later to acclaim. It told a story of southern street life punctuated by Patton's slick rhymes, Benjamin's smooth, relaxed musings, and sharp, powerful beats.

"Git Up, Git Out" was a highlight that called on listeners to make more of their lives.

Outkast's successful debut—with its live instrumentals, snare beats and thick bass—helped put Atlanta on the map as a hip-hop power alongside New York and Los Angeles. At the Source awards in 1995, after Outkast was named "Best Newcomer," they were initially booed—the New York-biased crowd wanted to see a local group win instead.

Benjamin wasn't having it.

"The South got something to say," he told the crowd. And it did.

As he explained later, "When you listen to hip-hop music here, growing up, you had influences from all kinds of music. There were no 'Atlanta's own TLC' and all that. So we've just come up with our Southern interpretation of all that we heard."

Their subsequent albums—*ATLiens* in 1996 and *Aquemini* in 1998—saw

Outkast taking more production control and exploring their musical influences of funk, southern soul, gospel, and country. It also saw them trying to steer clear of negative influences and pitfalls.

While Outkast was primarily thought of as a hip-hop group, there was always more there. Their style was tough to define; thus, *ATLiens*, a blend of their Atlanta influences and "aliens for our status as foreigners in the hip-hop game," as Benjamin said in a 1996 interview.

The 2000s iconic *Stankonia* album saw them diving deeper beyond traditional. The song "B.O.B." ("Bombs Over Baghdad") took the listener on a journey through hip-hop, gospel, and rock music, while "Ms. Jackson" was an ode to the "baby mamas' mamas" and being there for your child, even when the relationship doesn't last.

By 2003, Patton and Benjamin were drifting in different directions, and they chose to release a double album to reflect their styles—*Speakerboxxx* is Patton's ode to southern hip-hop and P-funk, while André 3000's *The Love Below* is a Prince-inspired eclectic journey through pop, jazz, and R&B influences.

The album spawned the smash hits "The Way You Move," a soul-infused appreciation of women, and "Hey Ya!," which explored the doubts and concerns in relationships and the fears we have of being alone.

"Hey Ya!" also served as a microcosm for the group—two people with lots of respect for each other who were going in very different directions.

The album would clean up, selling 13 million copies and winning the Grammy for album of the year, along with other awards.

The pair teamed back up for 2006's *Idlewild*, a companion to the movie of the same name, but in terms of Outkast albums, that was that.

Patton continued carrying the mantle of southern hip-hop forward, releasing his own material and guesting on other tracks, while Benjamin remained more elusive. It took 17 years for him to release another LP—but instead of hip-hop, his album *New Blue Sun* was an instrumental record featuring his flute recordings.

Benjamin had some fun with the song titles. The first track is named "I Swear, I Really Wanted to Make a 'Rap' Album but This Is Literally the Way the Wind Blew Me This Time." At 12:20, it became the longest song to chart on the *Billboard* Hot 100.

♔ GRAMMY NOMINATIONS: 16
♔ GRAMMY WINS: 6

- ✹ Best Rap Album: *Stankonia*
- ✹ Best Rap Performance by a Duo or Group: "Ms. Jackson"
- ✹ Best Rap Performance by a Duo or Group: "The Whole World"
- ✹ Best Rap Album: *Speakerboxxx/The Love Below*
- ✹ Best Urban/Alternative Performance: "Hey Ya!"
- ✹ Album of the Year: *Speakerboxxx/The Love Below*

Musical Artists Big Boi (left) and André 3000 of Oukast pose with their six Grammys backstage in the Pressroom at the 46th Annual Grammy Awards held on February 8, 2004, at the Staples Center, in Los Angeles, California. (Photo by Frederick M. Brown/Getty Images)

Billboard Hot 100 CHARTING SINGLES

Here is a list of Outkast's *Billboard* Hot 100 hits in chronological order.

Song	Year Released	Billboard Hot 100 Peak Position
"Player's Ball"	1993	37
"Southernplayalisticadillacmuzik"	1993	74
"Elevators (Me & You)"	1996	12
"ATLiens"	1996	35
"Jazzy Belle"	1996	52
"Rosa Parks"	1998	55
"Ms. Jackson"	2000	1
"So Fresh, So Clean"	2001	30
"The Whole World" (with Killer Mike)	2002	19
"Hey Ya!"	2003	1
"The Way You Move" (with Sleepy Brown)	2003	1
"Roses"	2004	9
"Mighty 'O' "	2004	77
"Morris Brown" (with Scar and Sleepy Brown)	2006	96
"Idlewild Blue (Don'tchu Worry 'Bout Me)"	2006	100

🔥 *My Favorite Outkast Songs*

❯ "SpottieOttieDopaliscious" ❯ "So Fresh, So Clean"
❯ "Crumblin' Erb"

♥ *My Favorite Outkast Samples*

- •• "Man I Is" by Logic sampled "SpottieOttieDopaliscious"
- •• "Through the Wire" by Kanye West sampled "Player's Ball"
- •• "Comfortable" by Lil Wayne feat. Babyface sampled "Player's Ball"

⊙ *My Take*

I know it is a serious stretch to consider Outkast an R&B group, but after months of debate with other musicologists, producers, and DJs, I decided to include them for a variety of reasons. Their last few albums had distinct R&B origins, so the decision was made. I understand if you disagree, but we can continue the discussion! I give all props to my college roommate Chico, who turned us on to Outkast way before they made it big.

Chapter 60

. . . .

THOUGHTS AFTER REACHING THE FINAL GROUP

WHILE WRITING THIS BOOK AND REVIEWING THE STORIES of each group included, I found several overarching themes.

First, there was always a dominant set of producers that pushed the sound of the era. The first one that comes to mind is the sound and production skills of Gamble and Huff, with their Philadelphia sound that numerous Black R&B groups would seek out to create hit after hit. Overall, this production team created over 3,000 songs, which makes them one of the most prolific songwriting teams of all time. Of course, the Motown production team led by Berry Gordy also produced some of the biggest Black R&B groups of all time as they thrived throughout the 1960s and most of the 1970s. Specifically, Holland–Dozier–Holland had a run of hits from 1962–1967 that is staggering. Twenty-five number 1 hit singles later, they made their mark on the music industry, specifically in the Black R&B category.

As we got to the 1980s, Jimmy Jam and Terry Lewis started to produce countless R&B hits, and their sound took over. New Edition broke out when Jam

& Lewis produced "Heartbreak." Teddy Riley, first with Guy and then with Blackstreet, created a whole new subgenre, new jack swing. He led two groups to prominence with his sound and production skills. While he struggled a bit during his famous Verzus show, that shouldn't reduce his accomplishments to popular memes. Riley is legendary.

The producers who took us through the 1990s and into the 2000s were Babyface, Diddy, and Jermaine Dupri. These three dominated the sound and hits from the groups in this era. We could create a timeline that shows how each producer from every decade subconsciously passed the torch to the next in line, who took it and ran with it.

Second, there was a common issue of revenue distribution and money. From the very first decade we researched until the mid-2000s, money always became an issue, and very few groups could survive once it become a topic.

The scary part for me is that, in my opinion, the overwhelming majority of these groups had limited knowledge of how the music business operated, so they left substantial money on the table. For example, each member of each group should have had a choice to get songwriting credits and a share of the publishing revenue, which could have paid them (or their estates) for years to come. Lack of knowledge is a big issue in our current environment, so I imagine it was worse back in the day.

I listened to an interview with the Whispers on the *R&B Money Podcast*, and they spoke about how they weren't given many choices in terms of songwriting credits and publishing. They were just lucky to have their songs put on the radio and on an album. I imagine this was the deal for many, many artists. My goal is to continue to do the work so this knowledge gap is closed, particularly for Black and brown artists.

Every decade is littered with groups whose run of success was cut short due to internal issues that stemmed from contracts, money, and other grievances. The story that hurts me the most is En Vogue's because they had an opportunity to make great strides during the golden era of R&B music. They could sing, write, and even dance a little.

The third takeaway is how much drug usage affected groups and cut individual careers short while destroying groups' chemistry. Drug use continued to be a consistent theme throughout the decades up until the 1990s. This is not the most surprising fact (think of the saying "sex, drugs, and rock and roll"), but seeing how it affected group after group really hit home. The drugs spared no type of group (male or female), and they completely destroyed some groups.

As I mentioned before, many of the groups written about in this book showed an incredible amount of resilience as they fought for their moment in the spotlight. Some groups had to put in work for over 20 years before getting their moments. That in itself is very inspiring. That would never happen in the present day. Today, people are here one month and gone two months later. That is a radical shift to the business and has caused other groups to miss their time. This fact is one of the primary reasons why I feel that groups will never reach the level of success witnessed in the 1970s–1990s. The record labels have no patience and don't have enough money to see groups spend seven to 10 years putting out music and building their audiences large enough to then recoup the investment placed in them. I don't see this shifting any time in the future. The new model is being an independent group and signing with a label once you are about to hit it big, and that model will be followed in the future.

Let's take a closer look at the reasons for the disappearance of Black R&B groups and make a quick prediction for what the future holds. Hint: the outlook for the future is bleak, unfortunately.

Part Seven
WHAT HAPPENED?

NOW THAT WE HAVE REVIEWED A THOROUGH HISTORY of the top R&B groups from the 1950s to the 2000s, it is time to examine what exactly happened to cause such a severe drop-off in the quantity and quality of R&B groups and appearances on the *Billboard* Hot 100 chart. This research continues and updates will be included in future editions of the book. My goal is to continue to acquire interviews with music professionals who are part of the R&B world and can contribute their stories and reflections to add further context to what occurred.

This section of the book discusses what happened and why it happened and gives a quick glimpse of what the future could hold. All the research was completed with the assistance of my student volunteers from California State University, Fullerton, and with the guidance of my professors at Berklee College of Music.

Chapter 61

·······

THE EMERGENCE OF HIP-HOP

HIP-HOP MUSIC CONTINUED TO EVOLVE. WHILE IT WAS first thought of as a fad, it became an overwhelming success. The industry shift from keeping hip-hop and R&B music separate to including hip-hop influences on every track (with a guest appearance at a minimum) was complete. As Elias Leight mentions in a 2018 article for Genius, in the year 2002, 45 top 20 airwave hits were by rappers or featured an emcee. This continued the subtle push of singers off the radio and out of listeners' minds and pockets. Hip-hop had taken over, and there was no sign of any letup.

By 2004, hip-hop acts dominated the *Billboard* charts, with acts such as Ludacris, 50 Cent, and Jay-Z spending multiple weeks charting with numerous number 1 hits. Ironically, Destiny's Child had the last of their top hits during this year, and the exodus of R&B groups would quickly commence. One of the first indicators that hip-hop was hitting the mainstream and being taken seriously by the public was when Sean "Diddy" Combs was listed in *Forbes's* 2002 rankings of 40 entrepreneurs under 40. The two most popular hip-hop artists of this time were Eminem and 50 Cent, who dominated all of the *Billboard* charts with hit after hit.

Let's take a look at the shift in the charts from 1993 to 2004.

The week of July 24, 1993, on the *Billboard* Hot 100 charts, R&B groups dominated the top 20. SWV was just coming off of a number 1 hit with "Weak." H-Town was at number 5 with "Knockin' da Boots." Jodeci was at number 11 with "Lately." Tony! Toni! Toné! was at number 16 with "If I Had No Loot." Twenty percent of the top 20 hits were R&B groups. Also, take note of how many hip-hop songs were in the top 20. Twenty-five percent of the top 20 hits were hip-hop songs. Tag Team, Onyx, Duice, Dr. Dre, and 95 South all had strong positions on the *Billboard* Top 20. This is a prime example of how, in 1993, R&B groups *and* hip-hop acts were coexisting and dominating almost 50% of the *Billboard* Hot 100 charts. Why did this change in only 10 short years?

Fast-forward to the same week 11 years later. There were zero R&B groups in the top 20. For some perspective, the first R&B groups didn't appear on the Hot 100 charts for the week until the Isley Brothers at number 85 ("What Would You Do?") and Floetry at number 86 ("Say Yes"). On the flip side, there were between 8 and 10 hip-hop songs within the top 20 for the week. The dominance was evident, and momentum only continued as the decade's end approached.

Hip-hop music is now the most dominant genre of music, with no signs of slowing down. The majority of record labels that influence the charts have completely shifted their support, promotions, and scouting to hip-hop acts. The money that was once reserved for promoting R&B groups has dried up and is now focused on hip-hop. According to Deryck Vanderbilt-Nicholson, "Hip-hop artists can churn out three albums in a year, but R&B artists cannot churn out three albums in a year. Writing a song just takes so much more than putting together a hip-hop album. You don't necessarily need vocal training to put together a rap album. You don't necessarily need to layer vocals to the same degree when you are making R&B music."

This is the perfect segue to an additional direct correlation. Another growing trend that accelerated the hip-hop "takeover" starting in the late 1990s and moving into the early 2000s was the fact that R&B songs were rarely sent to the radio without a verse featuring a rap/hip-hop artist. This was the price of admission to popular radio, so R&B groups had to deviate from their previous formula for success. In essence, they were letting the fox (rap) into the hen house, and slowly but surely, hip-hop had taken over the very market (and charts) that R&B groups had dominated for over three decades. Producers such as Dr. Dre, Jermaine Dupri, J Dilla, 9th Wonder, and Pete Rock were at the peak of their game, producing hits that would overrun the *Billboard* charts with song after song. This work led us to the Neptunes, a now-legendary music-producing duo who continued the momentum by consistently creating hits for hip-hop acts nationwide. The Neptunes dominated most charts for a stretch of time from 2002 to 2007.

That raises the question, "Why can't R&B groups coexist on the charts with hip-hop groups?" Hip-hop finally hit the mainstream in the early 2000s, and most record labels were faced with a decision. Should they continue to fund and support R&B groups, or should they focus their time, energy, and money on hip-hop groups, which were proving to be less expensive and easier to manage? After looking closely at more apparent challenges, including massive choreography budgets, group members who didn't get along, and the emotional difficulties of managing three to four different personalities over a decade, other questions begin to emerge.

Did executives within the music industry purposefully stop promoting and supporting R&B groups to limit the amount of diversity seen on the charts? According to DJ Junior, "I think executives and the people running the music business were getting tired of so many black performances happening at these award shows. They were trying to figure out how they could change the narrative. I think the thing with the award shows is that it's an actual visual piece like music videos. So, many people are watching the Grammys. They were looking at the solo artists and also groups like Destiny's Child, and every damn thing (award) they were winning. Then I think people were like, 'How can we not have so many brown faces on the screen?' And I think that is a piece that changed the narrative."

Although this question may seem a little drastic in the "progressive" era of race relations that is currently promoted in the mainstream media, it needs to be addressed and answered. Several record executives spoke of a time when record labels chose to put money toward hip-hop groups and not R&B groups. Why not work to promote and support both genres of music? Why was there a choice made to support one or the other? According to Angie Moon, "Record labels don't take the same chances that they used to. And it's even more about money than ever before and record labels, they like safety, they like formulas." The question came up frequently in my research, and there was never a definitive answer given. This shortfall could be compared to microaggressions in numerous racism cases that are now discussed in civil courtrooms across the country. The common thought based on conversations I have had with numerous music industry professionals off the record is that the leaders of record labels made a conscious choice to only promote hip-hop artists and not promote both hip-hop artists and R&B acts. There are subtle and under-the-radar examples of small things that labels did to diminish promotion and exposure of R&B groups. This is a potential topic for another research study and an additional book.

The most recent whispers from record labels are that "R&B doesn't sell." In a day and age where a star can be born from a single viral TikTok video and can just as quickly fade from memory, the R&B group who might need to simmer for years (see: the Whispers) is not even allowed in the game. Instead, the hip-hop star who produces a beat from their bedroom and uploads themselves rapping over it online with the hopes of catching a hungry A&R's attention is the current norm.

Unfortunately, if this financial disparity trend continues, R&B groups may disappear forever from the *Billboard* charts. If this happens, then the primary foundations of all music today will be extinct. This would be a tragic conclusion to a genre of music that has spanned over 70 years and has birthed numerous other genres of music. This would create a void in modern music that would stifle creativity, bleed the industry of diversity, and continue to minimize the importance of group harmony throughout all of the music world.

Chapter 62

....

THE DECLINE OF AFRICAN AMERICAN MAGAZINES

HISTORY SHOWS US THAT R&B GROUPS ARE CLOSELY tied to African American culture. Also, African American media is the primary source of news and information on all subjects for African Americans. In their heyday, *Ebony*, *Jet*, and *Essence* magazines were the most popular sources of information for the African American community. Those magazines are now shells of their former selves. Unable to adjust to rapid changes in technology (sound familiar?), these magazines have all gone through a steep decline in subscribers and experienced various forms of bankruptcy. In a 2020 *USA Today* article, Robert Hill speaks to how the digital reincarnations of these crucial publications "lack the depth of reporting and coverage of the Black American landscape." Within the entertainment portion of their coverage, it is the R&B groups who have been hurt the most.

AFRICAN AMERICAN MONTHLY MAGAZINE SUBSCRIPTIONS (2002)

Magazine	# of monthly subscriptions
Ebony	2,500,000
Jet Magazine	2,800,000
Essence	1,600,000
Vibe Magazine	1,400,000

Source: TBD.

Mainstream media, combined with the rise of social media, tends to focus on singular stars when covering entertainment, thus leaving groups to be discovered on their own. The modern-day voices of the press, whether popular bloggers, journalists, live streamers, or podcasters, need to continue this discussion and assist in the research. If we look at the most popular African American magazines from the past 70 to 80 years, we discover some startling trends that mirror the decline of R&B groups, which adds fuel to the fire of this discussion.

AFRICAN AMERICAN MONTHLY MAGAZINE SUBSCRIPTIONS (2021)

Magazine	# of monthly subscriptions	Date of last issue
Ebony	0	May 2019
Jet Magazine	0	June 2024
Essence	1,050,000	n/a
Vibe Magazine	0	June 2009

Source: TBD.

The purpose of highlighting the top four African American magazines is to show the parallels in terms of their decline, which was directly in line with the decline of R&B groups. Also, these same publications were the main drivers of earned media and press coverage for R&B groups. Frequently, the mainstream consumer and media would learn about these groups through various articles and features. By the time the year 2010 arrived, there were over 10 million magazines no longer sold to consumers every month that consistently promoted, featured, and highlighted R&B groups through written and visual methods.

Losing a reach of 10 million people was a massive decline in potential audience for all of the groups and is an essential factor to discuss when evaluating why there are no longer R&B groups in existence. If consumers don't have a variety of ways to learn about groups and their latest albums, singles, or collaborative projects, how will they purchase, stream, and support those groups? One of the most important promotional sources had been cut off in a drastic way. The common belief is that the content can be discovered online, but due to the digital divide and slow internet adoption in the African American community, the lag factor is dramatic.

What can happen now to address this shortfall? Unfortunately, magazines are not returning to newsstands or mailboxes. Many of the publications mentioned above are currently (or planning to) operate in a full-service digital capacity. A mixture of experienced writers (perhaps former journalists from *Vibe*, *Jet*, *Ebony*, etc.) and new writers need to be hired with a focus on bringing the spotlight back to R&B groups. Established R&B groups that are still releasing music (the Isley Brothers, New Edition, SWV, etc.) and new R&B groups (Silk Sonic) need to be a primary focus to raise the awareness levels of mainstream consumers.

EBONY MAGAZINE

Ebony magazine was first published in 1945 and was the primary lifestyle magazine documenting the African American experience, publishing for more than seven decades. The rise of *Ebony* magazine coincided with the rise of R&B groups to prominence, starting in the 1950s and continuing all the way through the early 2000s. This magazine was the Black voice of many professionals, authors, actors, musicians, and government officials for over 70 years. Then, like the music industry, this magazine struggled in the digital age and saw a severe decline in monthly circulation throughout the late 2000s and early 2010s.

This publication was one of the main promotional vehicles for R&B groups, with numerous features, covers, and articles dedicated to R&B groups. Marketers in the 1980s estimated that *Ebony* was reaching over 40% of African American adults at that time. In 2000, *Ebony* reached its peak circulation of 2.5 million people. From that date, the circulation declined to approximately 1.2 million in the late 2000s and then ceased print operations in 2019. *Ebony* filed for bankruptcy in 2019 and recently sold out of bankruptcy with a digital launch in late 2021. The story of *Ebony* magazine's rise and fall is synonymous with the rise and "fall" of R&B groups. This publication was the most impactful and influential voice for African Americans, but over time it dwindled away to a skeleton of what it had been in the '80s and '90s. It was a massive promotional vehicle for R&B groups that disappeared and directly impacted the popularity, record sales, and recognition of R&B groups.

VIBE MAGAZINE

The next publication that had a massive impact on R&B groups in a relatively short period of time was *Vibe* magazine. This magazine helped launch hip-hop and R&B music into the mainstream with the partnership of Quincy Jones and Steve Ross. Steve Ross was the CEO of Time Warner and Warner Communications. Ross wanted his companies (and himself) to get more involved with authentic stories of African American artists and entertainers. Thus, the partnership with Quincy Jones was born. The magazine was initially called *Noise* magazine, then *Volume*, and it was finally changed to *Vibe* magazine right before the first issue.

From the first test issue in 1992 to its final print issue in 2009, *Vibe* magazine was the ultimate source of information on hip-hop and R&B music and culture. Over 16 years, this publication was another prominent voice for hip-hop and R&B music and promoted individual and group acts alike. In a 2018 article for *Billboard*, Dan Charnas speaks about the impact of various stories that *Vibe* magazine broke, including the first interview with Prince in over five years (1994), R. Kelly's underage marriage to Aaliyah (December 1994/January 1995), and an exclusive interview with 2Pac from Rikers Island (April 1995). This magazine gave a more honest view of what was happening in the music community and frequently featured the good and bad sides of R&B groups' stories.

The peak circulation for *Vibe* magazine was during the early 2000s, during which time they had approximately 1.4 million subscribers. At the time of its last print issue in 2009, its circulation was 800,000. When the magazine first shut down in June 2009, it was a massive loss to the Black music community. Although it came back briefly as a print publication and then as a more permanent digital community, the damage was done.

This is another critical publication that was a crucial voice for R&B groups and that ceased to exist rather abruptly. When, in 2009, as R&B groups were already disappearing, *Vibe* magazine disappeared from the landscape, that meant fewer eyes and less attention on the groups and also a dearth of articles, reviews, and earned media coverage for this segment of the music industry. The acceleration of digital media, an economic recession, and another cloud in this imperfect storm hurt R&B groups more than it harmed groups in any other genre.

JET MAGAZINE

The third publication that played a major role in promoting African American culture and African American R&B groups was *Jet* magazine. *Jet* magazine was first published in 1951, at the same time that groups were beginning to impact *Billboard* charts. From the dawn of the civil rights movement to President Obama's two terms in office, *Jet* magazine served as a consistent and reliable source for fashion, beauty, and entertainment news, politics, and health tips for the African American community every week. With over two million copies sold monthly, *Jet* magazine was an essential source of information and data for the African American community. But, as the other weekly or monthly publications suffered in the digital age, *Jet* was no different and eventually ceased publication in 2014.

With another reliable and important source of information gone from the African American community, the options for R&B groups to gain press coverage, reviews, and exposure continued to dwindle at a shocking pace.

ESSENCE MAGAZINE

The final publication that must be discussed is *Essence* magazine. This publication was created by four African American men with a core demographic of affluent African American females. This demographic was ignored in 1970 when *Essence* published its first issue. Extremely successful for almost 30 years and reaching a peak circulation of five million, *Essence* was a place where R&B groups would discuss other aspects of themselves besides the music. Grooming routines, spiritual practices, fashion ideas, and entrepreneurial pursuits were common topics discussed during in-depth interviews with R&B groups, particularly with the Black female groups that dominated the charts in the 1970s–1990s. A by-product of the magazine's work is the Essence Festival, which takes place in New Orleans during 4th of July week. This event is one of the largest African American cultural events in the United States and is a haven for R&B groups to perform and interact with fans new and old (Fernandez, 2019).

The shift to digital has hurt *Essence* magazine's circulation numbers (dropping them to one million), but this magazine still has a presence in the community and an influence on the buying decisions of African American consumers.

CONCLUSION

These publications were some of the most effective earned media elements for R&B groups and had a long history of introducing the world to the next big groups. Although they are rarely discussed, the parallels between the decline of these publications and the disappearance of Black R&B groups from the charts are striking.

CONCLUSION

Chapter 63

. . . .

TECHNOLOGY TAKES OVER

THE EFFECT OF TECHNOLOGY

The introduction of the MP3 and portable music devices like the iPod and the move toward downloading of individual songs turned the music industry on its head. This resulted in fewer consumers visiting local record stores to search for and purchase music. Local music stores in traditionally urban neighborhoods had been where many R&B acts would first perform, host meet and greets, and get radio airplay that would not have occurred on mainstream radio.

Technology also negatively affected R&B groups' ability to maintain their place on the charts. Throughout my research, I found several startling similarities between technology taking over the music industry and the digital divide in urban communities. According to Oxford Languages, the proper definition of the digital divide is as follows: "The gulf between those who have ready access to computers and the internet, and those who do not."

THE DIGITAL DIVIDE

The digital divide affected mom-and-pop record stores that were historically the primary way that R&B groups would first be introduced to fans and gain momentum on an organic level. According to Carolyn Owens, "In the past, many R&B groups or acts, in general, would start to perform at high schools, smaller gyms, churches, and community-based centers. This is how they would get fans and create a community. They would generally do little tours with the retail mom-and-pop shops, and that is how you would kind of really start getting known by the community and the neighborhood. Due to the fact that you were known by this method, generally, that mom-and-pop owner would be a really influential person in the community of that neighborhood or that city. And so when you no longer have a lot of record stores to go to, and we don't even have a bigger record store to go to in conjunction with the mom and pops being gone, then we no longer have a community connection to growing music groups."

Once a group reached moderate success on this level, they would progress to radio appearances, followed by appearances on television shows such as *Video Soul*, *The Arsenio Hall Show*, *The Oprah Winfrey Show*, *Total Request Live*, etc. If this foundational level was never met, then the cycle could not begin, and groups were not discovered. While Tuesday mornings were a time when you would see lines around the corner at the local record stores in all communities, Saturday mornings were prime time for groups to appear at local record stores for their meet and greets. These meet and greets created exposure and buzz for all types of groups, particularly R&B groups. With the ability to sing and harmonize on cue, these groups had a low lift to break out into a mini concert while at the store signing autographs.

The impact of these consistent appearances over the years helped numerous groups ascend the *Billboard* charts and earn substantial sales numbers. A rapid shift from MP3s to the current streaming model left mom-and-pop record stores with boarded-up windows and R&B groups searching for answers. According to Bianca Gracie, "When you think of R&B, you always think of albums, right? You never think, of course, they had tons of hit singles. But when you look at the genre as a collective entity, you always think of individual albums, whether it's the artist Beyoncé's *Dangerously In Love*, [Lauryn Hill's] *The Miseducation of Lauryn Hill*, or Mary J. Blige's *My Life*. There are always albums that stand out, and the singles fall behind. So I think with the rise of Napster and LimeWire, people were more so downloading singles rather than albums, and I think that's what affected the genre because people were either stealing the songs [(ripping them off of these platforms)] or with the rise of iTunes, they were buying individual singles. And that affected the sales of the albums themselves."

What are some potential solutions? It is not impossible for local arts organizations and other music-focused nonprofit organizations to push for the re-emergence of mom-and-pop record stores focused on the local artists within their communities. Small business owners would win. The arts community would win. And, in the long term, R&B groups would win. Even with the digital divide present in many urban communities, this grassroots effort would appeal to a local music community that grew up listening to the harmonization of groups such as the Isley Brothers, Boyz II Men, and Klymaxx.

YOUTUBE

As iTunes became more dominant and publicly accepted, a singular social media platform that allowed up-and-coming musicians to create a following was quickly growing. At this time, we had the birth of YouTube and the creation of the "YouTube star." To prove how serious this phenomenon was, we can look to the year 2009 when Usher introduced us to young teen phenom Justin Bieber, who was singing "Baby" on YouTube. Even though "Baby" was one of the most disliked videos on YouTube, Bieber's success showed artists the power of appearing as a singular act on YouTube and gaining rapid exposure and fame.

By this time, monetization of videos was available, and many artists (and record labels) saw the amount of revenue that was generated from this one video. The mindset that was already shifting continued to morph at an increased pace, and there was no looking back. The shift was considered to be complete when the video for "Gangnam Style" by the artist Psy became the first YouTube video to reach 1 billion views. Unsurprisingly, this song reached number 2 on the *Billboard* Hot 100 charts.

Despite releasing seven more singles after this massive hit, Psy never achieved nearly the success of "Gangnam Style" again. However, record executives quickly took notice of the "Gangnam Style" phenomenon and began to search for, develop, promote, and release singular acts while following this formula of releasing a potential hit single with a video right away for primarily singular acts.

While working on this book, I learned many lessons. The most startling was how disruptive the technological innovations of the early 2000s were, including the creation and adoption of the MP3 file, Napster/torrent sites, iTunes, and finally, streaming services. This rapid technological evolution left R&B groups behind other genres of music, and they have yet to catch up. As social media became more prominent, fans became interested in hearing from individual members of groups instead of from groups as a whole. According to A. Moon, "I think we're in an era of solo musicians. Like I looked at the *Billboard* charts, and everything seems to be a solo artist or some sort of collaboration. It's not groups anymore, in any genre." YouTube hit the mainstream, and it became significantly easier to share content on an individual basis. There was no more need to get the entire group together, record a performance together, and then release a video. It was as simple as hitting record with just one performer and then uploading that video.

Chapter 64

. . . .

EDM HITS THE MAINSTREAM

AS THE ENTIRE WORLD WAS EXPERIENCING A MASSIVE disruption to how they discover, consume, purchase, and share music, a sleeping giant of a genre was finally hitting the mainstream. This genre is called electronic dance music (EDM).

EDM is a genre of music characterized by its reliance on electronic instruments and technology for composition and production. Anchored by pulsating rhythms and infectious beats, EDM captivates listeners with its energetic and danceable nature. Its diverse subgenres—ranging from techno and house to dubstep and trance—each bring unique sonic signatures to the genre. Using synthesizers, samplers, drum machines, and digital software, EDM artists craft soundscapes that often feature repetitive structures, driving home the music's hypnotic allure. EDM's widespread popularity is evidenced by its dominance on dance floors, in clubs, and at music festivals worldwide, where live performances by DJs and electronic artists create an immersive sonic experience that resonates with a global audience.

EDM has evolved over the years, adapting to changes in technology, production techniques, and cultural trends. It has become a dominant force in the music industry and has significantly influenced popular music, fashion, and youth culture.

The history of EDM can be traced back to 1970s New York disco and 1980s Detroit techno music. Ironically, EDM gained momentum and popularity overseas, primarily in Europe. The evolution of EDM has traveled through the techno, acid house, rave, trance, jungle, drum and bass, dubstep, electro house, and trap music genres. This evolution coincided with the heyday of R&B groups and was like a younger, quieter sister to hip-hop, growing up before our very eyes.

For the longest time, mainstream media and the record industry did not classify EDM as a legitimate genre of music. Radio refused to play EDM due to its diverse song structure. EDM was also associated with drug culture, which led to governments passing legislation to halt the spread of rave culture; several laws and acts were passed or enforced in the early 2000s in particular that indirectly affected rave-related events.

But after battling public perception and successfully getting the description of the EDM events to use the word "festival" instead of "rave," the EDM genre experienced a few breakthroughs that further pushed down Black R&B groups from the *Billboard* Top 100. After years of momentum, in 2010, the Electric Daisy Carnival sold out the LA Coliseum.

This was a watershed moment for EDM and another major blow to R&B groups. This event caused the music industry and music press to further promote and push EDM into the mainstream. This effort was finally realized when Skrillex's "Scary Monsters and Nice Sprites" entered the *Billboard* Top 200 charts in 2012. If there were a graph comparing EDM chart success to R&B chart success, it would be like two ships passing in the night. EDM was on its ascension, and R&B groups were quickly becoming an afterthought.

What caused the music industry to promote EDM acts and step away from R&B groups?

Generally speaking, EDM groups are singular acts that focus on various guest appearances across different tracks. The best example of this was the massive 2011 hit "We Found Love" by Rihanna and Calvin Harris. This song was number 1 on the U.S. *Billboard* 100 charts for 10 weeks and cemented EDM as the third most popular genre in music (after hip-hop and country). When different singers are featured on an album, specific EDM acts capitalize on each guest's appearance with their audience crossover while still remaining singular acts. Therefore, decisions about touring, videos, television show appearances, and so on fall to one person.

The simplicity and high revenue from a small team of people instantly became more attractive to record labels than the tried-and-true model of R&B groups. The emergence of EDM was the equivalent of the final nail in the coffin for R&B groups. Like the old guy at the party who gets pushed out by a younger and more attractive attendee, R&B groups continued their exodus from the *Billboard* charts as more and more EDM acts took over.

Chapter 65

. . . .

THE TELECOMMUNICATIONS ACT OF 1996

IT IS NECESSARY TO REFLECT ON THE IMPACT of the Telecommunications Act of 1996 and how often R&B groups were played. As Brian Josephs mentions concerning Black music in a 2020 *Vice* article, the Telecommunications Act of 1996 was an absolute failure.

The United States Congress enacted the Telecommunications Act of 1996 to promote competition and foster innovation in the telecommunications industry. The act, signed into law by President Bill Clinton on February 8, 1996, represented a comprehensive overhaul of the nation's telecommunications laws, addressing various aspects of the industry including telephone service, cable television, and the emerging field of the internet.

Here is a detailed summary of the key provisions and objectives of the act:

1. **Promoting Competition:** One of the primary goals of the act was to promote competition in the telecommunications industry. It aimed to remove barriers to entry and reduce monopolistic

practices. The act encouraged the development of competitive local telecommunications markets, allowing new companies to enter the market and compete with established regional and local providers.

2. **Deregulation of Telecommunications:** The act sought to deregulate certain aspects of the telecommunications industry to encourage innovation and investment. It eliminated restrictions on the entry of long-distance companies into the local telephone service market and vice versa. It also removed the restrictions on Regional Bell Operating Companies, commonly known as the "Baby Bells," which were created after the breakup of AT&T in 1984. This allowed them to enter the long-distance market.

3. **Universal Service:** The act aimed to promote universal service by ensuring that affordable telephone service was available to all Americans, regardless of their location. It established the Universal Service Fund to support providing telecommunications services in underserved areas, such as rural and low-income communities. The USF is funded through contributions from telecommunications carriers.

4. **Spectrum Allocation:** The act included provisions for allocating radio spectrum, which is essential for wireless communication services. It aimed to promote efficient and effective spectrum use by reallocating it through competitive bidding. This allowed for increased competition in the wireless industry and facilitated the growth of cellular and mobile communications.

5. **Media Ownership Rules:** The act addressed the issue of media ownership consolidation. It sought to promote diverse voices and prevent excessive concentration of media ownership. However, subsequent court rulings and regulatory changes have modified some of these provisions.

6. **Internet and E-Commerce:** The Telecommunications Act of 1996

recognized the importance of the internet and sought to promote its development. It included provisions to facilitate the growth of internet access and e-commerce. The act prohibited restrictions on providing internet services and sought to promote the deployment of advanced telecommunications services, including broadband internet.

7. **Privacy and Consumer Protection:** The act included provisions to protect consumer privacy in the context of telecommunications services. It required telecommunications carriers to protect the confidentiality of customer information and to disclose their privacy policies. It also established the Federal Communications Commission (FCC) as the primary regulatory authority for enforcing these privacy protections.

Initially intended to promote competition and diversity, the act ended up creating a never-ending stream of repetitive songs with no local flavor. Even worse, what now gets played on the radio rests in the hands of advertisers and playlists mandated by the few corporations that own radio stations. Digging deeper, most of the boards of directors for the top five radio corporations have minimal racial or gender diversity among each roster.

Several subsequent court rulings and regulatory changes have modified specific provisions of the Telecommunications Act of 1996. Here are some notable examples:

1. *Prometheus Radio Project v. FCC* (2004): In this case, the United States Court of Appeals for the Third Circuit ruled against the FCC and overturned specific ownership rules established by the Telecommunications Act. The court found that the FCC had failed to adequately justify its decision to relax restrictions on media ownership, particularly cross-ownership rules that allowed a single

company to own multiple media outlets (such as newspapers, radio
stations, and television stations) in the same market. The court's
ruling prompted the FCC to reevaluate and modify its media
ownership rules. Below are the impacts of the *Prometheus Radio
Project v. FCC* on the radio industry.

    a.   **Ownership Limits:** The court ruling in *Prometheus Radio
Project v. FCC* highlighted concerns about media consolidation and the need to maintain diversity of voices in the
local media landscape. As a result, the FCC was required to
reassess and modify its ownership limits to prevent excessive concentration of media ownership. The ruling prompted a reevaluation of the restrictions on cross-ownership,
which refers to the ownership of multiple media outlets by
a single entity in the same market.

    b.   **Cross-Ownership Restrictions:** The court ruling chal-
lenged the FCC's decision to relax the cross-ownership
rules under the Telecommunications Act of 1996. The
ruling emphasized the importance of preventing undue
concentration of media ownership and maintaining
a diversity of viewpoints. As a result, the FCC had to
reevaluate and impose restrictions on cross-ownership,
particularly the ownership of multiple media outlets in the
same market. These restrictions aimed to preserve localism
and ensure a variety of perspectives and sources of news
and information.

    c.   **Preservation of Localism and Diversity:** The *Prometheus
Radio Project v. FCC* case underscored the significance of
localism and diversity in the radio industry. The court rul-

ing recognized the value of local radio stations as a source of community-focused content, diverse programming, and locally relevant information. As a result, the FCC was prompted to reconsider and reinforce policies that promote localism and diversity, including ownership limits and restrictions on cross-ownership, to preserve a vibrant local radio landscape.

d. **Opportunities for Low-Power FM (LPFM) Stations:** The *Prometheus Radio Project v. FCC* case indirectly benefited low-power FM (LPFM) stations. LPFM stations are small-scale, noncommercial stations with limited coverage areas that serve specific local communities. The ruling prompted the FCC to create more opportunities for LPFM stations by opening up licensing windows and reducing regulatory barriers. This allowed nonprofit organizations and community groups to establish and operate LPFM stations, providing additional avenues for local voices and community-based programming.

2. **2007 Media Ownership Revisions:** In response to court rulings and public concerns, the FCC revised its media ownership rules in 2007. These revisions included retaining the ban on a single company owning both a daily newspaper and a television or radio station in the same market (cross-ownership rules) but allowing waivers on a case-by-case basis. The revisions also established restrictions on the number of radio and television stations a company could own in a single market based on the size of the market and the number of stations available.

3. **FCC Quadrennial Reviews:** The FCC conducts periodic reviews of its media ownership rules through quadrennial reviews. These

reviews assess the current state of the media landscape and determine whether any changes to the ownership rules are necessary. The quadrennial reviews provide opportunities for public input and allow for modifications to be made to the media ownership regulations. The most recent quadrennial review was conducted in 2016, and subsequent reviews have been scheduled.

4. **Local Community Radio Act (2010):** This act, signed into law in 2010, amended the Telecommunications Act and expanded opportunities for the establishment of LPFM radio stations. The Local Community Radio Act aimed to increase localism and diversity in the radio industry by allowing nonprofit organizations and community groups to operate LPFM stations. This act provided more opportunities for independent and local voices to be heard on the radio.

5. **Proposed Changes and Ongoing Debates:** The FCC has continued to propose and consider changes to its media ownership rules. For example, in 2017, the FCC under Chairman Ajit Pai proposed further relaxation of the ownership restrictions, including eliminating the cross-ownership ban and other regulations. However, these proposed changes faced significant public opposition and legal challenges, leading to delays and modifications to the proposed rules.

The only hope is that college and independent radio stations continue to be able to curate radio programming that can resist the demands of their advertisers.

Back in 2001, then CEO of Emmis Communications, Jeffrey Smulyan, told the *Chicago Tribune*, "It is very hard to us to be arbiters of taste, especially when we're responsible for shareholders." These signaled the first storm clouds on the horizon.

An additional report by the Future of Music Coalition in 2006 saw the writing on the wall as the industry was reeling from this act. As Brooks Boliek reported in an article for the *Hollywood Reporter*, "Putting more radio stations in fewer hands has reduced listener choices and made it harder for musicians to get airplay." The importance of this report is that it was shared in 2006, which was at the exact time that R&B groups were beginning their decline. The genres that were noted as being in danger were classical, jazz, Americana, bluegrass, and folk. R&B music was not mentioned. Even in 2006, the impact of the Telecommunications Act was not yet realized within this genre. A common question that has come up in interviews is, "If there are no adjustments or revisions to this act, what is the next genre of music that could become irrelevant to the *Billboard* charts?"

THE IMPACT OF THE TELECOMMUNICATIONS ACT OF 1996 ON RADIO

The Telecommunications Act of 1996 had a significant impact on radio stations in the United States. The act brought about changes in ownership restrictions, market competition, and the regulatory framework for radio broadcasting. Here are some of the critical effects:

- **Relaxation of Consolidation and Ownership Rules:** The act relaxed ownership restrictions, allowing for increased consolidation in the radio industry. Before the act, there were limits on the number of radio stations a single entity could own nationwide and in a local market. The act removed these restrictions, leading to many mergers and acquisitions among radio companies. As a result, a few large corporations began to dominate the radio market, leading to concerns about a lack of diversity of voices and local programming.

- **Increased Market Competition:** The act aimed to promote competition by reducing barriers to entry and fostering a more competitive marketplace. It allowed for increased cross-ownership between radio stations, television stations, and newspapers within a local market. This change was intended to encourage new players to enter the radio industry and to promote diverse media ownership. However, some argue that the increased consolidation led to a decrease in competition and local programming.

O **Increased Format Diversity:** Following the act, radio stations had more freedom to experiment with different formats and programming. The relaxation of ownership rules allowed for specialized formats to emerge, targeting specific demographics or musical genres. This led to the proliferation of formats such as talk radio, all-news, sports, and niche music stations, providing listeners with a broader range of options.

O **Challenges for Independent and Local Stations:** The consolidation resulting from the act presented challenges for independent and locally owned radio stations. Smaller stations often found it difficult to compete with giant corporations with greater resources and market power. Many independent stations were bought out or forced to change formats to remain financially viable. This trend raised concerns about losing local programming and diverse airwave voices. The impact of the Telecommunications Act of 1996 on independent and local radio stations was significant. The relaxation of ownership restrictions and the subsequent consolidation in the radio industry presented challenges for these stations.

O **Increased Competition:** The consolidation resulting from the act intensified competition in the radio industry. As conglomerates acquired multiple stations, they gained increased market power, resources, and bargaining leverage with advertisers. Independent and local stations, with their limited resources and smaller market shares, often needed help to compete with the conglomerates for advertising revenue and audience attention. The increased competition posed challenges for independent stations to sustain their operations and profitability.

O **Limited Access to Advertising Revenue:** Independent and local stations faced difficulties in securing advertising revenue. As conglomerates offered advertisers a larger audience reach across their stations, independent stations often needed to be more recognized. Advertisers seeking broad national or regional coverage were more inclined to work with conglomerates, which could offer more extensive and cost-effective advertising packages. This limited access to advertising revenue placed financial strain on independent and local stations.

O **Changes to Format and Programming:** The consolidation trend also led to changes in programming formats. Conglomerates, seeking economies of scale and standardized programming, often implemented formats that could be replicated across their stations. This standardized approach typically focused on formats with broad appeal, such as popular music genres or syndicated talk shows. As a result, there was a decrease in locally produced and unique programming, a hallmark of independent and local stations. This shift limited the diversity of programming options and reduced the localism that was a distinguishing feature of these stations.

O **Reduced Local Content and Voices:** Independent and local stations had traditionally played a vital role in reflecting local communities' interests, culture, and news. However, as conglomerates gained control over more stations, there was a decline in locally produced content and a loss of local voices on the airwaves. Syndicated programming and centralized operations became more prevalent, diluting the distinct local flavor and reducing the opportunity for community-focused content.

O **Increased Financial Pressures and Ownership Changes:** Many independent and local stations faced financial pressures after consolidation. Some were acquired by larger conglomerates, resulting in changes to their programming, format, and local identity. Others were forced to change formats or cease operations altogether due to the inability to compete effectively in the consolidated market. The consolidation trend often led to a decrease in the number of independent and locally owned stations, raising concerns about the diversity of voices and viewpoints available to listeners.

O **New Regulatory Challenges:** The impact on independent and local stations prompted concerns among policymakers and regulators. The consolidation trend raised questions about preserving localism, diversity, and competition in the radio industry. However, subsequent changes in regulations and court rulings have modified some of the ownership restrictions, leading to ongoing debates and challenges regarding media ownership and the protection of independent and local voices.

O **Challenges to Regulation and Enforcement:** The act also impacted the regulatory framework for radio broadcasting. It required the FCC to review its rules and policies to ensure they aligned with the goals of promoting competition and localism. The act also introduced penalties for violations of FCC regulations, including fines and license revocation, which aimed to encourage compliance with broadcasting standards and regulations.

How did the urban contemporary format change across the United States after the Telecommunications Act of 1996?

O **Consolidation and Ownership Changes:** The relaxation of ownership restrictions under the Telecommunications Act led to increased consolidation in the radio industry, including stations with urban contemporary formats. Larger conglomerates, such as Clear Channel Communications (now iHeartMedia) and Entercom Communications (now Audacy), acquired numerous urban contemporary stations nationwide. This consolidation resulted in a more centralized approach to programming and a shift toward national syndication rather than localized content.

○ **Standardization of Playlists:** With consolidation came a greater emphasis on research-driven programming and standardized playlists. National conglomerates implemented playlist optimization strategies to maximize ratings and advertising revenue. This often led to a narrower selection of songs being played on urban contemporary stations, as they focused on proven hits with broad appeal. The standardization of playlists reduced the diversity of music played and limited opportunities for local and regional artists. The standardization of playlists in urban contemporary radio following the Telecommunications Act of 1996 reduced the diversity of music played and limited opportunities for local and regional artists due to several factors:

○ **Shift to Research-Driven Programming:** With consolidation and the rise of larger conglomerates, urban contemporary stations increasingly relied on market research and data analysis to shape their playlists. This research-driven approach aimed to maximize ratings and advertising revenue by playing songs that had proven to be popular across a broad audience. As a result, there was a greater emphasis on a limited number of chart-topping hits that appealed to the mainstream, often resulting in a narrower selection of songs being played.

○ **Implementation of Top-Down Programming Decisions:** The standardization of playlists often involved centralized programming decisions made by corporate executives and programming departments at the conglomerate level. These decisions were driven by national trends and market research rather than local or regional considerations. As a result, there was less flexibility for individual DJs or local program directors to curate their playlists based on local tastes or to showcase emerging local and regional artists.

O **Decreased Airplay for Niche and Local Artists:** The standardization of playlists made it more challenging for niche or local artists to gain airplay on urban contemporary stations. As conglomerates focused on promoting well-established hits with broad appeal, limited airtime was available for lesser-known or emerging artists. This reduced the exposure and opportunities for local and regional talent, as stations primarily prioritized nationally recognized artists with major label backing.

O **Limited Label Influence:** Standardized playlists often favored major record labels and their established artists. Major labels had more resources and connections to promote their artists to national conglomerates, resulting in increased airplay for their releases. Independent and regional labels with smaller marketing budgets and lesser-known artists found it more difficult to compete for airtime on stations with standardized playlists.

O **Fewer Opportunities in Local Music Scenes:** With fewer opportunities for local and regional artists to receive airplay on urban contemporary stations, it became more challenging for them to gain exposure and build a local following. This limited the growth and vibrancy of local music scenes and reduced the diversity of voices and styles represented on the airwaves.

O **Emphasis on Syndicated Programming:** The consolidation trend, combined with advancements in technology and syndication capabilities, led to an increased reliance on syndicated programming in urban contemporary radio. Syndicated shows hosted by popular

personalities gained prominence, allowing for consistent programming across multiple stations. This shift reduced the presence
of local on-air talent and reduced the variety of voices on urban
contemporary stations.

O **Integration of Hip-Hop:** The urban contemporary format evolved
to integrate more hip-hop music. Following the Telecommunications Act, urban contemporary stations started to embrace the
growing popularity of these genres. Hip-hop became a significant
component of the format, reflecting the changing musical landscape
and the preferences of the target audience. This shift helped urban
contemporary stations stay relevant and appeal to a younger
demographic.

O **Challenges for Independent and Local Stations:** Independent and
local urban contemporary stations faced challenges in the wake of
consolidation. The increased dominance of conglomerates made it
difficult for smaller stations to compete for advertising revenue and
attract top talent. Independent stations often had to differentiate
themselves by focusing on hyper-local content, community engagement, and specialized programming to retain their audience and
attract advertisers.

O **Digital Disruption and Transition to Online Streaming:** With
the advent of the internet and digital technology, the Telecommunications Act coincided with the rise of online streaming platforms
and digital radio. This allowed independent and local urban
contemporary stations to reach a global audience and compete with
larger conglomerates. Digital platforms allow for the creation of
more niche programming, the discovery of independent artists, and
the cultivation of loyal online communities.

This legislation was supposed to breed more competition in the radio indus-

474 THE QUIET STORM

try and allow for more diversity in the music being played across the country. The exact opposite occurred. Companies like iHeartMedia, Cumulus Media, and Townsquare Media purchased numerous radio stations nationwide.

According to Angie Moon, "Radio stations are a lot more commercialized and more homogenous than ever before. You know, it's a lot more concentrated ownership which limits the diversity of songs played." With these radio station purchases came required playlists from board members and not DJs, who are the true selectors. When the power of curating the music played is taken out of the DJs' hands and placed in the hands of a "vanilla" board of directors, R&B groups will quickly disappear.

Why, you ask? According to a 2020 Nielsen study, 91% of Black adults 18 and older listen to the radio weekly. This is a major source of information and taste within the African American community. And radio plays are dictated by advertising dollars in an age where radio is trying to stay afloat and fend off streaming services. The popular songs will get the most "ear traffic," and this drives up the value of an advertising spot. Therefore, the radio stations are playing for the advertisers and not for the listeners.

An R&B group singing about love and heartbreak does not fit the typical ad spots (outside of those for online dating companies). The cycle continues, and R&B groups lose in this equation. This is true for radio stations nationwide in every major metropolitan area. From 1997 until approximately 2004, this process continued until you could no longer hear R&B groups consistently on the most popular radio stations across the country. The impact was devastating. This was another (or probably the first) cloud in the imperfect storm we witnessed.

. . . .

Chapter 66

THE MUSIC RECESSION OF 2008-2013

THE GREAT RECESSION, WHICH BEGAN IN 2008 AND resulted from the global financial crisis, significantly affected the music industry. The recession impacted various industry sectors, including record sales, live music, and overall revenue.

Here are some areas in which the music industry was affected by the Great Recession:

O **Record Sales:** The music industry was already grappling with declining physical album sales due to the rise of digital music and online piracy. The recession exacerbated this decline, as consumers had less disposable income to spend on nonessential items, including music purchases. This led to a further decline in physical album sales and contributed to the industry's ongoing shift to digital distribution.

O **Major Record Labels:** Major record labels faced financial challenges as consumer spending decreased. This led to budget cuts, staff layoffs, and restructuring within these companies. Major labels were already dealing with the effects of the digital music transition, and the recession compounded these challenges.

- **Live Music and Touring:** The live music sector, which had been relatively resilient to economic downturns in the past, was not immune to the effects of the recession. Consumers cut back on discretionary spending, which affected attendance at concerts and music festivals. Some artists faced difficulties in filling venues and selling tickets, impacting their touring revenue.

- **Music Publishing and Licensing:** The recession led to reductions in advertising budgets, affecting the demand for music licensing in commercials, films, and TV shows. This had implications for music publishers and composers who relied on licensing deals for revenue.

- **Independent Artists:** Independent musicians and smaller labels often rely on consumer spending for merchandise and album purchases and for concert attendance. The economic downturn limited their ability to generate income from these sources.

- **Digital Music:** The recession accelerated the ongoing shift from physical music formats to digital downloads and streaming services. As consumers sought more affordable entertainment options, legal digital music platforms gained traction. This accelerated transition reshaped how music was consumed and monetized.

- **New Business Models:** The challenges posed by the recession prompted the music industry to explore new business models and revenue streams. Subscription-based streaming services gained prominence as a way for consumers to access music affordably, albeit at lower revenue per stream for artists and labels than traditional sales.

Overall, the Great Recession had a complex and multifaceted impact on the music industry. It highlighted the need for adaptation to changing consumer behaviors and technological shifts. In response to the challenges posed by the recession, the industry continued to evolve and experiment with new approaches to distribution, consumption, and revenue generation.

In 2008, the major record labels were reeling, as they were in the midst of losing significant money to online digital piracy.

Online digital piracy exerted a profound and multifaceted impact on the music industry, fundamentally altering the landscape of music consumption, distribution, and revenue generation. Among its notable effects, piracy triggered a decline in physical album sales, as freely accessible music reduced consumers' incentive to purchase CDs or other tangible formats. This resulted in significant revenue losses for artists, record labels, and industry stakeholders, prompting a shift toward digital distribution models.

The concurrent rise of legal digital music platforms was a response to both piracy and the growing popularity of digital music formats. Moreover, piracy fostered the emergence of streaming services that offered legitimate and convenient alternatives to illegal downloads, consequently transforming how listeners accessed music.

To combat piracy, the industry invested resources in copyright enforcement, often resorting to legal action against file-sharing platforms and individuals engaged in piracy. Creative challenges also arose, affecting artists' financial viability and influencing the diversity and quality of music production. On a global scale, piracy transcended geographical boundaries, necessitating international efforts to address the issue. In response, artists began emphasizing fan engagement through live performances, exclusive releases, merchandise, and special content. These adaptations reflected a broader industry transformation, as the music sector navigated the complex terrain of online piracy to establish new distribution models and engage with evolving consumer behaviors.

Stock prices of the top three record labels were at historically low levels, and this would eventually lead to takeovers and purchases.

In 2011, Universal Music's acquisition of EMI marked a pivotal moment in the music industry, characterized by the consolidation of two influential record labels. EMI Group, a prominent British music company encompassing record labels and publishing divisions, faced financial challenges and debt by this time. Universal Music Group, a global music corporation under the umbrella of French media conglomerate Vivendi, recognized an opportunity to expand its influence and catalog by acquiring EMI. The purchase agreement, announced in November 2011, outlined Universal's intention to acquire EMI's recorded music division for approximately $1.9 billion.

However, due to concerns over potential antitrust implications and monopolistic tendencies, regulatory authorities in various countries, including the United States and the European Union, closely examined the deal before granting approval. To address these concerns, Universal agreed to divest certain assets from both EMI and its own portfolio, ensuring a competitive market landscape. Notably, a portion of EMI's European catalog, including Parlophone Records, was divested to Warner Music Group to meet European Union regulations. With regulatory approvals secured and divestitures completed, Universal finalized the acquisition of EMI's recorded music division in September 2012.

This strategic move solidified Universal's status as the world's largest record label, redefining the music industry's structure and dynamics. As the music sector grappled with the challenges of digital transformation, piracy, and shifting consumer behaviors, the acquisition illustrated the industry's quest to adapt and thrive amidst a rapidly changing landscape.

In addition, labels had acquired debt throughout the previous year and had difficulty paying it back. The labels also had trouble securing more money from creditors, which led to lower profits. Music subscription models were just beginning to appear and gain momentum. This movement started to devalue music in general and the record album specifically. The shift was on to a more singles-forward environment.

By the time the year 2007 had come to a close, digital singles had overtaken CD sales by a wide margin of $819 million to $500 million. Steve Jobs, cofounder of Apple, is celebrated in many business circles, but the music industry owes a significant amount of pain to Steve Jobs and his negotiations with record labels in 2003.

In 2003, Steve Jobs embarked on negotiations with record labels that would shape the landscape of the music industry. These discussions were pivotal in bringing to life the iTunes Store, a groundbreaking digital music platform that would redefine how music was consumed. At the heart of these negotiations was Jobs's proposal for a single pricing model, advocating for a flat rate of $0.99 per song, simplifying the purchasing process for consumers regardless of a song's popularity. A key aspect of these talks was Jobs's stance on digital rights management (DRM), which he believed should be minimized or eliminated to encourage accessibility and interoperability of music across devices.

Working closely with major record labels like Universal Music Group, Warner Music Group, Sony Music Entertainment, and EMI, Jobs secured the necessary licensing agreements that enabled Apple to offer an extensive catalog of music on the iTunes Store. He emphasized seamless integration with Apple's iPod, a popular portable media player at the time, further enhancing the user experience. Revenue-sharing agreements were negotiated, allocating a portion of the $0.99 song price to record labels and the rest to Apple, departing from the traditional album-based pricing structure. Remarkably swift negotiations resulted in the iTunes Store's rapid launch, marking a turning point in digital music distribution. This launch set the stage for the legal, user-friendly alternative to music piracy and laid the foundation for the future growth of music streaming services, profoundly impacting the entire music industry.

The Great Recession was a massive blow to the popularity of R&B groups. Record labels were in the process of going from their peak in terms of revenue earned to their lowest revenue-earning years in decades. After losing such a staggering amount of money, record labels redistributed their spending to cheaper and more singular acts such as hip-hop and pop stars. R&B groups were left out of the big spend. According to D. Vanderbilt-Nicholson, "If I'm planning a video, I'm spending $20,000 and $30,000 on two people. Imagine if it's four people. That's a $40,000 expense. That is now on that group to recoup that money. In addition to the money you're borrowing, you do need other things for the video, like styling four outfits for four separate members. If you're a group of females, you need to spend on hair and makeup every time you step onto a set nowadays. Hair can run you $15,000 or $20,000 a video shoot, depending on the stylist who the group selects. Even traveling with wigs makes this overall a very costly situation."

Chapter 67

. . . .

WHAT DOES THE FUTURE HOLD FOR R&B GROUPS?

ACCORDING TO BIANCA GRACIE, "IN THE MAINSTREAM SENSE, pop groups are dying. Fifth Harmony broke up a few years back, and all of the members went solo. Little Mix recently took a hiatus. Several of the group members from One Direction left the group. They're the biggest pop group coming from the UK since probably the Beatles. They all broke up and went solo. So if the pop group can't withstand this trend, why do we think the R&B groups can?" Many industry professionals that we interviewed feel that the cycle will turn around, and eventually, groups will reenter the charts and the limelight. Others feel that R&B groups are headed the way of the dinosaur—extinction.

According to D. Vanderbilt-Nicholson, "R&B music can't die as long as people are taking the music and the samples." Somewhere in the middle is what our research shows us. Groups like Silk Sonic made up of established artists coming together after experiencing a large amount of success to create a unique album appear to be the most likely trend moving forward. L.S.G.

was one of the first groups that has made this idea a reality in the 21ˢᵗ century.

L.S.G. was formed in the late 1990s, bringing together three accomplished R&B artists: Gerald Levert, Keith Sweat, and Johnny Gill. The name L.S.G. was a fusion of the initials of these members' last names. Levert, known for his soulful vocals and musical legacy, was the son of Eddie Levert from the O'Jays. Keith Sweat, recognized for his smooth R&B ballads, had already made a mark on the R&B scene with successful albums. Johnny Gill, a former member of New Edition who was renowned for his versatile vocal range, added his own distinct flair.

The collaboration in 1997 led to the release of their debut album, *Levert. Sweat. Gill.* This album, containing hit singles like "My Body" and "Door #1," was warmly received and showcased their collective musical prowess. While another album followed, *LSG2*, their inaugural release remained a standout in their discography. When Gerald Levert died in November of 2006, his father, Eddie Levert, took over for him in the group. Throughout their journey, these artists continued their individual solo careers alongside their collaborative work in L.S.G.

Why did no other artists choose to follow this model until Silk Sonic? Artists such as H.E.R., Kehlani, Leela James, and SZA could create a group, release a few albums, return to their solo careers, and alternate back and forth.

Understanding that many things run in cycles, it would be easy to assume that R&B groups will eventually return to the level of success and prominence that they experienced in their previous 50-plus-year run. However, I am concerned that this trend will never "correct" itself, and we have lapsed into a much more singular world—*singular* regarding how we buy music and how branding, marketing, and performances are done. Despite the fact that there have been minor blips on the radar (Silk Sonic) with regard to

R&B groups, the future seems bleak. Financially, it does not seem prudent for groups to stay together for decades while trying to earn a living making music. Additionally, record labels no longer have the patience to wait for groups to find their stride and develop into successful acts. I can't imagine a label waiting 16 years for a group to get a *Billboard* Hot 100 song like we saw with the Whispers. Hip-hop isn't slowing down, and the playlist era will dominate as streaming services evolve and the algorithms continue to get in tune with what people are listening to.

CONCLUSION

THE FUTURE IS NOT BRIGHT FOR R&B GROUPS. I hope with all of my heart that there is a miraculous transformation and that they reappear on a more consistent level. I am saddened at the outlook, but I am further emboldened to continue to spread the history of R&B groups and how they have birthed many of the popular acts and genres (*ahem, K-pop!*) that are popular today. And remember, the majority of the samples that you hear across all music come from R&B groups. They are tied within the fabric of all music, and we can never forget that.

The soundtrack of my entire life is filled with song after song from R&B groups. There were countless songs by New Edition ("Can You Stand The Rain"), Whistle ("Still My Girl"), SWV ("I'm So Into You"), and Jodeci ("U And I") that I would play over the phone to young ladies I was interested in. I would make slow-jam mixtapes filled with R&B groups on every volume.

I want the soundtrack for the rest of my life to be filled with new songs from new R&B groups.

ACKNOWLEDGMENTS

I want to acknowledge my students at California State University, Fullerton, who helped me complete the research shared in this book over the four years it took to write it. The students include Ashley Landa, Landy Waight, Jasmin McDowell, Aaron Acero, Jade Manese, Rachel Heinz and Brandon Eggleston.

I want to thank the team at Book Launchers for guiding me along the way and helping me stay true to the book's pure message. Specifically, I want to thank John Schlimm II, Dan Good, and Yna Davis.

RESOURCES

"1960: The Payola Scandal Heats Up." History. Last updated February 9, 2024. https://www.history.com/this-day-in-history/the-payola-scandal-heats-up.

"2010-2019: A Timeline of the EDM Decade." EDM.com. December 30, 2019. https://edm.com/features/2010-2019-edm-decade-timeline.

"About FMC." Future of Music Coalition. Accessed May 21, 2024. https://www.futureofmusic.org/about.

Anderson, Trevor. "Silk Sonic 'Stake' Rolls into Top 10 on Hot R&B/ Hip-Hop Songs Chart." *Billboard*. August 11, 2021. https://www.billboard.com/pro/silk-sonic-skate-top-10-rb-hip-hop-songs-chart/.

Ankeny, Jason. "Ohio Players Biography." AllMusic. Accessed May 24, 2024. https://www.allmusic.com/artist/ohio-players-mn0000390390#biography.

Aquila, Richard. *Rock & Roll in Kennedy's America: A Cultural History of the Early 1960s.* Baltimore, MD: Johns Hopkins University Press, 2022.

Benitez-Eves, Tina. "Behind the Song Lyrics: 'Be My Baby,' Performed by Ronnie Spector and the Ronettes." American Songwriter. Accessed May 24, 2024. https://americansongwriter.com/be-my-baby-performed-by-ronnie-spector-and-the-ronettes/.

Blavat, Jerry. "The O'Jays." Rock & Roll Hall of Fame. Accessed May 28, 2024. https://rockhall.com/inductees/ojays/.

Boliek, Brooks. " '96 Act Killed Radio's Star." *Hollywood Reporter*. December 14, 2006. https://www.hollywoodreporter.com/business/business-news/96-act-killed-radios-star-146401/.

Bordowitz, Hank. "Ahmet Ertegun and the History of Atlantic Records." TeachRock. 1991. https://teachrock.org/article/ahmet-ertegun-and-the-history-of-atlantic-records/.

Bowman, Rob. "The Ronettes." Rock & Roll Hall of Fame. Accessed May 28, 2024. https://rockhall.com/inductees/ronettes/.

Breihan, Tom. "The Number Ones: Lisa Lisa and Cult Jam's 'Lost in Emotion.' " Stereogum. March 19, 2021. https://www.stereogum.com/2120952/the-number-ones-lisa-lisa-and-cult-jams-lost-in-emotion/columns/the-number-ones/.

"Brick-and-Mortar Record Stores Are Trying to Get Their Groove Back." *PopMatters*. February 23, 2009. https://www.popmatters.com/70763-brick-and-mortar-record-stores-are-trying-to-get-their-groove-back-2496056189.html.

"Cameo." Soul Tracks. Accessed May 24, 2024. https://www.soul-tracks.com/cameo.

Channick, Robert. "*Ebony*, the Voice of Black America +75, Set for Digital Relaunch Monday." *Chicago Tribune*. February 26, 2021. https://www.chicagotribune.com/2021/02/26/ebony-the-voice-of-black-america-for-75-years-set-for-digital-relaunch-monday/.

Charnas, Dan. " 'We Changed Culture': An Oral History of *Vibe* Magazine." *Billboard*. September 27, 2018. https://www.billboard.com/music/rb-hip-hop/vibe-magazine-oral-history-8477004/.

"The Coasters." Billboard Database. Accessed May 23, 2024. https://elpee.jp/artist/The%20Coasters/.

Cochrane, Naima. "Music Sermon: The Evolution and Extinction of Male R&B Groups." *Vibe*. February 18, 2019. https://www.vibe.com/features/editorial/music-sermon-evolution-extinction-of-male-rb-groups-635624/.

"El DeBarge." *Rolling Stone*. January 1, 2023. https://www.rollingstone.com/music/music-lists/best-singers-all-time-1234642307/el-debarge-1234642964/.

Erlewine, Stephen Thomas. "The Penguins Biography." AllMusic. Accessed May 23, 2024. https://www.allmusic.com/artist/the-penguins-mn0000893719#biography.

Erlewine, Stephen Thomas. "Sly & the Family Stone Biography." AllMusic. Accessed May 23, 2024. https://www.allmusic.com/artist/sly-the-family-stone-mn0000033161#biography.

Fox, Ted. *In the Groove: The People Behind the Music.* New York: St. Martin's Press, 1986.

"George Clinton." GeorgeClinton.com. Accessed June 19, 2024. https://georgeclinton.com/bio/.

"Gladys Knight & the Pips." Biography. May 17, 2021. https://www.biography.com/musicians/gladys-knight.

Granditsky, Maria. "The Lionel Richie Interview." Miss Funkyflyy's Web Pages. December 1996. Archived February 20, 2016, at the Wayback Machine. https://web.archive.org/web/20160220074828/http:/hem.bredband.net/funkyflyy/commodores/richie.html.

Hall, Josh. "From the Bronx to the World: The Birth and Evolution of Hip-Hop." Red Bull. April 6, 2020. https://www.redbull.com/ie-en/history-of-hip-hop.

Harrington, Richard. "MCA to Pay Royalties to RB Greats." *Washington Post.* December 6, 1989. https//www.washingtonpost.com/archive/lifestyle/1989/12/07/mca-to-pay-royalties-to-rb-greats/63714098-29be-481e-915f-cb43f6bdf07c/.

Herbison, Bart, and Jim Weatherly. "The Story Behind the Song 'Midnight Train to Georgia.' " *Tennessean.* July 15, 2016. YouTube video, 4:40. https://www.youtube.com/watch?v=TNjBZTl6h84.

Hickey, Andrew. "Episode 68: 'Yakety Yak' by the Coasters." *A History of Rock Music in 500 Songs*, podcast. February 4, 2020. https://500songs.com/podcast/episode-68-yakety-yak-by-the-coasters/.

Hill, Michael. "The Coasters." Rock & Roll Hall of Fame. Accessed May 23, 2024. https://rockhall.com/inductees/coasters/.

Hill, Michael. "The Drifters." Rock & Roll Hall of Fame. Accessed May 28, 2024. https://rockhall.com/wp-content/uploads/2024/03/The_Drifters_1988.pdf.

Hill, Michael. "The Supremes." Rock & Roll Hall of Fame. Accessed May 28, 2024. https://rockhall.com/inductees/supremes/.

Hill, Michael. "The Temptations." Rock and Roll Hall of Fame. Accessed May 24, 2024. https://rockhall.com/wp-content/uploads/2024/03/The_Temptations_1989.pdf.

Hill, Robert. "The Titan of Black Media, John H. Johnson, Shaped How African American Got the News." *USA Today.* September 20, 2020. https://www.usatoday.com/story/opinion/voices/2020/09/20/black-media-jet-ebony-jounalism-john-johnson-column/3485589001/.

Hutchinson, Lydia. "Alan Freed and the Radio Payola Scandal." Performing Songwriter. August 20, 2015. https://performingsongwriter.com/alan-freed-payola-scandal/.

"History." Kool & the Gang. Accessed May 24, 2024. https://www.kooland-thegang.com/history.

Hogan, Ed. "The S.O.S. Band Biography." AllMusic. Accessed May 24, 2024. https://www.allmusic.com/artist/the-sos-band-mn0000495366#biography.

Howard, Jackson. "Wonderland Lost." The Ringer. June 7, 2019. https://www.theringer.com/music/2019/6/7/18655225/earth-wind-fire-maurice-white-i-am-boogie-wonderland-disco-demolition.

Jordan, Chris. "How the Isley Brothers' Mom Made Jimi Hendrix Feel Right at Home in New Jersey." *Asbury Park (NJ) Press.* https://www.app.com/story/entertainment/music/2022/05/05/the-isley-brothers-jimi-hendrix-nj-home-mothers-day-concert/9617106002/.

Josephs, Brian. "This 1996 Law Was Meant to Save Radio. Instead, It Decimated Popular Black Music." *Vice.* October 21, 2020. https://www.vice.com/en/article/n7vjqm/this-1996-law-was-meant-to-save-radio-instead-it-decimated-popular-black-music.

"The Jackson 5, 'I Want You Back.' " *Rolling Stone.* February 16, 2024. https://www.rollingstone.com/music/music-lists/best-songs-of-all-time-1224767/the-jackson-5-i-want-you-back-2-1225234/.

Kelly, D. B. "The Messed Up Truth About the 1950s Music Industry." Grunge. Last updated February 28, 2022. https://www.grunge.com/388043/the-messed-up-truth-about-the-1950s-music-industry/.

Kelly, Ken. "The Commodores of Tuskegee Sail on a Golden Sea of Hits." *People.* February 20, 1978. https://people.com/archive/the-commodores-of-tuskegee-sail-on-a-golden-sea-of-hits-vol-9-no-7/.

Knight, Gladys, and Oprah Winfrey. "Who Discovered the Jackson 5?" OWN. April 16, 2016. YouTube video, 4:13. https://www.youtube.com/watch?v=1GfnYiRJdnk.

"Kool & the Gang." *Rolling Stone.* 2004. Archived August 21, 2009, at the Wayback Machine. https://web.archive.org/web/20090821005118/http:/www.rollingstone.com/artists/koolthegang/biography.

Koskoff, Ellen. *Music Cultures in the United States: An Introduction.* Abingdon, Oxfordshire, UK, 2005.

LeDonne, Rob. "Frankie Beverly Responds to Beyonce Covering His Maze Hit 'Before I Let Go.' " *Billboard.* April 24, 2019. https://www.billboard.com/music/music-news/frankie-beverly-beyonce-homecoming-8508606/.

Leiber, Jerry, Mike Stoller, and David Ritz. *Hound Dog: The Leiber and Stoller Autobiography.* New York: Routledge, 2005.

Leight, Elias. "Can R&B Groups Make a Comeback in the Streaming Era?" Genius, February 8, 2018. https://genius.com/a/can-r-b-groups-make-a-comeback-in-the-streaming-era.

Leskin, Paige. "YouTube Is 15 Years Old. Here's a Timeline of How YouTube Was Founded, Its Rise to Video Behemoth, and Its Biggest Controversies Along the Way." Business Insider. Last modified May 30, 2020. https://www.businessinsider.com/history-of-youtube-in-photos-2015-10.

"The Life and Legacy of Essence." *Essence.* September 15, 2020. https://www.essence.com/feature/essence-50th-anniversary-legacy/.

McEwen, Joe. "The '5' Royales." Rock & Roll Hall of Fame. Accessed May 28, 2024. https://rockhall.com/inductees/5-royales/.

"The Miracles." Classic Motown. Accessed May 23, 2024. https://classic.motown.com/artist/the-miracles/.

Misha. 2023. "It is with great sadness that I have to let you know that my beautiful sister and friend has passed away this evening."

Instagram. September 16, 2023. https://www.instagram.com/p/CxRsLNWsB3x/.

Mitchell, Gail. "O'Jays Celebrate 40th Anniversary of First Hit 'Back Stabbers.'" *Billboard.* August 17, 2012. https://www.billboard.com/music/music-news/ojays-celebrate-40th-anniversary-of-first-hit-back-stabbers-480384/.

Molanphy, Chris. "I Know You Got Soul: The Trouble with *Billboard*'s R&B / Hip-Hop chart." Pitchfork. April 14, 2014. https://pitchfork.com/features/article/9378-i-know-you-got-soul-the-trouble-with-billboards-rbhip-hop-chart/.

Murphy, Keith. "After Success and Then Struggle, R&B Legends New Edition Finally Enjoy a Victory Lap." *Los Angeles Times.* March 18, 2022. https://www.latimes.com/entertainment-arts/music/story/2022-03-18/new-edition-bobby-brown-bell-biv-devoe-culture-tour.

Murray, Sonia. "Hip-Hop with a Southern Sensibility Makes Atlanta Rap Twosome One to Watch—and Listen To." *Atlanta (GA) Journal-Constitution.* September 15, 1996. https://philly.newspapers.com/article/the-atlanta-constitution/136460802/.

"National Recording Preservation Board," Library of Congress. Accessed May 17, 2024. https://www.loc.gov/programs/national-recording-preservation-board/recording-registry/frequently-asked-questions/.

Parks, Andrew. "Types of Sync Placements & Uses." *Songtrust* (blog). Last modified December 7, 2023. https://blog.songtrust.com/types-of-sync-placements-uses.

Petrarca, Emilia, "TLC Annotates Their 10 Best Looks from the 1990s, from Boxer Shorts to Track Pants." *W.* June 20, 2017. https://www.wmagazine.com/gallery/tlc-best-90s-fashion-style.

Powell, Herb. "The Spinners." Rock & Roll Hall of Fame. Accessed May 28, 2024. https://rockhall.com/inductees/spinners/.

"RIAA." Recording Industry Association of America. Accessed May 17, 2024. https://www.riaa.com/.

Rizik, Chris. "Atlantic Starr." Soul Tracks. Accessed May 24, 2024. https://www.soultracks.com/atlantic_starr.htm.

Robinson, Smokey. "The Story Behind 'The Tracks of My Tears.' " AARP. June 3, 2021. Video, 2:41. https://www.youtube.com/watch?v=9IvA5sGOLAw.

Ross, Janell. "Ebony and Jet Magazines Transformed the Narrative of Black America. Now, Their Photo Archive is Up for Sale." NBC News. July 17, 2019. https://www.nbcnews.com/news/nbcblk/ebony-jet-magazines-transformed-narrative-black-america-now-their-photo-n1030771.

Shaffer, Paul. "The Shirelles." *Rolling Stones.* April 21, 2005. Archived February 6, 2007, at the Wayback Machine. https://web.archive.org/web/20070206065556/http:/www.rollingstone.com/news/story/7248611/76_the_shirelles.

Sheffield, Rob. "Danity Kane." *Rolling Stone.* September 7, 2006. Archived October 2, 2007, at the Wayback Machine. https://web.archive.org/web/20071002075402/http:/www.rollingstone.com/reviews/album/11113996/danity_kane.

Staples, Brent. "The Radical Blackness of *Ebony* Magazine." *New York Times.* August 11, 2019. https://www.nytimes.com/2019/08/11/opinion/ ebony-jet-magazine.html.

Stevens, Jenny. "How We Made TLC's Waterfalls." *Guardian* (U.S.). May 15, 2018. https://www.theguardian.com/culture/2018/may/15/ how-we-made-tlc-waterfalls.

"Still Spinning." *Honolulu Star-Bulletin*, March 8, 1976. https://www. newspapers.com/newspage/271801985/.

"Sweet, Sweet Soul," *Montreal (QC) Star*, June 23, 1972, https://www. newspapers.com/newspage/743098186/.

"Telecommunications Act of 1996." Federal Communications Commission. Accessed May 17, 2024. https://www.fcc.gov/general/telecommuni-cations-act-1996.

Trust, Gary. "How the Charts Have Evolved Across Billboard's History: The Hot 100, Billboard 200 & More." *Billboard.* November 14, 2019. https://www.billboard.com/pro/billboard-chart-history-evolu-tion-milestones/.

Warner, Jay. *American Singing Groups: A History from 1940s to Today.* Milwaukee, WI: Hal Leonard Corporation, 2006.

Was, Don. "Sly and the Family Stone." *Rolling Stone.* December 3, 2010. https://www.rollingstone.com/music/music-lists/100-greatest-art-ists-147446/sly-and-the-family-stone-89455/.

Watkins, Grouchy Greg. "For 2010: The Death of the Mom and Pop Record Store." AllHipHop.com. December 22, 2009. https://

allhiphop.com/uncategorized/for-2010-the-death-of-the-mom-and-pop-record-store/.

"The Whispers' Biographical Summary." The Legendary Whispers. Accessed May 25, 2024. https://thelegendarywhispers.com/epk.

Whitall, Susan. "Martha and the Vandellas." Rock & Roll Hall of Fame. Accessed May 28, 2024. https://rockhall.com/inductees/martha-and-the-vandellas/.

Whitburn, Joel. *Joel Whitburn's Top Pop Singles 1955-2012*. Menomonee Falls, WI: Record Research Inc, 2013.

White, Adam. *The Billboard Book of Gold & Platinum Records*. New York: Billboard Books, 1990.

Wilson, Charlie. "We Named the Gap Band After Greenwood Archer & Pine Streets in Tulsa, OK." July 11, 2023. YouTube video, 0:34. https://www.youtube.com/shorts/N74U0d2yRDM.

www.ingramcontent.com/pod-product-compliance
Lightning Source LLC
LaVergne TN
LVHW012147180225
804059LV00034B/757